H O T E L S
of Character and Charm
I N   P A R I S

Hunter Publishing, Inc.
www.hunterpublishing.com

HUNTER PUBLISHING, INC.

130 Campus Drive, Edison NJ 08818
(732) 225 1900, (800) 255 0343; fax (732) 417 0482

IN CANADA
Ulysses Travel Publications
4176 Saint-Denis
Montreal, Quebec H2W 2M5 Canada
(514) 843 9882, ext. 2232; fax 514 843 9448

ISBN 1-55650-901-4
Third Edition

Copyright © 2001 by Payot/Rivages

For complete information about the hundreds of other travel guides offered by Hunter Publishing, visit our website at **www.hunterpublishing.com**

**Hotels of Character
and Charm in Paris**

Translator: Dominique Bach, Richard Willett,
Anne Norris, Oliver Langhorne
Front cover photograph: Hôtel Garden Élysées (Paris, 16e)
photo by François Tissier
Back cover: Hôtel de Banville (Paris, 17e)
photo by Dannie A. Launay

Special Sales
Hunter Travel Guides can be purchased in quantity at special discounts. For more information, contact us at the address above.

Printed in Italy by Litho Service
10 9 8 7 6 5 4 3 2 1

HUNTER RIVAGES

HOTELS
of Character and Charm
IN PARIS

Conceived by
Jean and Tatiana de Beaumont,
and Michelle Gastaut

Project editor
Tatiana de Beaumont

Hunter Publishing, Inc.
www.hunterpublishing.com

Photographic Credits

Important

FOREWORD

Once again this year, we have sought out those small hotels that perpetuate the "Paris of poets" and bring delight to a regular clientele.

The 283 addresses featured in this fifth edition are therefore the fruit of rigorous fieldwork, from which we have selected some additional hotels, eliminated others and updated the practical information and descriptions.

All these hotels were carefully visited, and then selected according to a criterion not easy to define, but which more and more of you are looking for: charm.

A hotel of charm retains eloquent signs of the past such as a beautiful stone stairway, beamed ceilings or high windows opening onto a garden. It offers a number of rooms at reasonable prices, all different and beautifully decorated with elegant fabrics, engravings and antique pieces of furniture. It is regularly renovated, notably with regard to the bedding, and avoids the pitfall of out-of-date decor. The bathrooms are equipped with the best modern comforts. The quality of the welcome, a lounge inviting guests to read or have a drink near the fire, a dining room where guests enjoy breakfast when the weather does not allow them to sit outside, all these make for a home-like feeling.

The hotels presented in this guide all have something in common with this ideal model. Some have all the features, others have the affable welcome, the irreproachable upkeep and the charming decoration details to compensate for its sometimes too standard appearance. Whether they marvelously take advantage of contemporary trends, or appeal to us with their calm and greenery, they are the proof that charm goes hand in hand with diversity.

Simple or luxurious, classic or contemporary, the selected establishments have real qualities. If you read the description of each hotel carefully, you will no doubt find those corresponding to your taste. And if you do not expect the same service from a two-star hotel as from a palace, you have a chance to discover, as we did, some true gems.

PRACTICAL ADVICE

The hotels are classified by district (arrondissement) and alphabetical order (you will find a table of contents at the beginning of the guide). The flags on the map of Paris indicate the hotel location and the page where its photo and description are to be found.

At the end of the guide, there are various indexes to help you in your research. We have grouped the hotels according to:
- touristic areas
- low prices (double rooms from 295 to 500F)
- the presence of a restaurant in the hotel
- name (alphabetical index)

Do not forget that the stars mentioned in the practical information correspond to the hotel's classification by the Ministry of Tourism, not to a standard set by this guide's authors.

We have given the prices current at the time of printing. However, these are always likely to be modified by the owners during the year. Therefore we recommend that you check them when you reserve. We have also taken care to indicate the high and low season rates. The hotel low season is particularly well suited to the tourist calendar: it usually varies from July to August and November to February (except during trade fair and convention periods). Before reserving, do not hesitate to ask for those exact dates. Likewise, many hotels offer promotional rates for weekends. In these cases, the price reduction can be significant.

Some hotels may charge preferential rates to the readers of our guide; the details are indicated in the practical information for each hotel. In order to benefit from this reduction, let them know when you reserve.

YOUR OPINION INTERESTS US

Do not hesitate to write and let us know your appreciation of the places we recommend. You can also inform us about hotels you have liked and which are not featured in this guide. We can visit them, and perhaps integrate them into the next edition (of course, there is no financial participation on the part of hotel owners; we thus retain the freedom to select an address or to remove it from the guide).

Please send all comments about individual hotels to:

Tatiana de Beaumont
Guide des hôtels de charme à Paris
Éditions Payot & Rivages
106, boulevard Saint-Germain - 75006 Paris

You can also contact us on the Guides Rivages' website at:
http://www.guidesdecharme.com

Or get in touch via our US website at
http://www.hunterpublishing.com

Thank you very much.

C O N T E N T S

Table of Contents
General Map of Paris
Individual Maps

Hotels:

Index of Hotels by Quarter
Index of Hotels with Low Rates
Index of Hotels with Restaurants
Index of Hotels in Alphabetical Order

TABLE OF CONTENTS

P R E M I E R

D E U X I E M E

T R O I S I E M E

QUATRIEME

CINQUIEME

S   I   X   I   E   M   E

S E P T I E M E

H U I T I E M E

N E U V I E M E

D I X I E M E

O N Z I E M E

D O U Z I E M E

T R E I Z I E M E

Q U A T O R Z I E M E

Q U I N Z I E M E

S E I Z I E M E

D I X – S E P T I E M E

DIX - HUITIEME

DIX - NEUVIEME

BOULOGNE - NEUILLY - LA DÉFENSE

Map for the Hotels of Paris

The following map of Paris is divided into eleven double pages, with two "zoom" maps of the most heavily visited *arrondissements* (Ie, IIe, IIIe, Ve, VIe, and parts of IVe and VIIe).

The doubled pages are arranged as follows: two "zoom" maps (1 and 2) with a scale of 1:12,500, and nine large-scale maps (3 to 11) covering the entire Paris area with a scale of 1:15,500.

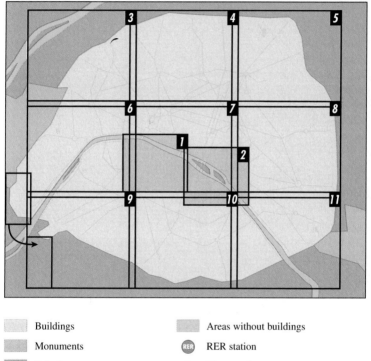

	Buildings		Areas without buildings
	Monuments	RER	RER station
	Suburbs	M	Metro station
	Garden	92	Hotel
	Water (Rivers, lakes, ponds, canals)		

All the hotels in this guide are marked on the map with the page number of the hotel's review.

Hotels referred to in the "zoom" maps are not recorded on the corresponding, large-scale maps: these "zoom" areas are indicated on the large maps by a darker background color.

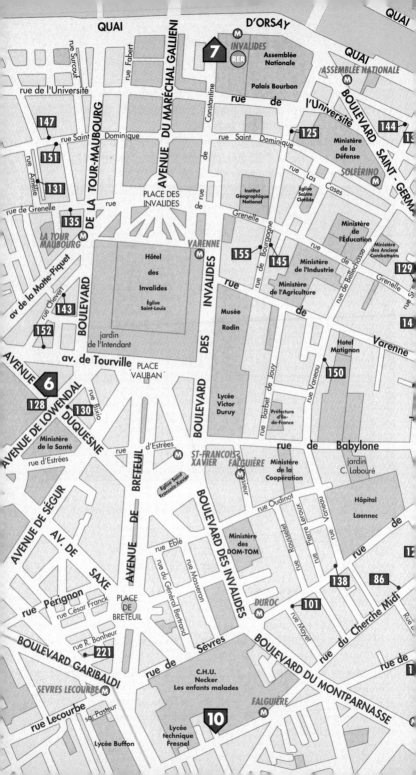

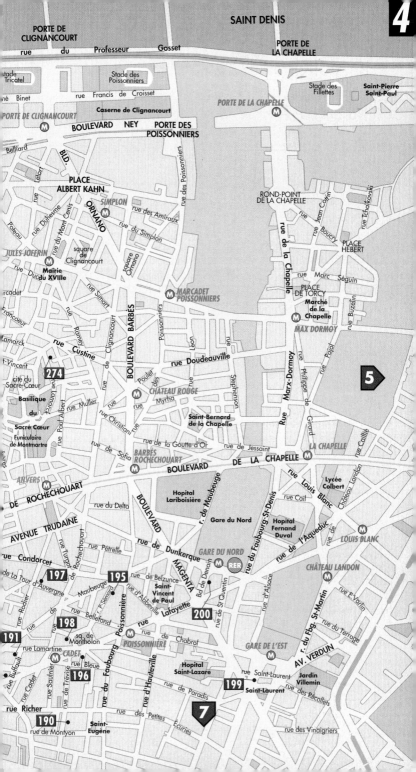

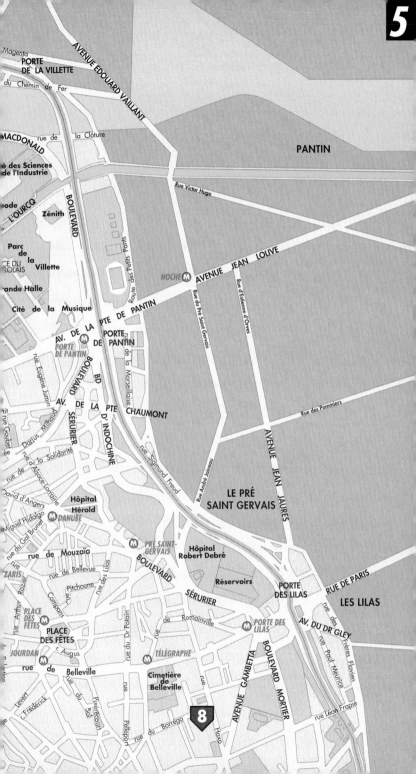

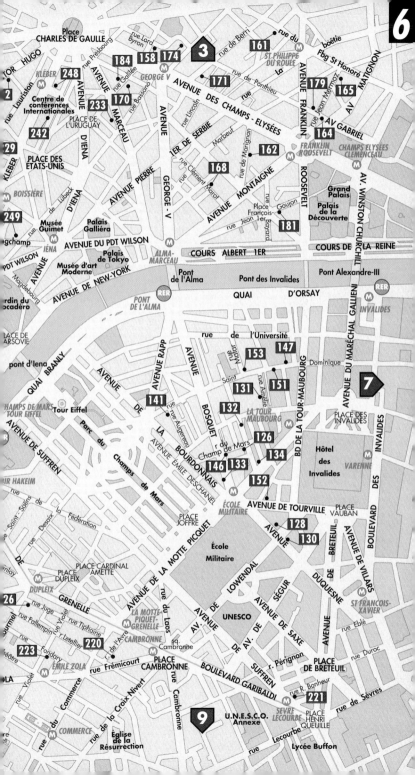

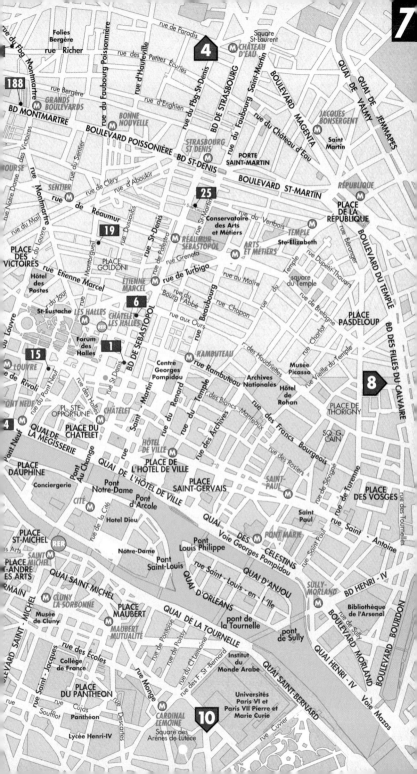

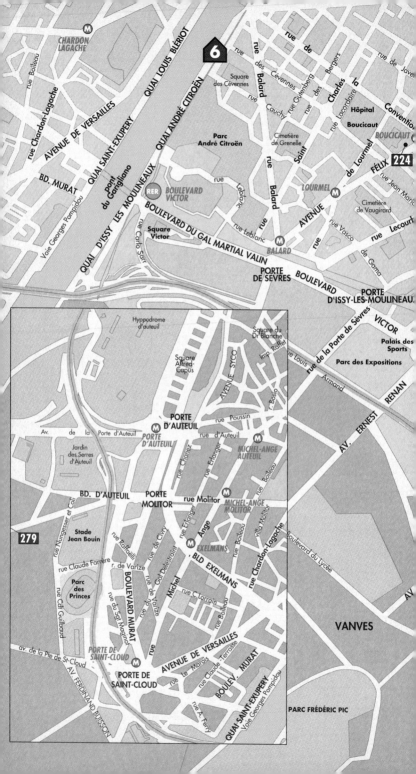

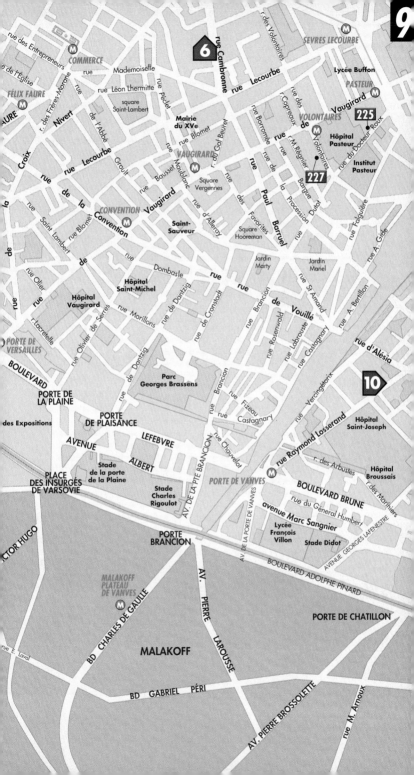

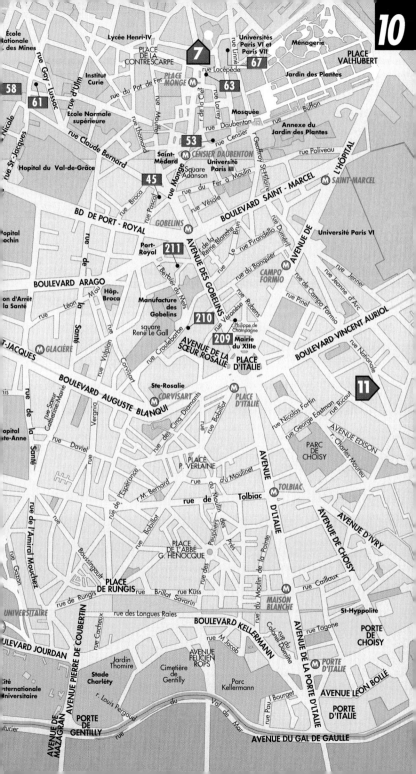

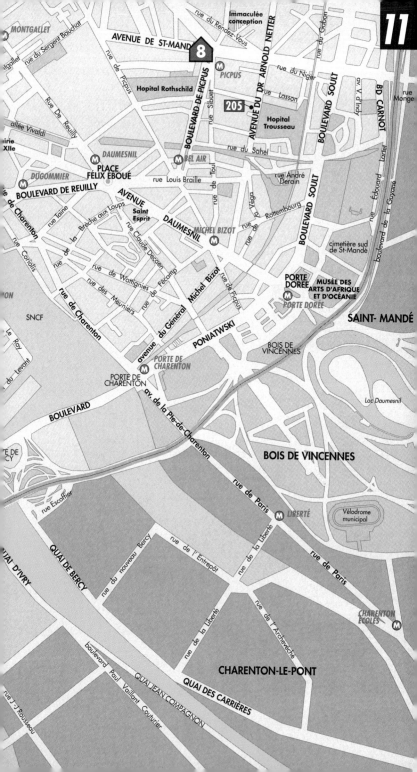

Hôtel Agora

7, rue de la Cossonnerie
75001 Paris
Tel. 01 42 33 46 02 – Fax 01 42 33 80 99
M. De Marco

Category ★★ **Rooms** 29 with soundproofing, bath or shower, WC, satellite TV, safe. **Price** Single 360-595F / 54,88-90,71€, double 540-710F / 82,32-108,24€; extra bed 100F / 15,24€ – Special rates in Jul and Aug –10%. **Meals** Breakfast 40F / 6,10€, served 7:00-9:30. **Credit cards** Amex, Visa, Eurocard, MasterCard. **Pets** Dogs not allowed. **Facilities** Elevator. **Parking** Forum des Halles. **How to get there** (Map 7) Bus: 29, 38, 47, all to Châtelet – Metro and RER: Châtelet-Les Halles. **Open** All year.

The Agora is on a bustling street in Les Halles, very near the Les Innocents Square and Fountain, where trendy clothes shops rub elbows with lively restaurants. The Centre Beaubourg (George Pompidou Modern Art Center) is also in this area, one of the most touristed quarters of Paris. A stairway leads to the reception area and the lounge-corner where breakfast is served. A very small, embellished elevator takes you to the bedrooms; they also have individual touches: an old-fashioned chest of drawers, a pretty painted closet, a gilt mirror, a carved wood headboard, a painting or an ancient engraving. Unquestionably full of charm. On the other hand, washrooms are more basic. Rooms ending in 1, 2 or 6, have more pleasant proportions. All overlook the pedestrian street. In winter, double-glazed windows effectively soundproof the rooms, but in good weather, it's best to stay on the top floors. This simple, surprising hotel should delight antique hunters and flea market hounds.

Hôtel Brighton

218, rue de Rivoli – 75001 Paris
Tel. (0)1 47 03 61 61 – Fax (0)1 42 60 41 78
M. Lebouc
E-mail: hotel.brighton@wanadoo.fr

Category ★★★ **Rooms** 69 and 1 suite with soundproofing, bath or shower, WC, telephone, TV, minibar. **Price** Single 685-915F / 104,43-139,49€, double 720-950F / 109,76-144,83€, triple 1025-1125F / 156,26-171,5€; suite 1400F / 213,43€. **Meals** Breakfast (buffet) 50F / 7,62€, served 7:00-11:00. **Credit cards** All major. **Pets** Dogs not allowed. **Facilities** Room service. **Parking** Place Vendôme and Place du Marché Saint-Honoré. **How to get there** (Map 7) Bus: 68, 72 – Metro: Tuileries and Concorde. **Open** All year.

The Brighton is undergoing an important renovation program that will, in the end, give it back its charm. Overlooking the arcades on rue de Rivoli, the lounge where breakfast is now served has retained its columns, its carpets, its mirrors, and its Louis XVI medallion-back chairs, which make it look like a Grand Hotel. The renovation is not totally finished, but the rooms we have seen are really well done, and have retained their large initial size. The new paintings and tapestries reinforce the classical style of the hotel: *toile de Jouy*, white *piqué* bedspreads, heavy curtains. These are the only rooms we recommend, but on the upper floors, simpler and not yet renovated rooms offer an exceptional view from balconies overlooking the Tuileries Gardens along with a view stretching from Notre Dame cathedral to the La Défense district. The creation of a new lounge and new suites is underway. Considering its location and kind welcome, you will easily show leniency for what is left to be done.

Hôtel Britannique

20, avenue Victoria – 75001 Paris
Tel. (0)1 42 33 74 59 – Fax (0)1 42 33 82 65
M. Danjou
Web: www.hotel-britannique.fr – E-mail: mailbox@hotel-britannique.fr

Category ★★★ **Rooms** 40 with soundproofing, telephone, bath, WC, hairdryer, TV satellite, minibar, safe. **Price** Single 750F / 114,34€, double 895-1025F / 136,44-156,26€; extra bed 135F / 20,58€. **Meals** Breakfast (buffet) 62F / 9,46€, served 7:00-10:30. **Credit cards** All major. **Pets** Dogs not allowed. **Facilities** Elevator, bar, laundry service. **Parking** Hôtel de Ville and Quai de Gesvres. **How to get there** (Map 2) Bus: All to Châtelet and Hôtel de ville – Metro and RER: Châtelet-Les Halles. **Open** All year.

A plaque at the entrance to the Hotel Britannique informs you that it was built in 1840 and has been run to this day by a family of English origin. It has always been a favorite hotel with Anglo-Saxon tourists. The lounge downstairs is faithful to this British influence, with leather chesterfield and Turner reproductions. The cozy, elegant atmosphere is heightened by figured carpets in the corridors and bouquets of fresh flowers throughout the hotel. The bedrooms are of varying sizes, from singles and small doubles to more spacious rooms on the courtyard. But all are pleasant, comfortable, bright, and well-decorated. The Hôtel Britannique is next door to the *Cèdre Rouge,* one of the most famous garden stores in Paris, and near many other flower and horticultural shops off the Place du Châtelet and the Quai de la Messagerie. Scattered among the flower shops on the quay are other shops selling billy goats, roosters, rabbits, turtles, rods and reels–you name it. Tourists and Parisians alike love it.

Hôtel du Continent

30, rue du Mont-Thabor – 75001 Paris
Tel. (0)1 42 60 75 32 – Fax (0)1 42 6152 22
M. Siméon
E-mail: continent@cybercable.fr

Category ★★★ **Rooms** 26 with air-conditioning, soundproofing, bath or shower, telephone, hairdryer, WC, cable TV and minibar. **Price** Single 756-956F / 115,42-145,95€, double 962-1062F / 146,87-162,13€, extra bed 206F / 31,45€; in Jul and Aug, double from 862F / 131,60€. **Meals** Breakfast (buffet) 55F / 8,38€, served 7:00-10:30. **Credit cards** All major. **Pets** Dogs not allowed. **Facilities** Elevator, laundry service. **Parking** Place Vendôme. **How to get there** (Map 7) Bus: 24, 42, 72, 73, 84, 94 – Metro: Concorde. **Open** All year.

It is certainly true that with the Tuileries, Opera and Place Vendôme as neighbors, this small hotel can boast of its location. It has been entirely renovated this year in a contemporary style; the new decoration is all in soft tones, with gray and sea-green as the dominant colours. The space on the ground floor is nicely laid-out. Behind the reception area one finds a pleasant breakfast room and a lounge where abundant woodwork helps make the atmosphere warm. The rooms have been redone in the same spirit. They are clear, comfortable and well-arranged (some even have large closets). The pretty bathrooms are very pleasant. The only thing one could hold against this small hotel is the small size of some of the rooms, especially singles and rooms ending with a number 2. On the other hand, air-conditioning and a quiet street guarantee your tranquillity. A successful renovation. Good welcome.

Hôtel Costes

239, rue Saint-Honoré
75001 Paris
Tel. (0)1 42 44 50 00 – Fax (0)1 42 44 50 01
M. Costes and M. Lordonnois

Category ★★★★ **Rooms** 81 and 2 suites with air-conditioning, soundproofing, bath, WC, hairdryer, telephone and fax, TV, CD player, safe and minibar – 4 for disabled persons. **Price** Double 2000-3500F / 304,90-534,35€, duplex 3500-4000F / 534,35-610,68€, suite 5500-12 500F / 838,46-1905,61€; rooms with terrace +250F / 38,11€. **Meals** Breakfast 170F / 25,92€, served from 7:00. **Credit cards** All major. **Pets** Dogs allowed. **Facilities** Elevator, laundry service, swimming pool, sauna, health center. **Restauran** à la carte; tea room. **Parking** Place Vendôme. **How to get there** (Map 7) Bus: 24, 42, 52, 72, 73, 84 and 94 – Metro: Concorde. **Open** All year.

On the rue Saint-Honoré close to the Place Vendôme, only the name Costes indicates that this discreet façade is a hotel. A gallery of red-trimmed windows leads you to the reception area where lounges open onto a large courtyard in the Italian style of terraces decorated with antique statues. This well of light contrasts with the cozy and theatrical ambiance of the small lounges around the patio. The decor comes from the *La Traviata* opera, with deep armchairs and "confidante" chairs in dark pearwood arranged around the lampstands, and an imposing ceramic fireplace to create cozy corners for conversation. The same *fin de siècle* decor is in the rooms with cases in red brocade, a subtle mix of colours for the topstitched bedspreads, beautiful monogrammed bathroom linen and an amusing reusage of former *bourgeois* furniture. The suites are more luxurious and even more baroque.

Hôtel du Cygne

3, rue du Cygne
75001 Paris
Tel. (0)1 42 60 14 16 – Fax (0)1 42 21 37 02
Mme Rémont

Category ★★ **Rooms** 20 with telephone, satellite TV, safe, hairdryer, 18 with bath or shower and WC; 2 with washstand **Price** Single 410F / 62,50€, double 460F / 70,13€, triple 560F / 85,37€. **Meals** Breakfast 40F / 6,10€, served 7:30-10:00. **Credit cards** All major. **Pets** Dogs not allowed. **Parking** Saint-Denis, rue Turbigo. **How to get there** (Map 7) Metro: Étienne-Marcel – RER: Châtelet-Les Halles – Bus: 29, 38 and 47. **Open** All year.

Located on a pedestrian street (which is not to say a quiet street) in the Les Halles quarter, the Hôtel du Cygne has the feel of a provincial hotel. With a Louis Philippe writing desk and various nick-nacks, the rooms in the reception area resemble those of a private house. The stairway (there is no elevator) has retained its original 17th-century half-timbering. While the carpeting is brand-new, the wall covering deserves to be changed (the two charming sisters who have taken over the hotel will no doubt consider it). The pleasure of personalizing the rooms is shown in an antique piece of furniture or painting. The rooms are of reasonable size on the whole, number 35 is the largest (it easily sleeps 3), and our favorite remains Room 41. Generally speaking, in this district one had better sleep on the courtyard side, even though the street is pedestrian. The bathrooms are still quaint, but the price takes that into account, and the whole effect does not lack charm.

Demeure Hôtel Castille

33, rue Cambon – 75001 Paris
Tel. (0)1 44 58 44 58 – Fax (0)1 44 58 44 00
Mme Vallelian
E-mail: hotel@castille.com

Category ★★★★ Rooms 107 with air-conditioning, bath, telephone, hairdryer, WC, satellite TV, minibar, safe. **Prices** Rooms 2427-3332F / 370-508€, duplex and suite 4500F / 687€. **Meals** Breakfast 150F / 22,87€, served 7:00-10:30. **Credit cards** All major. **Pets** Dogs allowed. **Facilities** Elevator, laundry service, room service. **Restaurant** *Il Cortile* closed on weekends; à la carte (about 300F / 45,73€). Specialties: Italian cooking. **Parking** Garage (8 spaces) 150F / 22,87€. **How to get there** (Map 7) Bus: 24, 42, 52, 84, 94 – Metro: Concorde, Madeleine. **Open** All year.

The Hotel Castille adjoins the famous couture house of Coco Chanel on the rue Cambon. The Opera wing was once the annex of the equally famous Ritz Hotel. The hotel was extensively redesigned in an Italian style, with engraved mirrors, clouded patinas, painted furniture and lamps, and a large Roman mosaic. Vivid salmon and green colours were chosen for the decoration of the bedrooms, matching the bathrooms' majolica and marble. The largest are duplex rooms. Common to both hotels is the bar on the ground floor, with dark wood and dim light, an atmosphere foreshadowing the minimalist chic decor chosen by Jacques Granges for the Rivoli wing. There, bedrooms are decorated in green and burgundy stripes, checks or plaids, with dark, 19th-century–style furniture and photos of Paris by Robert Doisneau. One should mention the excellent restaurant which has earned one Nicolas Vernier star. Summer meals are served in a charming courtyard painted in *trompe-l'œil*, beautified with a fountain and cypress trees.

Grand Hôtel de Champagne

13, rue des Orfèvres
75001 Paris
Tel. (0)1 42 36 60 00 – Fax (0)1 45 08 43 33
M. Herbron – M. and Mme Lauferon

Category ★★★ **Rooms** 40 and 3 suites (with minibar) with telephone, bath, WC, satellite TV. **Price** Single 590-785F / 89,94-119,67€, double 640-880F / 97,57-134,16€, triple 810-970F / 123,48-147,88€, suite 990-1430F / 150,92-218€. **Meals** Breakfast (buffet) 60F / 9,15€, served 7:00-11:00. **Credit cards** All major. **Pets** Dogs allowed (+50F/7,62€). **Facilities** Elevator, laundry service, bar. **Parking** Rue du Pont-Neuf. **How to get there** (Map 2) Bus: All to Châtelet – Metro: Châtelet – RER: Châtelet-Les Halles. **Open** All major.

Dating from 1562, the Grand Hôtel de Champagne has an inviting entrance and reception area, leading to a convivial bar and lounge. The adjacent breakfast room is in a Louis XIII style, which harmonizes well with the hotel's architecture. Little by little, renovations have brought about more unity. White and red *toile de Jouy* has given the rooms on the *deuxième étage* the light they lacked. The *troisième étage* is in a Louis XIII style. The rest is more surprising, including the suites which vary from Japanese to 1970s styles, while paintings and frescos depicting Paris women add color to other bedrooms. The top floor rooms are our favorites, with mansard roofs and large balconies with a view over the Paris rooftops. Good service and warm welcome. Note that to get to the small rue des Orfèvres (meaning goldsmiths, who were located here from the 15th to the 19th centuries), you take the rue Jean-Lantier. History buffs will be interested to know that the hotel was once home to tailors belonging to the prestigious skilled-workers guild called the *Compagnons du Tour de France*, which still exists.

Hôtel Louvre Saint-Honoré

141, rue Saint-Honoré
75001 Paris
Tel. (0)1 42 96 23 23 - Fax (0)1 42 96 21 61
M. Toulemonde

Category ★★★ **Rooms** 40 with air-conditioning, soundproofing, telephone, bath, WC, hairdryer, safe, cable TV, minibar. **Price** Single 750-850F / 114,34-129,58€ (820-920F / 125,01-140,25€ during trade fair periods), double 900-1000F / 137,20-152,45€ (960-1080F / 146,35-164,64€ during trade fair periods). **Meals** Breakfast (buffet) 75F / 11,43€, served 7:00-10:30. **Credit cards** All major. **Pets** Dogs allowed. **Facilities** Elevator, bar, laundry service. **Parking** Louvre, Louvre des antiquaires, rue Croix des Petits Champs. **How to get there** (Map 1) Bus: 21, 67, 69, 72, 74, 75, 76, 81, 85 – Metro: Louvre-Rivoli – RER: Châtelet-Les Halles. **Open** All year.

Next to the Louvre and Les Halles, this hotel comprises two buildings connected by a skylight under which an "honesty bar" bar has been set up where clients can serve themselves drinks. The breakfast room is also found here and small exhibitions of pictures are organized. The decor and accommodations are modern without being austere. The bedrooms are bright, quiet (20 overlook the courtyard) and the bathrooms are well-equipped. In the rooms you find a tray set for tea or coffee so that you can relax in full privacy when returning home in the late afternoon. The staff is very friendly. The hotel is in an extremely picturesque neighborhood where, on Sunday morning, an open-air market takes place on the rue Montorgueil. Nearby, around the Place des Victoires, you will find the fashionable boutiques of the city's leading *créateurs*.

9

Hôtel Mansart

5, rue des Capucines – 75001 Paris
Tel. (0)1 42 61 50 28 – Fax (0)1 49 27 97 44
M. Dupain
E-mail: hotel.mansart@wanadoo.fr

Category ★★★ **Rooms** 57 (20 with air-conditioning, some with soundproofing) with telephone, bath or shower, WC, satellite TV, safe, minibar. **Price** Single and double 700-990F / 106,71-150,92€, "chambre Vendôme" 1300F / 198,18€, "chambre Mansart" 1600F / 243,92€. **Meals** Breakfast 60F / 9,15€, served 7:00-11:00; snacks available. **Credit cards** All major. **Pets** Dogs not allowed. **Facilities** Elevator. **Parking** Place Vendôme. **How to get there** (Map 7) Bus: All to Opéra – Metro: Opéra, Madeleine, Concorde – RER: Auber. **Open** All year.

On the corner of the Place Vendôme and the rue des Capucines, the Hôtel Mansart has an idyllic location. The refurbishment was conceived in homage to Louis XIV's architect, Jules Mansart; you will find tasteful baroque decor in the lobby, with mauve damask-covered 18th-century furniture and large paintings inspired by the famous formal gardens of Le Nôtre, Mansart's contemporary. The spacious bedrooms are comfortable, as are their bathrooms which have kept their original sizes. The flowery wallpaper and rustic furniture pieces give the rooms a certain provincial charm. For more style, and if you want to enjoy the view over Place Vendôme, ask for the Mansart suite with its *Grand Siècle* styling.

Hôtel Opéra-Richepanse

14, rue Richepanse - 75001 Paris
Tel. (0)1 42 60 36 00 - Fax (0)1 42 60 13 03
Mme Laporte - M. Jacques
Web: www.hotel-opera-richepanse.fr - E-mail: richepanseotel@wanadoo.fr

Category ★★★★ **Rooms** 35 and 3 suites, with air-conditioning, soundproofing, bath, WC, hairdryer, telephone, satellite TV, minibar and safe. **Price** Single 1370-1560F / 208,86-237,82€, double 1560-1820F / 237,82-277,46€, suite 2390-2700F / 364,35-411,61€. **Meals** Breakfast (buffet) 105F / 16,01€, served 7:00-10:30; snacks available on request. **Credit cards** All major. **Pets** Dogs allowed (+75F/11,43€). **Facilities** Elevator, laundry service, room service, sauna. **Parking** Place de la Madeleine. **How to get there** (Map 7) Bus: 24, 42, 52, 84, 94 – Metro: Madeleine. **Open** All year.

This new luxury hotel is two paces away from Madeleine and Concorde, and displays the full aesthetics and opulence of Art Deco. All the acajou furniture was especially designed for the hotel from drawings that copied the typical forms of the 1920s. Their brown-red tones perfectly harmonize with the two other dominant colours, royal-blue and a golden-orange. Very comfortable and perfectly soundproofed, the rooms vary in size, and it seems that the bigger ones with two beds are a better deal. You will also appreciate the comfort and beauty of the bathrooms with their white faience enhanced by a frieze of gilt, silver or colored cabochons, large three-panelled mirrors and perfect lighting. A small vaulted room for the copious breakfasts, a sauna and a very warm little lounge on the ground floor are also available to you in this welcoming hotel.

Hôtel de la Place du Louvre

21, rue des Prêtres-Saint-Germain-l'Auxerrois - 75001 Paris
Tel. (0)1 42 33 78 68 – Fax (0)1 42 33 09 95
M. Dupain
E-mail: hotel.place.louvre@wanadoo.fr

Category ★★★ **Rooms** 20 with telephone, bath, WC, satellite TV, safe, hairdryer. **Price** Single 540-740F / 82,32-112,81€, double 740-840F / 112,81-128,06€, duplex 880F / 134,15€. **Meals** Breakfast 55F / 8,38€. **Credit cards** All major. **Pets** Dogs allowed. **Facilities** Elevator, bar. **Parking** Place du Louvre, Saint-Germain-l'Auxerrois. **How to get there** (Map 1) Bus: 21, 24, 27, 67, 69, 74, 76, 81, 85 – Metro: Louvre-Rivoli, Pont-Neuf – RER: Châtelet-Les Halles. **Open** All year.

A room with a view awaits you at this hotel – and what a view! Rooms overlook the famous Louvre itself (which you can see by leaning out of the windows) along with the gargoyles and spires of the church of Saint-Germain-l'Auxerrois. Although it is few steps away from the Louvre Museum and Gardens, the Pont des Arts, the Ile de la Cité, the Beaubourg museum and Chatelet, nothing troubles the quietness of this hotel. A few vestiges of this ancient building have been preserved and successfully incorporated with modern decorative elements. The lounge and bar are located beneath a glass roof and breakfast is served in a beautiful vaulted cellar called the *Salle des Mousquetaires,* which once was connected with the Louvre. Bright, comfortable and functional, the rooms are decorated in elegant shades of beige and white. Each has the name of a modern painter and lithographs on the walls. As always, the quieter rooms are on the courtyard, but they lack the view. The service is attentive.

Hôtel Regina Paris

2, place des Pyramides - 75001 Paris
Tel. (0)1 42 60 31 10 - Fax (0)1 40 15 95 16
M. Jean Viguier
Web: www.regina-hotel.com - E-mail: sales@regina-hotel.com

Category ★★★★ **Rooms** 105 and 15 suites with air-conditioning and soundproofing with telephone, bath, WC, hairdryer, satellite TV, safe and minibar. **Price** Single 1720-2020F / 262,21-307,95€, double 2020-2350F / 307,95-358,26€; suite (2 pers.) 3 850-4150F / 586,93-632,66€; extra bed 400F / 60,98€. **Meals** Continental breakfast 100F / 15,24€, buffet 150F / 22,87€, served 7:00-10:00. **Credit cards** All major. **Pets** Dogs allowed. **Facilities** Elevator, bar, laundry service, patio, room service. **Restaurant** Mealtime specials 135-270F / 20,58-41,16€, also à la carte. **Parking** Pyramides. **How to get there** (Map 7) Metro: Tuileries and Palais-Royal – Bus: 68 and 72. **Open** All year.

The Regina is one of the mythical Parisian palaces, yet without their usual gigantic size. With its 120 rooms, it could rather be qualified as a "palace of charm". It opened in 1900 for the Universal Exhibition. It has retained its Art Nouveau decoration in the great hall and the series of reception rooms. The rooms and apartments have recently been entirely renovated in a more classical style – Louis XV, Louis XVI or *Directoire* - all very elegant. While some open onto the inner patio, most rooms offer a choice view overlooking the Palais du Louvre and Tuileries gardens (the hotel is of course equipped with air-conditioning and is well-soundproofed; therefore the traffic on the rue de Rivoli is easily forgotten). The bar and restaurant, much appreciated by the Parisians themselves, add to the charm of this beautiful hotel where comfort, hospitality and discretion are the notes of a faultless service.

Le Relais du Louvre

19, rue des Prêtres-Saint-Germain-l'Auxerrois
75001 Paris
Tel. (0)1 40 41 96 42 - Fax (0)1 40 41 96 44
Mlle Aulnette

Category ★★★ **Rooms** 18 with soundproofing and 2 junior suites and 1 apartment with air-conditiong and soundproofing, telephone, bath or shower, WC, cable TV, safe, hairdryer, minibar. **Price** Single 650-800F / 99,09-121,96€, double 880-1000F / 134,16-152,45€; suite 1300-1500F / 198,18-228,67€; apart. (1-4 pers.) 2400F / 365,88€ – Weekends (including Sunday night) and long stays: −10%; August: −20%. **Meals** Breakfast 60F / 9,15€, served from 6:30. **Credit cards** All major. **Pets** Dogs "tolerated". **Facilities** Elevator, room service. **Parking** 2 private locations (70F / 10,67€ per day) and Place du Louvre, Saint-Germain-l'Auxerrois. **How to get there** (Map 1) Bus: All to Châtelet – Metro: Louvre-Rivoli, Pont-Neuf; RER: Châtelet-Les Halles. **Open** All year.

One can guess the charm of the hotel from the reception area's pretty lighting and warm colours, which complement the chairs and antique furniture to a lovely effect. The rooms are not particularly large, apart from those designated suites, where particular attention has been given to both decor and comfort. Most rooms can be converted into small apartments for families. The hotel is in one of the most prestigious areas of Paris, near the Grand Louvre and in the shadow of the church of Saint-Germain-l'Auxerrois, the former parish of the kings of France. Lastly, breakfasts are prepared with great care and the welcome is very friendly

Tonic Hôtel Louvre

12-14, rue du Roule - 75001 Paris
Tel. (0)1 42 33 00 71 - Fax (0)1 40 26 06 86
M. Frédéric Boissier
E-mail: tonic.louvre@wanadoo.fr

Category ★★★ **Rooms** 34 with soundproofing (14 in the Roule section) telephone, bath with whirlpool and steam bath, WC, hairdryer, satellite TV, minibar – 1 for disabled persons. **Price** Single 590-750F / 89,94-114,34€, double 690-850F / 105,19-129,58€, triple 850F / 129,58€. **Meals** Breakfast (buffet) 45F / 6,86€, served 7:00-11:00. **Credit cards** All major. **Pets** Small dogs allowed. **Facilities** Elevator, laundry service, patio, room service. **Parking** Les Halles, access: rue du Pont-Neuf. **How to get there** (Map 7) Bus: All to Châtelet – Metro and RER: Châtelet-Les Halles. **Open** All year.

The Tonic Hotel was formed out of two earlier hotels. In the section known as the *Roule,* the rooms are decorated identically, with beautiful beamed ceilings and walls of exposed stone behind the bed. The dark, Spanish-style furniture goes well with the predominantly red color scheme. The rooms are spacious, and have very modern bathrooms where you can relax with a jacuzzi or steam bath. As for the "Tonic" section, it has just been renovated, with much improved decor in the bedrooms (yellow walls and floral fabrics) and comfort in the bathrooms. The reception area and breakfast room are in the "Tonic" section. Down on the rue du Roule, you will have a beautiful view of the Les Halles Gardens and Saint-Eustache Church. Looking the other way, you'll see the busy rue de Rivoli with its large department stores.

Hôtel des Tuileries

10, rue Saint-Hyacinthe - 75001 Paris
Tel. (0)1 42 61 04 17 - Fax (0)1 49 27 91 56
Famille Poulle-Vidal
E-mail: htuileri@aol.com

Category ★★★ **Rooms** 26 with air-conditioning, telephone, bath, WC, hairdryer, cable TV. **Price** Single 690-990F / 105,19-150,92€, double 790-1400F / 120,43-213,43€ – Special rates on request. **Meals** Breakfast 70F / 10,67€, served 6:30-12:00. **Credit cards** All major. **Pets** Dogs allowed. **Facilities** Elevator, laundry service, room service. **Parking** Place du Marché Saint-Honoré. **How to get there** (Map 7) Bus: 21, 27, 29, 68, 69, 72 and 95 – Metro: Tuileries, Pyramides. **Open** All year.

The Hôtel des Tuileries is tucked away behind the rue Saint-Honoré. The street is somewhat dark and sad, but very quiet; the bustling Palais-Royal and Les Halles are but a few steps away. The reception area is very inviting, leading to the basement sitting rooms, a small reading room and the breakfast room where guests can enjoy a buffet with favorite foods from their own country (cereals, toast, cheeses, etc.). This hotel is much fussed over by its owners, who have just equipped all the rooms with excellent bedding, and set up a superb suite on the last floor. All the bedrooms are uniquely decorated, some with Polish-style beds and tapestries in an 18th-century Chinese style, others with painted furniture and pastel colours, or a "Gustavian" atmosphere. Rooms are quiet because of double-glazing and air-conditioning, and they can be combined to form an apartment for four people. It is said that Marie-Antoinette stayed in this pleasant place. Note the proximity of the Saint-Roch Church, one of the most beautiful baroque churches in Paris.

Hôtel Violet

7, rue Jean-Lantier - 75001 Paris
Tel. (0)1 42 33 45 38 - Fax (0)1 40 28 03 56
M. Hakim Sifaoui
Web: www.franceparishotelviolet.com - E-mail: hotel.violet@wanadoo.fr

Category ★★★ **Rooms** 30 with soundproofing, telephone, bath or shower, WC, hairdryer, cable and satellite TV, minibar, safe – 1 for disabled persons. **Price** Single 606-726F / 92,51-110,83€, double 812F / 123,96€, triple 1010F / 153,97€; Jul and Aug −100F / 15,24€ and one night free of charge for any stay 4 nights or longer. **Meals** Breakfast (buffet) 55F / 8,38€, served 7:30-10:00. **Credit cards** All major. **Pets** Dogs not allowed. **Facilities** Elevator, laundry service. **Parking** Hôtel de Ville and Quai de Gesvres. **How to get there** (Map 2) Bus: All to Châtelet – Metro: Châtelet – RER: Châtelet-Les Halles. **Open** All year.

Via an alternating combination of windows and glass doors, the Hôtel Violet is wide open onto the quiet rue Jean Lantier running between the Châtelet Theater and the rue de Rivoli. Reception, lounge and bar are on the large and airy ground floor, along with a winter garden. The rooms, regularly freshened up, are all decorated on the same model: painted classical-style furniture and quilted cottons for the bedsteads, along with matching curtains. Some will comfortably sleep three people without need of the traditional emergency bed, usually uncomfortable and takes up space. These are genuine "triples" with the "double" part giving onto the street, and the "single" area onto the courtyard. This allows sharing without too much proximity. The breakfast buffet is laid out in a 16th-century, cut-stone vaulted room. The welcome is charming.

Hôtel Washington Opéra

50, rue de Richelieu - 75001 Paris
Tel. (0)1 42 96 68 06 – Fax (0)1 40 15 01 12
M. Boudaa
Web: www.hotel-wo.com - E-mail: info@hotel-wo.com

Category ★★★★ **Rooms** 36 with air conditioning and soundproofing, bath, WC, hairdryer, telephone, satellite TV, radio, minibar and safe – 2 for disabled persons. **Price** Single 980-1180F / 149,40-179,89€, double 1180-1400F / 179,89-213,43€; extra bed 300F / 46€. **Meals** Breakfast 80F / 13€, served 7:00-12:00. **Credit cards** All major. **Pets** Dogs not allowed. **Facilities** Elevator, bar, laundry service, room service, terrace. **Parking** Carrousel du Louvre **How to get there** (Map 7) Metro: Palais-Royal-Musée du Louvre – Bus: 29, 39, 48 and 67. **Open** All year.

Jean-Philippe Nuel has beautifully decorated the new Hôtel Washington Opéra. The luminous, elegant entrance is divided between the reception area and a lounge in pearl gray and straw-colours, the tones of the panoramic painting decorating the wall. On each floor a spacious corridor leads to the bedrooms. Most of them have been laid out with furniture in a *Directoire*-style, harmonizing with the beautiful beige and red fabrics. While the storage space is rather small, the red marble bathrooms are quite comfortable. The upper floors offer larger, "Gustavian" rooms, with canopied four-poster beds. The blue and white tones reinforce the atmosphere of elegance and refinement which is present all around the hotel. The same spirit can be found in the lower level bar, where breakfast is served in the morning. This level opens onto rue Montpensier. The hotel's double access gives it the advantage of being even closer to the Palais-Royal Gardens.

Grand Hôtel de Besançon

56, rue Montorgueil – 75002 Paris
Tel. (0)1 42 36 41 08 –Fax (0)1 45 08 08 79
M. Boudaa
Web: www.gd-besancon.com – E-mail: info@gd-besancon.com

Category ★★★ **Rooms** 9 and 11 junior suites, with soundproofing, telephone, bath or shower, WC, hairdryer, satellite TV, radio. **Price** Single 680F / 103,67€, double 720-980F / 109,76-149,40€, extra bed 150F / 22,87€. **Meals** Breakfast 40F / 6,10€, served 7:00-11:30. **Credit cards** All major. **Pets** Dogs not allowed. **Facilities** Elevator, laundry service. **Parking** Saint-Eustache (rue de Turbigo) and rue Saint-Denis. **How to get there** (Map 7) Bus: 20, 29, 39 – Metro: Étienne-Marcel, Sentier – RER: Châtelet-Les Halles. **Open** All year.

The rue Montorgueil is one of those historical streets of the capital that you should visit in this district once known as the "Belly of Paris"; it has kept all the life and noises of Parisian markets. If you decide to stay at the Grand Hôtel de Besançon you will have to cope with the robust street noises, unless you take a room on the courtyard. The hotel has acquired an adjoining store in which they will place the reception area (formerly located up a steep staircase). This expansion also includes the construction of six more bedrooms. At present identically decorated, the rooms are simple and in good taste. Louis Philippe-style furniture and floral cotton fabrics give them an incontestable provincial charm. Those on the back are light and attractive. A new breakfast room should also see the light of day. Meanwhile, go and have coffee and *tartines* on the rue Montorgueil where you may see the last street urchins of Paris.

Hôtel Lautrec et Marivaux

8-10, rue d'Amboise
75002 Paris
Tel. (0)1 42 96 67 90 – Fax (0)1 42 96 06 83
M. Franck du Chapelet

Category ★★★ **Rooms** 60 with air-conditioning and soundproofing, with telephone, bath or shower, WC, hairdryer, satellite TV, minibar and safe. **Price** Single 900-1200F / 137,20-182,94€, double 940-1200F / 143,30-182,94€. **Meals** Breakfast (buffet) 75F / 11,43€, served 6:30-10:00. **Credit cards** All major. **Pets** Dogs allowed. **Facilities** Elevator, bar, laundry service. **Parking** Place de la Bourse. **How to get there** (Map 7) Metro: Richelieu-Drouot – Bus: 20, 39, 48, 67, 74 and 85. **Open** All year.

The Opera Comique is just a few steps away, the Drouot auction rooms hardly any further: this is an interesting location for this hotel, which has just been entirely redone. Behind its 18th-century façade (put on the historical register) are small, comfortable and functional bedrooms. Their modern decoration blends smooth, light-colored wood furniture with blue and yellow fabrics, forming a cheerful ensemble of Scandinavian spirit. People looking for a little extra charm should book the rooms with exposed old beams and freestone walls (the only reference to the age of the place). Let us also mention the "privilege" rooms with such pleasant services as fresh flowers, free mini-bar and Internet access on television. The abundant buffet breakfast is served in the vaulted basement. Very elegant oak-cased lounges with a real library, comfortable Napoleon III armchairs and some beautiful contemporary paintings. A welcoming hotel, very professional and seriously run.

Hôtel Libertel l'Horset Opéra

18, rue d'Antin
75002 Paris
Tel. (0)1 44 71 87 00 – Fax (0)1 42 66 55 54
M. Antoine Fanton

Category ★★★★ **Rooms** 53 and 1 suite with soundproofing and air-conditioning, telephone, bath, WC, hairdryer, cable TV, minibar and safe. **Price** Single 1340F / 204,28€, double 1480F / 225,62€, suite 2800F / 426,86€. **Meals** Breakfast (buffet) 80F / 12,20€, served 6:30-11:00. **Credit Cards** All major. **Pets** Dogs allowed (+100F / 15,24€). **Facilities** Elevator, bar, laundry service, room service, snacks available at lunchtime (mealtime special 90F / 13,72€). **Parking** Place du Marché Saint-Honoré. **How to get there** (Map 7) Bus: All to Opéra – Metro: Opéra – RER: Auber. **Open** All year.

On a quiet street near Opera Garnier, a location which tourists like for both shopping and culture, the Libertel Horset Opera is a good, classic 4-star hotel. The building is chic, with a beautiful 1900 base. The oak-paneled reception rooms open wide onto the street; they have recently been redecorated in warm rust-brown colors. The bar, restaurant and lounge provide constant service. The bedrooms, decorated in the same monochromes, are spacious, cozy, pleasant and comfortable beyond reproach. Efficient room service. A hotel of discreet and elegant professionalism.

Hôtel de Noailles

9, rue de la Michodière – 75002 Paris
Tel. (0)1 47 42 92 90 – Fax (0)1 49 24 92 71
Mme Falck
E-mail: tulip.inn.hotel.de.noailles@wanadoo.fr

Category ★★★ **Rooms** 61 with soundproofing and air-conditioning, telephone, bath, WC, hairdryer, cable TV. **Price** Single and double 650-950F / 99,09-144,83€; extra bed 200F / 30,49€ (free until 12 year). **Meals** Breakfast (buffet) 50F / 7,62€, served 7:00-11:00; snacks available, room service until 22:00. **Credit cards** All major. **Pets** Dogs allowed. **Facilities** Elevator, laundry service, patio and terraces. **Parking** Rue de la Chaussée-d'Antin. **How to get there** (Map 7) Bus: All to Opéra – Metro: Opéra, Quatre-Septembre. **Open** All year.

The neighborhood around the Opéra is popular with tourists for its proximity to the Grand Louvre as well as to the large department stores. The Noailles, centered around a small garden and a terrace on the *troisième étage*, is a refuge of peace and comfort. It is decorated in a contemporary Japanese style. The already vast reception area has just been enlarged; it now comprises a lounge-library with a fireplace, a bar and, as before, a breakfast area opening onto a garden where you can be served when the weather is nice. The same modern decor can be found in the bedrooms, which have been entirely redecorated (including the bathrooms) with wood and a discreet touch of color. Some open onto terraces and those on the top floor have a balcony. On each floor, there is a small lounge for entertaining guests, with a soft drink machine. The staff is friendly and attentive. The same can be said of the house dog, Nils.

Le Stendhal Hôtel

22, rue Danielle-Casanova - 75002 Paris
Tel. (0)1 44 58 52 52 - Fax (0)1 44 58 52 00
Mlle Anne Onno
E-mail: h1610@accor-hotels.com

Category ★★★★ **Rooms** 17, 1 suite and 2 junior suites with air-conditioning, soundproofing, telephone, bath or shower, WC, hairdryer, minibar, safe, cable TV. **Price** Single and double 1470-1660F / 224,10-253,07€, suite 1850-2050F / 282,03-312,52€. **Meals** Breakfast 100F / 15,24€, served from 6:30 (weekend: from 7:00). **Credit cards** All major. **Pets** Dogs allowed. **Facilities** Elevator, laundry service, bar, room service. **Parking** Place Vendôme. **How to get there** (Map 7) Bus: All to Opéra — Metro: Opéra and Tuileries — RER: Auber. **Open** All year.

Rue Saint-Honoré, Place Vendôme and rue de la Paix - the whole district stands for the French luxury and chic of the leading *couturiers* and prestige jewelers. The Stendhal Hôtel is in a discreet building on the quiet rue Danielle-Casanova, right next to this world center for window-shopping. In this small hotel, a lot of care has been given to decor quality and the well-being of the guests. The bedrooms differ in size; those with a number ending in a 3 are in yellow and blue with large window-lit bathrooms. Just as pretty are others in reds and greens, along with the suites; one of them plays on "The Red and the Black" theme in tribute to Stendhal. Double-glazing and air-conditioning guarantee quiet. Room service helps you relax and enjoy your room, since the pretty lounge of the hotel shares its small space with the reception desk. Along with a beautiful room in the basement for breakfast service, this is a refined hotel.

Hôtel des Chevaliers

30, rue de Turenne
75003 Paris
Tel. (0)1 42 72 73 47 - Fax (0)1 42 72 54 10
Mme Truffaut

Category ★★★ **Rooms** 24 with soundproofing, telephone, bath, WC, hairdryer, satellite TV and safe. **Price** Single and double (depending on the season) 660-750F / 100,62-114,34€, twin 700-840F / 106,71-128,06€, triple 874-1014F / 133,43-154,80€ – Special rates in Aug. Low season: Jan – end Feb, Jul – end Aug and Nov – end Dec. **Meals** Breakfast 50F / 7,62€ , buffet 80F / 12,20€, served 7:00-10:30. **Credit cards** Amex, Visa, Eurocard, MasterCard. **Pets** Dogs allowed. **Facilities** Elevator, laundry service, room service. **Parking** At 16 rue Saint-Antoine. **How to get there** (Map 2) Bus: 20, 29, 65, 76 and 96 – Metro: Chemin Vert, Saint-Paul. **Open** All year.

Very near the famous Place des Vosges, the Carnavalet Museum and the Picasso Museum in the historic Marais quarter, the Chevaliers occupies a 17th-century building of which there are still original vestiges, such as the half-timbering in the stairwell and the well in the cellar. The recent renovation has brightened up the lounge walls and chairs in their yellow and blue prints, which go well with the new style furniture in cherry wood. All the rooms are different and a discreet stylisation of the furniture pieces has been adopted, which gives full decorative effect to the prettily coordinated drapes and bedspreads. Many thoughtful details further add to guests' pleasure: fresh flowers in the rooms, baskets of fruit, chocolates on the pillows, toiletries in the bathrooms. These are touches you'd normally expect in a more luxurious hotel.

Little Palace Hôtel

4, rue Salomon-de-Caus - 75003 Paris
Tel. (0)1 42 72 08 15 - Fax (0)1 42 72 45 81
M. Lebail
E-mail : littlepalacehotel@compuserve.com

Categorie ★★★ Rooms 57 with soundproofing and air-conditioning, telephone, bath or shower, WC, hairdryer, minibar, cable TV – 1 for disabled persons. **Price** Single 720F / 109,76€, double 820F / 125,01€, triple 980F / 149,40€. **Meals** Breakfast (buffet) 60F / 9,15€, served 7:00-10:30. **Credit Cards** All major. **Pets** Small dogs allowed. **Facilities** Elevator, bar, laundry service, patio, restaurant, room service. **Parking** Rue Saint-Martin. **Hoaw to get there** (Map 7) Bus: 20, 38, 39 and 47 – Metro: Réaumur-Sébastopol and Strasbourg-Saint-Denis. **Open** All year.

Bordering Les Halles and Beaubourg, this small hotel had no qualms about calling itself Little Palace. In this lively district, the street alongside the Emile Chautemps public garden looks residential. The entrance is attractive, with an anteroom leading to the reception area, which extends into a library lounge. This is also where two dining rooms are found: the bistro under a glass roof, and the restaurant with neoclassical architecture, more elegant and suitable for taking one's time. The bedrooms have had a full face-lift: cerused furniture brightened by lively colors. All of them have improved in comfort, from air-conditioning to bathroom fixtures. The rooms on the upper floors are above the trees, and therefore have an open view. This is a good address, and nearby you can discover Passage Brady (at 33 boulevard de Strasbourg), full of Indian and Pakistani restaurants with their spicy fragrances under the glass roof.

Hôtel Pavillon de la Reine

28, place des Vosges - 75003 Paris
Tel. (0)1 40 29 19 19 - Fax (0)1 40 29 19 20
Mme Véronique Ellinger
Web: www.pavillon-de-la-reine.com - E-mail: pavillon@club-internet.fr

Category ★★★★ **Rooms** 34, 13 apartments and 8 duplexes, with air-conditioning, soundproofing, telephone, bath, WC, cable TV, hairdryer, safe and minibar – 4 for disabled persons. **Price** Single 1750-1900F / 266,79-289,65€, double 1950-2150F / 297,28-327,77€, "luxe room" 2150-2550F / 327,77-388,74€, suite 2600F-3950F / 396,37-603,05€. **Meals** Continental breakfast 115F / 17,53€, buffet 145F / 22,11€, served 7:00-11:00 (in room at any time). **Credit cards** All major. **Pets** Dogs allowed. **Facilities** Elevator, laundry service, bar, patio, room service (24h). **Parking** Private garage (25 spaces). **How to get there** (Map 2) Bus: 20, 29, 65, 69, 76, 96 – Metro: Bastille, Saint-Paul. **Open** All year.

This is an admirable hotel in a historic setting. The hotel consists of two buildings, one dating from the 17th century and the other harmoniously rebuilt around a small courtyard. The entry lobby is superb, all green with its Virginia creeper and geraniums. The *Haute Epoque* interiors reflect the architectural style, with carved oak covering the lounge walls, beautiful antique pieces and deep armchairs in smart polished leather. The rooms, and above all, the suites, have very fine fittings and offer warmth and comfort, with colors and materials of great refinement. Whichever side they are on, looking over the garden or the flowery courtyard, they are very quiet. The service is discreet and stylish, and the welcome personal. This is a very fine hotel on one of the most exceptional sites of all Paris.

Hôtel Beaubourg

11, rue Simon-Lefranc
75004 Paris
Tel. (0)1 42 74 34 24 - Fax (0)1 42 78 68 11
M. and Mme Morand

Category ★★★ **Rooms** 28 with telephone, bath or shower, WC, hairdryer, satellite TV, minibar. **Price** Single 590-630F / 89,94-96,04€, double 590-700F / 89,94-106,71€. **Meals** Breakfast 42F / 6,41€, served 7:00-11:00. **Credit cards** All major. **Pets** Dogs allowed. **Facilities** Elevator. **Parking** Beaubourg. **How to get there** (Map 2) Bus: 29, 38, 47 and 75 – Metro: Rambuteau - RER: Châtelet-Les Halles. **Open** All year.

Rue Simon-Lefranc is right behind the Georges Pompidou Center and its facade of colored piping, shafts and air-conditioning vents. In contrast, the Hôtel Beaubourg is in an old house that has conserved its ceiling beams, fine samples of exposed stonework and a vaulted basement. The decor is classical, with leather sofas and armchairs in the entrance-reception-lounge area. Most of the rooms are large and equipped with functional furniture, headboards in copper, cane, or bamboo. These are enhanced by the flowery fabrics of the curtains and bedspreads. The whole effect has a velvety feel and is well-maintained. On the ground floor, rooms number 1 and 2 seem a bit dark, but Room 4 has a small private terrace, particularly attractive in the summertime. If you are lucky to find it free then take it, but if not, do not embarrass the owners by insisting on it, since the others are all just as comfortable and pleasant (notably Room 51, under the roof, which is slightly smaller but really lovely). The welcome appears a little reserved, but this is only a first impression soon forgotten as M. and Mme. Morand are attentive to ensure that all goes well.

Hôtel de la Bretonnerie

22, rue Sainte-Croix-de-la-Bretonnerie - 75004 Paris
Tel. (0)1 48 87 77 63 - Fax (0)1 42 77 26 78
Mlle Valérie Sagot
Web: www.labretonnerie.com

Category ★★★ **Rooms** 24 and 6 junior suites with soundproofing, bath or shower, WC, hairdryer, telephone, cable TV, safe, minibar. **Price** Single and double 660-830F / 100,62-126,53€, junior suite 1050F / 160,07€. **Meals** Breakfast 60F / 9,15€, served 7:15-10:30. **Credit cards** Visa, Eurocard, MasterCard. **Pets** Dogs allowed. **Facilities** Elevator. **Parking** Place Baudoyer (rue de Rivoli), rue Lobau and garage nearby. **How to get there** (Map 2) Bus: All to Hôtel de Ville – Metro: Hôtel de Ville. **Closed** Aug.

In a private residence dating from the 17th century, just a few steps from the Pompidou Center and Picasso Museum, the Hôtel de la Bretonnerie has pleasant surprises in store for its visitors. In fact, each year the owners transform and redecorate a few rooms, and thus they all acquire their own special atmosphere and decor. Most rooms are vast, and those with mezzanine ceilings will sleep three people. Bright colors for some, softer lines for others, they are all decorated in a warm, refined style (numbers 17 and 31 a little less so, but then when everything is so lovely, one tends to be demanding.) The bathrooms are very well equipped, and some have large windows opening onto the courtyard. A cozy atmosphere of comfort reigns throughout the hotel. The very friendly reception and the constant efforts made for the well-being of guests make this a precious address in the heart of Paris.

Hôtel Caron de Beaumarchais

12, rue Vieille–du–Temple
75004 Paris
Tel. (0)1 42 72 34 12 – Fax (0)1 42 72 34 63
M. Bigeard

Category ★★★ **Rooms** 19 with air-conditioning, soundproofing, bath, WC, telephone, satellite TV, hairdryer and minibar. **Price** Single and double 730 and 810F / 111,29 and 123,48€. **Meals** Breakfast 54F / 8,24€, brunch 78F / 11,90€, served 7:30-12:00. **Credit cards** All major. **Pets** Dogs not allowed. **Facilities** Elevator. **Parking** Place Baudoyer (rue de Rivoli) and rue Lobau. **How to get there** (Map 2) Bus: 29, 67, 69, 75, 76 and 96 – Metro: Hôtel de Ville and Saint-Paul-Le Marais. **Open** All year.

This comfortable 18th–century house has been restored in homage to the famous author of "The Marriage of Figaro", who lived on this street in the Marais district. The decoration was carried out by Alain Bigeard, who researched and took inspiration from documents of the time. In the lobby, the walls are covered with embroidered fabric reproduced from original designs, and there are Burgundian stone floors, along with such curios as a plaster medallion, a well–worn chair, a backgammon table, etc. The same elegance is found in the comfortable bedrooms and the bathrooms, whose tiles are modeled on those made in Rouen and Nevers. They have good soundproofing and those onto the street are brighter. The welcome is sympathetic to your needs, and the location is ideal on the corner of rue de Rivoli, right between the Marais quarter and the Ile Saint-Louis.

Hôtel des Deux Iles

59, rue Saint-Louis-en-l'Ile
75004 Paris
Tel. (0)1 43 26 13 35 - Fax (0)1 43 29 60 25
M. Buffat

Category ★★★ **Rooms** 17 with air-conditioning, bath or shower, WC, telephone, cable TV and hairdryer. **Price** Single 760F / 115,86€, double 890F / 136,44€. **Meals** Breakfast 55F / 8,38€, snacks available. **Credit cards** Visa, Eurocard, MasterCard, Amex. **Pets** Dogs not allowed. **Facilities** Elevator. **Parking** 2, rue Geoffroy l'Asnier and the square in front of Notre-Dame. **How to get there** (Map 2) Bus: 24, 63, 67, 86, 87 and 89 – Metro: Pont-Marie. **Open** All year.

Monsieur and Madame Buffat have converted two buildings into hotels of charm: the Hôtel des Deux Iles and the Lutèce, set between a former archibishop's palace, the Church of Saint-Louis-en-l'Ile, and *Bertillon*, famous for its ice cream. We have chosen the Deux Iles for its atmosphere – English with a tinge of the exotic; flowery fabrics as well as painted cane and bamboo furniture are the main features of the decor. The small but delightful bedrooms have more light, and are slightly larger on the street side. Provençal fabrics replace the chintzes used in the lounge, and the bathrooms are lined with gleaming blue tiles. Everything here is comfortable, including the beautiful vaulted breakfast room. This hotel has maintained a clientele loyal to an establishment that is so much in harmony with the whole of Ile Saint-Louis. Considering its location, it is wise to book well in advance.

Grand Hôtel Jeanne d'Arc

3, rue de Jarente
75004 Paris
Tel. (0)1 48 87 62 11 - Fax (0)1 48 87 37 31
M. and Mme Mesenge

Category ★★ **Rooms** 36 with telephone, bath or shower, WC, hairdryer, cable TV. **Price** Single 320-410F / 48,78-62,50€, double 325-500F / 49,55-76,22€, triple 550F / 83,85€, 4 pers. 620F / 94,52€. **Meals** Breakfast 35F / 5,34€, served 7:00-11:00. **Credit cards** Visa, Eurocard, MasterCard. **Pets** Dogs allowed. **Facilities** Elevator. **Parking** 16, rue Saint-Antoine. **How to get there** (Map 2) Bus: 29, 69, 76, 96 – Metro: Saint-Paul-Le Marais. **Open** All year.

The Marais is famous for its historic Place des Vosges, prestigious town houses, and the Picasso and Carnavalet Museums. It is less known for the small "village" just off the noble square: the Place du Marché Sainte-Catherine and the rue de Jarente, where you'll find the small Hôtel Jeanne d'Arc. Named after the Jeanne d'Arc Convent, which was demolished in the 18th century to make way for a market, the hotel reflects the simple charm of the neighborhood, which abounds with picturesque cafés and outdoor restaurants on tree-lined sidewalks. The hotel's reception area-lounge and the breakfast room with white crocheted tablecloths give it the feel of a family home. The house provides several types of rooms: four are quite small but reasonably priced, especially if there are two of you. Other rooms are larger, some are very large and can accommodate four people. They are all nicely decorated, some with *trompe-l'œil* tiling in the bathrooms. From most of the rooms on the upper floors, you will have a view over the flower-filled inner courtyards and the rooftops of this enchanting neighborhood. An excellent little hotel.

Hôtel du Jeu de Paume

54, rue Saint-Louis-en-l'Ile - 75004 Paris
Tel. (0)1 43 26 14 18 - Fax (0)1 40 46 02 76
Mme Elyane Prache
Web: www.hoteldujeudepaume.com

Category ★★★★ **Rooms** 30 and 1 junior suite with terrace, bath, WC, telephone, cable TV, hairdryer, minibar. **Price** Single and double 950-1495F / 144,83-227,91€, junior suite 2625F / 400,18€. **Meals** Breakfast 80F / 12,20€; snacks available. **Credit cards** All major. **Pets** Dogs allowed (+50F / 7,62€). **Facilities** Elevator, office facilities, sauna, gym, patio, bar. **Parking** 2, rue Geoffroy l'Asnier and the square in front of Notre-Dame. **How to get there** (Map 2) Bus: 24, 63, 67, 86, 87 and 89 – Metro: Pont-Marie. **Open** All year.

This hotel is on the site of an authentic old palm-tennis court. The spacious interior has been entirely and artfully restructured by creating a series of galleries and mezzanines to form a dynamic and decorative architectural arrangement. On the ground floor is an intimate lounge-bar and a warm, inviting breakfast room decorated in a Provençal style; on the mezzanine you will find a reading room, and off the galleries are the elegant and comfortable rooms with beautiful bathrooms. Our favorite ones open onto the garden, with a special mention for Room 108 whose windows overlook the large magnolia tree. We are more reserved about the few duplex rooms; their staircase is quite steep. The delicious breakfasts include excellent homemade preserves. A highly available staff will welcome you.

Hôtel Libertel Grand Turenne

6, rue de Turenne
75004 Paris
Tel. (0)1 42 78 43 25 – Fax (0)1 42 74 10 72
Mme Biagini

Category ★★★ **Rooms** 36 and 5 junior suites with soundproofing, telephone, bath or shower, WC, hairdryer, minibar, cable TV – 2 for disabled persons. **Price** Single 918,34F / 140€, double 989,94F / 150€, junior suite (2-3 pers.) 1305,35F / 199€ – Special rates in Jul and Aug and Nov to end Mar (low season). **Meals** Breakfast 81,99F / 12,5€, served 7:00-10:30. **Credit cards** All major. **Pets** Dogs allowed. **Facilities** Elevator, laundry service. **Parking** 16, rue Saint-Antoine. **How to get there** (Map 2) Bus: 20, 29, 65, 69, 76, 96 – Metro: Saint-Paul-Le Marais, Bastille. **Open** All year.

There is nothing to criticize about this comfortable hotel in Le Marais, just a few steps from the Place des Vosges, with a welcoming reception area enlivened by energetic and qualified personnel. It leads into a colorful lounge opening wide onto the street. On the left, the especially pretty breakfast lounge puts you in a good mood to start the day. The rooms are rather standardized and not large, but again there is nothing to criticize, since they are well-maintained, pleasantly furnished with good comfort, as are the bathrooms. Please note that some are reserved for non-smokers and that two of them have a view over the gardens of the Hôtel de Sully (on the other hand, numbers 101 and 201 face a wall). Hardly more expensive, those on the last floor (with mansard ceilings) are more charming. Your should book them in priority; they are also larger. A friendly hotel, efficiently managed.

Hôtel de Lutèce

65, rue Saint-Louis-en-L'Ile
75004 Paris
Tel. (0)1 43 26 23 52 - Fax (0)1 43 29 60 25
M. Buffat

Category ★★★ **Rooms** 23 with air-conditioning, telephone, bath or shower, WC, cable TV. **Price** Single 750F / 114,34€, double 890F / 135,68€, triple 1000F / 152,45€. **Meals** Breakfast 60F / 9,15€, served 7:30-12:00. **Credit cards** All major. **Pets** Dogs not allowed. **Facilities** Elevator. **Parking** 2, rue Geoffroy l'Asnier and the square in front of Notre-Dame. **How to get there** (Map 2) Bus: 24, 63, 67, 86, 87 and 89 - Metro: Pont-Marie. **Open** All year.

The intimate lighting, the beautiful bouquet of fresh flowers, the ancient floor in polished tiles, the fire burning in the hearth - all tempt you to come in through the reception door. Everything has been thought out with taste and care. The rooms are not very big, and furnished *a minima* but always with a certain note to personalize each: a lithograph by Braun Van Velde or Nicki de Saint-Phalle, a fine mirror and so on. A choice of pretty fabrics livens up the rooms, which have kept their fine ceiling beams. The top floor has mansard ceilings, with number 661 the largest room and 662 the sunniest. Generally speaking, there is more light on the side of the courtyard. The other rooms are smaller, except those made to accommodate three people. To dine near the hotel, let us recommend *Le Monde des Chimères* and *Au Gourmet de l'Isle*; at tea-time, chocolate-lovers will enjoy *La Charlotte de l'Isle* or *Bertillon* with its famous ice-cream. This hotel and district summarize all the charms of Paris.

Hôtel de Nice

42 *bis*, rue de Rivoli
75004 Paris
Tel. (0)1 42 78 55 29 - Fax (0)1 42 78 36 07
M. and Mme Vaudoux

Category ★★ **Rooms** 23 with soundproofing, telephone, bath or shower, WC, TV. **Price** Single 380F / 58,01€, double 500F / 76,22€, triple 630F / 96,04€. **Meals** Breakfast 35F / 5,34€, served 7:00-10:00. **Credit cards** Visa, Eurocard, MasterCard. **Pets** Dogs not allowed. **Facilities** Elevator. **Parking** Hôtel de Ville. **How to get there** (Map 2) Bus: All to Hôtel de Ville – Metro: Hôtel de Ville. **Open** All year.

At first you cannot make out the entrance of the Hôtel de Nice with its reception on the *premier étage*. On the other hand, you realize straight away that you are in a hotel with atmosphere as the book-binding covering on the walls, with its graphics repeated on the kilims covering the floors, is a handsome backing for the numerous cover pages of *Le Petit Journal* that decorate the walls. The lounge also serves as breakfast room and has the same feeling as a private house, with its very personal choice of antique furniture as well as a fine collection of 19th-century paintings, including one very large portrait. The rooms also reflect the owners' whims with Napoleon III chairs, a Louis-Philippe desk, cupboards, old doors, and always lots of prints, pastels and so on. The top-floor rooms have mansard ceilings and a small balcony. Among the largest, they are able to put up several guests. Other rooms are usually smaller but also quieter (we were not impressed by 15 and 16, all set up lengthwise). You find here an unexpected atmosphere right in the center of Paris between Le Marais and the Hôtel de Ville.

Hôtel Rivoli Notre-Dame

19, rue du Bourg-Tibourg - 75004 Paris
Tel. (0)1 42 78 47 39 - Fax (0)1 40 29 07 00
Mme Capdeville
Web: hotelrivolinotredame.com - E-mail: rivoli.notre.dame@wanadoo.fr

Category ★★★ **Rooms** 31 with bath, WC, hairdryer, telephone, satellite TV, minibar, safe. **Price** Single 550F / 83,85€, double 700F / 106,71€, triple 760F / 115,86€. **Meals** Breakfast 45F / 6,86€, served 7:00-11:00. **Credit cards** All major. **Pets** Dogs not allowed. **Facilities** Elevator. **Parking** Hôtel de Ville. **How to get there** (Map 2) Bus: All to Hôtel de Ville – Metro: Hôtel de Ville. **Open** All year.

We have been charmed and seduced by the new oriental decoration of the reception area and lounge at Hôtel Rivoli Notre-Dame. Created by Jacques Garcia, it is inspired by the Alhambra, and it is a total success (room number 2 on the ground floor has also benefited from this flurry of renovation). The upper floors, which for the moment have retained their old decor, are charming and in good taste. There is a friendly feeling to the rooms with their white molded bases, fine stripes on the walls, bedspreads in quilted Vichy, and soft color tones. Everything is well-done apart from the single rooms facing a wall on the courtyard. The bathrooms are comfortably equipped and some have daylight. The rooms in the corner (ending in 6) are the largest, as are those on the last floor. Here you touly get your money's worth in a friendly district bordering Le Marais, Les Halles, Beaubourg and the Hotel de Ville.

Hôtel Saint-Merry

78, rue de la Verrerie
75004 Paris
Tel. (0)1 42 78 14 15 - Fax (0)1 40 29 06 82
M. Crabbe

Category ★★★ **Rooms** 11 and 1 suite with soundproofing, telephone, bath or shower, 9 with WC. **Price** Single or double 480-1200F / 73,18-182,94€, suite (2 pers., free for children under 12 years) 1800F / 274,41€; extra bed 250F / 38,11€. **Meals** Breakfast 55F / 8,38€. **Credit cards** Visa, Eurocard, MasterCard, Amex. **Pets** Dogs allowed. **Parking** Saint-Merry/Rivoli (access: rue Saint-Bon). **How to get there** (Map 2) Bus: All to Châtelet – Metro: Châtelet, Hôtel de Ville – RER: Châtelet-Les Halles. **Open** All year.

This hotel is named after the Saint-Merry Church, which was built in the Renaissance in the flamboyant Gothic style. The hotel occupies the building adjoining the church, once the residence of the canons of Saint-Merry. The owner, Monsieur Crabbe, has restored the hotel to its original splendor. He spent years buying period pieces from auctions and second-hand sales, suchas furniture and old panels, which were reconstructed as headboards and closet doors. Ironwork, another major Gothic art form, is also well-represented in the chandeliers and large candelabras that have been transformed into beautiful lamps. All this is excellently done with taste and discretion, so that certain outdated details can be forgiven. You should see Room 9, traversed by a magnificent flying buttress, or the huge suite, known as "The Apotheosis of Saint Merry", but this must not keep you from trying the other rooms with their *Haute Epoque* tonality and embroidered bed sheets. All are highly recommendable, except number 11. The whole effect is surprising and makes the Saint Merry an authentic, original work of art by a passionate man sure that his dream will soon come to completion.

Hôtel Saint-Paul-Le Marais

8, rue de Sévigné – 75004 Paris
Tel. (0)1 48 04 97 27 – Fax (0)1 48 87 37 04
Mme Leguide
Web: www.hotel-paris-marais.com – E-mail: stpaulmarais@hotellerie.net

Category ★★★ **Rooms** 27 with soundproofing, bath or shower, WC, telephone, cable TV, hairdryer, safe. **Price** Single 590-690F / 89,94-105,19€, double 690-790F / 105,19-120,43€, "De luxe" with jacuzzi 920-1090F / 140,25-166,17€, triple 890-990F / 135,68-150,92€, 4 pers. 990-1140F / 150,92-173,79€. **Meals** Breakfast (buffet) 60F / 9,15€, served 7:00-10:15. **Credit cards** All major. **Pets** Dogs not allowed. **Facilities** Elevator, laundry service, patio, bar, beauty parlor (and water therapy), whirlpool. **Parking** 16, rue Saint-Antoine. **How to get there** (Map 2) Bus: 29, 69, 76, 96 – Metro: Saint-Paul. **Open** All year.

For those who love the Marais district, its private mansions, craftwork boutiques next to the fashion stores and proximity to the world-famous Place des Vosges, this hotel is ideal. Only a few pillars and some worked wood remain from the earlier building. The reception area, bar and lounge have just been renovated, the cold modern style has been replaced by a warm, classical decor with red carpeting and shimmering fabrics highlighting the mahogany period furniture. The bedrooms, some of which still display their ancient ceiling beams, are more disappointing. Renovated in combined blues and pinks, they remain simple and rather standard, but there are welcome extras such as an electric kettle with tea and coffee bags. Only number 317 (called "De luxe") has a more successful decor (which in future should also be applied to the rest of the rooms). In addition, the hotel provides a beauty parlor in the basement. Family-style welcome.

Hôtel du Vieux Marais

8, rue du Plâtre
75004 Paris
Tel. (0)1 42 78 47 22 – Fax (0)1 42 78 34 32
Mme Marie-Hélène Rumiel

Category ★★ **Rooms** 30 with air-conditioning (24 with soundproofing) telephone, bath or shower, WC, hairdryer, satellite TV and safe. **Price** Single 550-660F / 83,85-91,47€, double 660-690F / 100,62-105,19€; extra bed 100F / 15,24€. **Meals** Breakfast 40F / 6,10€, served 7:30-10:00. **Credit cards** Visa, Eurocard, MasterCard. **Pets** Dogs not allowed. **Facilities** Elevator. **Parking** Hôtel de Ville, Place Baudoyer (rue de Rivoli) and Centre Pompidou. **How to get there** (Map 2) Bus: All to Hôtel de Ville – Metro: Hôtel de Ville – RER: Châtelet-Les Halles. **Open** All year.

We do not need to sing the praises of the Marais another time. This district deserves to be a place of sojourn just as much as the left bank. The Hôtel du Vieux Marais is located on a small and very quiet street between Beaubourg and the rue des Archives. This year, it has finally completed a renovation program which lasted quite a long time. Walls were moved, rooms suppressed, glass roofs added and so on. The hotel is now offering a sober, contemporary decor. There is air-conditioning, light-oak furniture, low-tension lamps for warm, diffuse light, soft tones enlivened by the red leather of a chair or a stool by Poltrona Frau, superb bathrooms with aged marble and brightly shining faucets. The owners obviously like modern design, but, above all, quality and comfort. The lounge and reception (where you will be amiably greeted by Jean-Philippe) were also part of this beautiful renovation.

Hôtel Abbatial Saint-Germain

46, boulevard Saint-Germain - 75005 Paris
Tel. (0)1 46 34 02 12 - Fax (0)1 43 25 47 73
M. Michel Sahuc
E-mail: abbatial@hotellerie.net

Category ★★★ **Rooms** 43 with air-conditioning and soundproofing, bath or shower, WC, telephone, minibar, safe, TV. **Price** Single 600-700F / 91,47-106,71€, double 740-880F /112,81-134,16€, triple 980F / 149,40€. **Meals** Breakfast (buffet) 50F / 7,62€, served 7:00-10:30; free breakfast for any stays 4 nights or longer, Jan to end Mar, Jul and Aug and Nov to Dec 23. **Credit cards** Visa, Eurocard, MasterCard, Amex. **Pets** Dogs not allowed. **Facilities** Elevator. **Parking** Maubert. **How to get there** (Map 2) Bus: 24, 47, 63, 86 and 87 – Metro: Maubert-Mutualité – RER: Saint-Michel. **Open** All year.

The Abbatial Saint Germain is only two hundred yards from Notre-Dame (six bedrooms overlook the cathedral, of which number 61 is the largest). The lobby, which has been expanded, sets the general tone with Louis XVI-style furniture, encouraging guests to enjoy the adjoining lounge and bar. The same attention to detail can be found in the bedrooms; pink wall fabrics are coordinated with thick *piqué* bedspreads and furniture also in a Louis XVI-style. The atmosphere is peaceful, protected from the street and boulevard by double-glazing on the windows. The bathrooms are comfortable, but closet space is a bit on the small side. Breakfasts are served in a barrel-vaulted room where the rustic stones have been softened with beautiful Louis-Philippe medallion-back chairs and a large mural landscape. The effect is lovely, and a welcome change from the rustic coldness of many hotels with an overdone decor of exposed stones.

Hôtel des Carmes

5, rue des Carmes
75005 Paris
Tel. (0)1 43 29 78 40 – Fax (0)1 43 29 57 17
M. Paul Dauban

Category ★★ **Rooms** 30 with soundproofing, bath or shower, WC, telephone and TV – 1 for disabled persons. **Price** Single 455-555F / 69,36-84,61€, double 510-610F / 77,75-92,99€, triple 780F / 118,91€ – Special rates in low season on request. **Meals** Breakfast 35F / 5,34€, served 7:00-11:30. **Credit cards** All major. **Pets** Dogs not allowed. **Facilities** Elevator. **Parking** Maubert. **How to get there** (Map 2) Bus: 24, 47, 63, 84, 86, 87, 89 – Metro: Maubert-Mutualité. **Open** All year.

After eight months of work, the Hôtel des Carmes has found its youth again. The entry hall is spacious with a corner lounge which is agreeable, but without surprises, and a breakfast room. The bedrooms are much warmer, while their vivid and attractive colors form the basis of a functional decor. Small furniture in yellow and Sienna red, both modern and practical, go well with the curtains and bedcovers mainly in blues. The rooms on the street are generally larger and also have an attractive view on the ancient Convent of the Carmelites. Don't be afraid of noise, as the street is narrow with little traffic. On the courtyard side the rooms are smaller and less expensive, apart from some which are designed for three people. Those on the *sixième étage* are nice and large. The small bathrooms have also been renovated, and most of them have showers. All is impeccably maintained. Hospitality and service are always available. On leaving of the hotel one has a very pleasant direct view of the Panthéon.

Hôtel Claude Bernard

43, rue des Écoles - 75005 Paris
Tel. (0)1 43 26 32 52 - Fax (0)1 43 26 80 56
M. Paul Bénichou
Web: hotelclaudebernard.com - E-mail: claudebernardhotel@minitel.net

Category ★★★ **Rooms** 34 with bath or shower, WC, telephone, minibar, cable TV.
Price Single 530-720F / 80,80-111,29€, double 660-980F / 100,62-149,40€, triple
800-1150F / 121,96-175,32€; extra bed 120F / 18,29€; −20-30% for stays 4 nights or
longer (excluding trade fair periods) in Jan, Feb and Aug. **Meals** Breakfast (buffet) 50F /
7,62€, served 7:30-10:30. **Credit cards** All major. **Pets** Small dogs allowed. **Facilities**
Elevator, room service 7:30AM to 9:30PM (3:00PM Sunday), sauna. **Parking** Private at
200m (150F/22,87€ /day). **How to get there** (Map 2) Bus: 24, 47, 63, 84, 86, 87 and
89 – Metro: Maubert-Mutualité. **Open** All year.

At number 43 rue des Ecoles, the ox blood red-lacquered front of
the Claude Bernard Hotel entices you to push the door and go
in. In the reception lounge you can see a superb Renaissance cabinet
and a major 17th-century painting; however you also notice the state
of the carpeting and the lack of upkeep (but we have been assured
that the lounge has been renovated this year). On the other hand, the
room where breakfast is served is very pleasant. Indeed, the hotel has
changed owners, and an important renovation program has been
going on since the winter of 1998. Thus, the last floor is entirely
renovated, as are two bedrooms on the *cinquième étage*, and the result
is completely satisfying. Rooms ending with numbers in 1 or 2 are
now being redone. Of course, these are the only rooms we
recommend since the others have only been "freshened up" in the
meantime. There is a great deal of contrast, but this is a promising
hotel and very well situated.

42

Hôtel Colbert

7, rue de l'Hôtel-Colbert
75005 Paris
Tel. (0)1 43 25 85 65 – Fax (0)1 43 25 80 19
Mme Sylvie Alvarez

Category ★★★ **Rooms** 36 and 2 suites with air-conditioning and soundproofing, with bath, WC, telephone, minibar, safe, satellite TV. **Price** Single 1890F / 288,13€, double 1990F / 303,37€, suite (1-4 pers.) 2500-2800F / 381,12-426,86€ – Special rates on request Nov to Christmas Day, Jan – end Feb, Jul and Aug). **Meals** Breakfast 95F / 14,48€, served 7:00-11:00. **Credit cards** All major. **Pets** Dogs not allowed. **Facilities** Elevator, laundry service, bar. **Parking** Rue Lagrange. **How to get there** (Map 2) Bus: 21, 24, 27, 38, 47, 85, 96 – Metro: Maubert-Mutualité – RER: Saint-Michel. **Open** All year.

The Colbert has the quiet air of a private hotel with its entry court and elegant reception rooms. You find this same elegance in the rooms with their *toile de Jouy* paper and Persian decor; they are assembled with a small alcove in molded wood. Rooms with a number ending with a 5 or 7 are decorated with furniture pieces in cerused oak and bathrooms in marble. They are pleasant and more modern, but rather lacking in character. Those with numbers ending with a 1 or 2 have a view of Notre-Dame and some of the Seine *quais*. In this previously working-class district, the rooms were often small, and this is also the case with those of the Colbert. For this reason, and because many of them could do with renovations (especially in the bathrooms), we only recommend this hotel in the low season. Until the planned redecoration is carried out, we find the prices too expensive. Nevertheless, the location of the hotel and the quality of its service should compensate for this inconvenience.

Hôtel du Collège de France

7, rue Thénard – 75005 Paris
Tel. (0)1 43 26 78 36 – Fax (0)1 46 34 58 29
M. Taltavull
E-mail: taltavul@club-internet.fr

Category ★★ **Rooms** 29 (certain ones adjoining) with soundproofing, bath or shower, WC, hairdryer, telephone, safe, TV satellite – 1 for disabled persons. **Price** Single 500F / 76,22€, double 550F / 83,85€; extra bed 100F / 15,24€ (free of charge for children under 14). Jan 5 – end Feb, Jul, Aug and Christmas Day (–50F / 7,62€). **Meals** Breakfast 35F / 5,34€, served 7:00-10:30. **Credit cards** All major. **Pets** Dogs not allowed. **Facilities** Elevator, laundry service. **Parking** Rue Lagrange. **How to get there** (Map 2) Bus: 21, 24, 27, 38, 47, 63, 85, 86, 87 – Metro: Maubert-Mutualité, Cluny-La Sorbonne – RER: Saint-Michel-Notre-Dame. **Open** All year.

Founded in 1530 by Francis I, the Collège de France allows free access to its classes by the best-known intellectuals and scientists of France. The hotel is very close by, hidden in a small street linking the boulevard Saint-Germain and the rue des Ecoles. A statue of Joan of Arc welcomes you in the entry hall that stretches into a very pleasing small lounge, with comfortable Louis XVI-style armchairs in front of a perfect fireplace for winter evenings. Right behind is a cozy dining room where the breakfasts make for a pleasant way to start your day. The small rooms are all in the same style: plain cream wallpaper with elegant gilded brass wall-lamps. Only the pretty fabrics of the curtains and bedcovers are varied. All is certainly very simple, but one feels at home and the prices are truly easy on the pocket.

Hôtel de l'Espérance

15, rue Pascal
75005 Paris
Tel. (0)1 47 07 10 99 - Fax (0)1 43 37 56 19
M. and Mme Aymard

Category ★★ **Rooms** 38 with soundproofing, bath or shower, WC, telephone, hairdryer, cable TV – 1 for disabled persons. **Price** Single 400F / 60,98€, double 450-500F / 68,60-76,22€; extra bed 100F / 15,24€. **Meals** Breakfast 35F / 5,34€, served 7:30-11:00. **Credit cards** All major. **Pets** Dogs not allowed. **Facilities** Elevator, bar, 2 patios. **Parking** Rue des Patriarches (at 50m). **How to get there** (Map 10) Bus: 27, 47, 83, 91 – Metro: Censier-Daubenton, Gobelins. **Open** All year.

In a quiet spot near the rue Mouffetard, this is one of the most pampered hotels in Paris, thanks to owners who have given it so many personal touches. The reception area, opening onto the vast lounge bar, shows the attention paid to detail: white crocheted doilies over the tables and armchairs, personal curios and photos, many green plants and flower bouquets. The same care stands out upstairs in the bedrooms: patinated furniture, beautiful figured carpets, solid-color wallpaper coordinated with fabrics in pastel shades of blue, yellow and salmon-pink; lovely marble baths. The twenty-two four-poster beds have elegantly draped cotton canopies, and the larger rooms have a convertible sofa convenient for families. The bedrooms are impeccably maintained and always look bright and gay. At the rear of the hotel they get the morning sun, on the street side the evening sun. You can enjoy your breakfast in the lovely dining room looking out on the garden, or on one of the flower-filled patios. The Espérance (meaning "expectation") offers excellent value for the price.

Familia Hôtel

11, rue des Écoles
75005 Paris
Tel. (0)1 43 54 55 27 - Fax (0)1 43 29 61 77
M. Éric Gaucheron

Category ★★ **Rooms** 30 with bath or shower, WC, telephone, minibar, cable TV – 1 for disabled persons. **Price** Single 390-580F / 59,46-88,42€, double 450-590F / 68,60-89,94€. **Meals** Breakfast 35F / 5,34€, served 7:00-10:00. **Credit cards** All major. **Pets** Small dogs allowed. **Facilities** Elevator. **Parking** Rue Lagrangen and Maubert. **How to get there** (Map 2) Bus: 24, 47, 63, 67, 86, 87 and 89 – Metro: Maubert-Mutualité, Jussieu. **Open** All year.

The Familia is a genuine small district hotel surrounded by *bouquinistes*, bistros and stores for colors and paints. Under the leadership of the young Eric Gaucheron and his family, the hotel is changing fast and in each room Eric has tried to add "that little extra touch" in order to personalize them. For half of them, he has got an artist to make some very pretty sepia wall frescos of Parisian scenes. They are being redecorated with elegant fabrics and small pictures bought in the flea markets hang in the redecorated corridors. In the staircases there are reproductions of ancient tapestries. Some rooms have a tiny little balcony; they have been given a table and two chairs, and you have the pleasure of having a horticultural breakfast, since there are flower boxes at every window. Our only reservations concerned the singles and Rooms 11, 31 and 41, a bit too small and not as well-done. Lastly, the breakfast room with its Louis-Philippe chairs and cherry bookcase has all the airs of a lounge, to give a final family touch to the particularly warm and attractive overall effect.

Grand Hôtel Saint-Michel

19, rue Cujas - 75005 Paris
Tel. (0)1 46 33 33 02 - Fax (0)1 40 46 96 33
M. Belaid
Web: grand-hotel-st-michel.com - E-mail: grand.hotel.st.michel@wanadoo.fr

Category ★★★ **Rooms** 39 and 7 suites with air-conditioning and soundproofing, telephone, bath or shower, WC, hairdryer, satellite TV, minibar, safe – 2 for disabled persons. **Price** Single 690F / 105,19€, double 890F / 135,68€, triple or suite 1290F / 196,66€. **Meals** Breakfast 55F / 8,38€, served 7:00-10:30. **Credit cards** All major. **Pets** Small dogs allowed. **Facilities** Elevator, bar, laundry service, room service. **Parking** 20, rue Soufflot. **How to get there** (Map 2) Bus: 21, 27, 38, 63, 82, 84, 85, 86, 87 and 89 – Metro: Cluny-La Sorbonne – RER: Luxembourg. **Open** All year.

At two paces from the Sorbonne and boulevard Saint-Michel, the Grand Hôtel Saint-Michel was fully renovated in 1997. Two lounges face the entry door while one also shelters the bar. The floor is in beige marble and there is stucco work on the ceiling for a very classical decor, with Directory-style furniture and reproductions of famous pictures. The whole effect is still rather stuffy and cold, but the rooms themselves are very attractive. With a blue, green or salmon dominant color, matching the painted furniture pieces, curtains and bedspreads, they have one or two elegant old prints of Parisian scenes. The bathrooms are white with just one touch of color from the large basins varying with the rooms. Breakfasts are served in the basement and, despite the lack of any window, the room is comfortable and bright – a good place to start any day. The service is friendly and attentive.

Hôtel des Grandes Écoles

75, rue du Cardinal-Lemoine – 75005 Paris
Tel. (0)1 43 26 79 23 – Fax (0)1 43 25 28 15
Mme Le Floch
Web: www.hotel-grandes-ecoles.com

Category ★★ **Rooms** 50 with bath or shower, WC, telephone – 3 for disabled persons. **Price** Double 550-710F / 83,85-108,24€; extra bed 100F / 15,24€. **Meals** Breakfast 45F / 6,86€. **Credit cards** Visa, Eurocard, MasterCard. **Pets** Dogs tolerated. **Facilities** Elevator, garden. **Parking** Private location, 12 spaces (120F / 18,29€ /day). **How to get there** (Map 2) Bus: 47, 84 and 89 – Metro: Cardinal-Lemoine, Monge. **Open** All year.

At the end of a private alleyway and sunk in its full garden (not just a patch of lawn but a genuine garden), this hotel is a small marvel. How indeed could one imagine that such a space could survive so close to the Panthéon and the Contrescarpe, true to itself and escaping the fevered attention of developers, and still hold its prices down. This is however the case with these three houses forming the Hôtel des Grandes Ecoles. The place still keeps its unchangeable air of the provinces, which gives it so much charm. There is 19th-century furniture in fruitwood in the reception lounge, lace-skirted tables, straw-seated chairs and a piano in the breakfast room. The rooms mostly have flowered wallpaper but if you do not like such a dated setting, you can choose from those recently installed in the annex buildings. You can have your breakfast outside in the greenery accompanied only by the twittering of the sparrows. Your welcome will be friendly, quite natural and family-style.

Hôtel des Grands Hommes

17, place du Panthéon
75005 Paris
Tel. (0)1 46 34 19 60 – Fax (0)1 43 26 67 32
Mme Moncelli – Mme Gernigon

Category ★★★ **Rooms** 32 with air-conditioning, bath, WC, telephone, cable TV, hairdryer, minibar. **Price** Single and double 650-800F / 99,09-121,96€. **Meals** Breakfast (buffet) 50F / 7,62€. **Credit cards** All major. **Pets** Dogs allowed. **Facilities** Elevator, laundry service, room service until 6PM. **Parking** 20, rue Soufflot. **How to get there** (Map 2) Bus: 21, 27, 38, 82, 84, 85 and 89 – Metro: Cardinal-Lemoine – RER: Luxembourg. **Open** All year.

If the Hôtel des Grands Hommes refers to those illustrious personages buried in the Panthéon, you should also not forget that in one of its rooms André Breton and Philippe Soupault invented so-called "automatic writing". The reception area has moulded pink-orange walls and 1930s armchairs covered in the same shades, expressing the *bourgeois* decoration and comfort of the hotel. Its former owners, vigorous inventors of surrealism, might well have objected to this but it still remains very attractive to passing guests. All decorated in pastel shades, the rooms are comfortable, bright and prettily furnished, often with metal or gilt aluminium bedsteads. In addition to a sublime view over the famous square, the *cinquième* and *sixième étages* offer a wide view over the roofs of Paris with Sacré-Coeur in the distance. Excepting these two floors, the room numbers ending in 4 are small, on the courtyard side and less welcoming. The *quatrième étage* is rather less well furnished. There is a breakfast room in the vaulted cellar with plenty of warmth, and the welcome is very friendly.

49

Hôtel-Résidence Henri IV

50, rue des Bernardins - 75005 Paris
Tel. (0)1 44 41 31 81 - Fax (0)1 46 33 93 22
Mme Moncelli - Mme Gernigon
E-mail: henri4@hotellerie.net

Category ★★★ **Rooms** 8 (2 with air-conditioning) and 5 apartments with bath, WC, minibar, safe, telephone, cable TV, kitchen – 1 for disabled persons. **Price** Double 700-900F / 106,71-137,20€, apart. (1-4 pers.) 1000-1200F / 152,45-182,94€; in low season: double 600-700F / 91,47-106,71€, apart. 800-1000F / 121,96-152,45€. **Meals** Breakfast 40F / 6,10€, served 7:30-10:30. **Credit cards** All major. **Pets** Dogs allowed. **Facilities** Elevator, laundry service. **Parking** Saint-Germain (at 200m). **How to get there** (Map 2) Bus: 24, 47, 63, 84, 86, 87 and 89 – Metro: Maubert-Mutualité. **Open** All year.

On the corner of the rue des Ecoles and Square Paul Langevin, the rue des Bernardins ends in *impasse* where you will find the Hôtel Résidence Henri IV. All the bedrooms overlook the lush public garden and, to the right, the façade of the former Ecole Polytechnique. The interior has been totally renovated. There are comfortable bedrooms and apartments decorated with cheerful colors thick carpeting. Especially designed for the hotel, the oak furniture includes molded headboards in the shape of antique pediments, framed on each side by shelves, and a beautiful painted wardrobe in some rooms. The immaculate baths are modern and functional, and a number of them overlook a small, flower-filled courtyard. The two-room apartments can accommodate up to four people. Like the bedrooms, they have a well-equipped kitchenette (intended to prepare small snacks). A elegant and comfortable hotel, particularly for longer stays.

Hôtel des Jardins du Luxembourg

5, impasse Royer-Collard
75005 Paris
Tel. (0)1 40 46 08 88 – Fax (0)1 40 46 02 28
Mme Touber

Category ★★★ **Rooms** 27 with air-conditioning, soundproofing, bath or shower, WC, telephone, minibar, satellite TV, safe – 2 for disabled persons. **Price** Single and double 810-860F / 123,48-131,11€. **Meals** Breakfast (buffet) 50F / 7,62€, served 7:00-11:00. **Credit cards** All major. **Pets** Dogs not allowed. **Facilities** Elevator, laundry service, sauna, patio, bar. **Parking** 20, rue soufflot. **How to get there** (Maps 1 and 2) Bus: 21, 27, 38, 82, 84, 85, 89 - RER: Luxembourg. **Open** All year.

Open since 1995, this hotel located in a small, cul-de-sac near the Luxembourg Gardens is a true success, as far as decoration is concerned. In the lobby, kilims brighten the pale oak parquet floors; next to the red mahogany reception desk are two Oriental-style armchairs, a Chinese *cloisonné* table and an incandescent fireplace (for once, the flames look quite real). The bedrooms are small but very comfortable and elegant, with textured wallpaper, friezes matching the drapes and bedspreads, bronze beds, contemporary wooden furniture, statuettes and handsome sconces. Except for the two on the ground floor, our favorites are those overlooking the street, where noise is not a problem because the windows are double-glazed and there is no traffic outside. The bathrooms are decorated with gleaming tiles as is the breakfast room, where you will find an extremely warm decor in tones of green and orange. Excellent welcome.

Hôtel du Levant

18, rue de la Harpe – 75005 Paris
Tel. (0)1 46 34 11 00 – Fax (0)1 46 34 25 87
Mme Sophie Abonnat
E-mail: hlevant@club-internet.fr

Categorie ★★★ Rooms 42 and 4 suites with air-conditiong and soundproofing, bath or shower, WC, hairdryer, telephone, minibar, safe, cable TV. **Price** Single 560F / 85,37€, double 760-850F / 115,86-129,58€, triple 960-1260F / 146,35-192,09€, suite (5 pers.) 1800F / 274,41€. **Meals** Breakfast 40F / 6,10€, served 7:00-10:30. **Credit cards** Visa, Eurocard, MasterCard, Amex. **Pets** Dogs allowed. **Facilities** Elevator, laundry service, room service. **Parking** Saint-Michel (70F / 10,67€ /day). **How to get there** (Map 2) Bus: 21, 24, 27, 38, 47, 63, 85, 86, 87 and 96 – Metro: Cluny-La Sorbonne and Saint-Michel – RER: Saint-Michel-Notre-Dame. **Open** All year.

The rue de la Harpe is a pretty paved street at the corner of Saint-Michel and Saint-Germain. In contrast to its neighbors, it has almost escaped the fast food stores and you can still find a few Parisian bistros among the Greek taverns. The Hôtel du Levant will soon have completed its renovation program. In the bedrooms, the result is good comfort and personalized decoration with brand new carpeting and fabrics. The lounge overlooking the boisterous street is luminous and convivial, and the red velvet *portière* gives it a theatrical look. The breakfast room, with photos relating the history of the hotel, will soon be enlarged. The only outdated aspect is the furniture in some rooms. But the assets of this hotel are a stay in the Quartier Latin at a reasonable price and the rooms, themselves, which for the most part are fairly large and which can be combined to accommodate up to five people. Here you are only a short distance from the RER leading to the airports.

Hôtel Libertel Maxim

28, rue Censier
75005 Paris
Tel. (0)1 43 31 16 15 – Fax (0)1 43 31 93 87
Mme Chantal Pécou

Category ★★ **Roopms** 36 with soundproofing, bath or shower, WC, telephone, minibar, cable TV – 1 for disabled persons. **Price** Single 570,70F / 87€, double 636,30F / 97€. **Meals** Breakfast (buffet) 45,92F / 7€, served 7:00-10:30. **Credit cards** All major. **Pets** Dogs not allowed. **Facilities** Elevator, laundry service, room service. **Parking** Rue Censier. **How to get there** (Map 10) Bus: 27, 47, 67 and 89 – Metro: Censier-Daubenton – RER and train station: Gare d'Austerlitz. **Open** All year.

The Hôtel Libertel Maxim has an attractive location right next to the Jardin des Plantes and the National Museum of Natural History, while also being close to the rue Mouffetard, the Gobelins and the *Grande Mosquée*, the great mosque of Paris, where you should not miss having tea. The entry hall sets the style of the decor: well-kept, comfortable and refined, mixing the classical with the modern. Classical with the old prints and *toile de Jouy* which are found both in the ravishing lounge in raspberry and in all the rooms, set in pinks, blues or grays. The carefully modern in the furniture makes best use of available space. The rooms are small (apart from two of them) but really sweet. The bathrooms are just as well-thought-out with pretty designer basins. Despite clever arrangement, some rooms with showers do seem a bit too small; but all are well-soundproofed. One third of the rooms have the advantage of opening onto the small patio. There is a pretty breakfast room lit by a glass roof. The welcome is quite aimiable.

Hôtel Libertel Quartier Latin

9, rue des Écoles
75005 Paris
Tel. (0)1 44 27 06 45 - Fax (0)1 43 25 36 70
M. Philippe Roye

Category ★★★ **Rooms** 29 with air-conditioning, soundproofing, bath or shower, WC, hairdryer, telephone, minibar, safe, cable TV – 1 for disabled persons. **Price** Single 1016,73F / 155€, double 1082,33-1213,52F / 165-185€; extra bed 196,79F / 30€. **Meals** Breakfast (buffet) 78,71F / 12€, served 7:00-10:30. **Credit cards** All major. **Pets** Dogs allowed. **Facilities** Elevator, laundry service, room service. **Parking** Boulevard Saint-Germain. **How to get there** (Map 2) Bus: 24, 47, 63, 86, 87 and 89 – Metro: Cardinal-Lemoine. **Open** All year.

Midway between the Panthéon and the Arab World Institute, this hotel is rather different from the traditional hotels of this quarter as it is completely contemporary with a sober and soothing decor, yet warmed by the velvet fabrics and sombre Lapacho ebony wood found throughout. The tall bookshelves in the entry-lounge, photos of writers and quotations printed on the carpeting - all celebrate the literary life of the quarter. The decorator Didier Gomez designed the furniture and lighting, as well as the desk-consoles in the rooms, the headboards rich in carved wood and a whole series of accessory furniture all in pure lines. The curtains are linen while the bathrooms are superb in white, heightened by a wide frieze in molten glass. There are three ambiances: vanilla, off-white and sky-blue. All the rooms have a very high standard of comfort, but we stress that the more expensive ones offer more for your money given their size. Breakfast is carefully prepared and served in the same atmosphere as the rest of the hotel. Both reception and service are fully competent.

Minerve Hôtel

13, rue des Écoles
75005 Paris
Tel. (0)1 43 26 26 04 / (0)1 43 26 81 89 – Fax (0)1 44 07 01 96
Sylvie and Éric Gaucheron

Categorie ★★ **Rooms** 54 with soundproofing on the street side, bath or shower, WC, telephone, satellite TV and 24 with hairdryer. **Price** Single 390-610F / 59,46-92,99€, double 460-610F / 70,13-92,99€, triple 640F / 97,57€. **Meals** Breakfast 37F / 5,64€, served 7:00-10:00. **Credit cards** All major. **Pets** Dogs not allowed. **Facilities** Elevator, drinks machine. **Parking** Boulevard Saint-Germain. **How to get there** (Map 2) Bus: 24, 47, 63, 67, 86, 87 and 89 – Metro: Cardinal-Lemoine and Jussieu. **Open** All year.

We already quite liked the small Familia Hôtel for its welcome and personality. Its owners have now bought the hotel next-door, and we trust they will endow this new acquisition with the same qualities. By now the main work has been achieved: public areas, soundproofing, security. What remains to be done is the renovation of the bedrooms, although twenty-one are already finished. For the moment, we only recommend these (to be specified when you reserve), knowing that the rest will soon be completed. Wool carpeting, wallpaper in delicate tones, quality fabrics, period furniture in carved cherry wood, all are of rather classical inspiration apart from rooms ending with a 3 or 4 which have cerused wood furniture. Generally speaking, the rooms have a pleasant size and have been made agreeable and comfortable. Some have a small, furnished balcony overlooking the street, where you can have breakfast (on the side of the courtyard the view is slightly limited). The prices charged and the great deal of attention given to comfort will soon make the Minerve one of the nice little hotels of charm in the Quartier Latin.

Hôtel de Notre-Dame

19, rue Maître–Albert
75005 Paris
Tel. (0)1 43 26 79 00 – Fax (0)1 46 33 50 11
M. J. P. Fouhety

Category ★★★ **Rooms** 34 with soundproofing, bath or shower, WC, telephone, cable TV, hairdryer, safe and minibar. **Price** Single and double 750-850F / 114,34-129,58€. **Meals** Breakfast 40F / 6,10€. **Credit cards** All major. **Pets** Dogs not allowed. **Facilities** Elevator, bar, laundry service. **Parking** Rue Lagrange. **How to get there** (Map 2) Bus: 21, 24, 27, 38, 47, 85, 96 – Metro: Maubert-Mutualité and Saint-Michel – RER: Saint-Michel-Notre-Dame. **Open** All year.

In this typical small street of the old quarter of Paris, one immediately notices the Hôtel de Notre-Dame which has retained its huge frontage, which in earlier days must have been a shop window. An assembly of modern panelling has now reshaped this area, with the original beams, some beautiful antique furniture pieces and a superb tapestry giving full character to the reception, bar and corner-lounges of the ground floor. The small rooms have retained their beamed ceilings from earlier times and some slabs of cut-stone walls. For the rest, some beautiful contemporary furniture in light oak mingles in full harmony with the pastel shades of the walls and the sanded glass of the panelling closing off the bathrooms. All is very comfortable and intimate. The place is in close proximity of Notre-Dame, the Seine and the small book stalls or *bouquinistes*.

Le Notre-Dame Hôtel

1, quai Saint-Michel
75005 Paris
Tel. (0)1 43 54 20 43 – Fax (0)1 43 26 61 75
M. J. P. Fouhety

Categorie ★★★ Rooms 23 and 3 junior suites with air-conditioning and soundproofing with telephone, bath, WC, hairdryer, cable TV, safe and minibar. **Price** Single and double 680-1100F / 103,67-167,69€, triple and junior suite (3-4 pers.) 1500F / 228,67€. **Meals** Breakfast 40F / 6,10€, served 7:00-10:00. **Credit cards** All major. **Pets** Dogs not allowed. **Facilities** Elevator. **Parking** Square in front of Notre-Dame. **How to get there** (Map 2) Bus: 21, 24, 27, 38, 47, 85 and 96 – Metro and RER: Saint-Michel. **Open** All year.

Just opposite Notre-Dame, this hotel is set in a corner, at the axis of the Seine river, which sparkles in the rising sun and caresses the banks of Ile Saint-Louis upstream. One could not dream of a better spot. The rooms with a number ending with a 2 or a 3 are the best-oriented to enjoy the view, but the others are well-situated all the same, apart from those ending with a 5 and overlooking the courtyard, which we advise against. They are all renovated (except perhaps on the *deuxième étage*). They are comfortable and well-soundproofed, decorated with beautiful mural fabrics enhanced with ancient engravings and designer furniture in light-colored wood. Behind frosted glass walls are delightful bathrooms blending green marble and white tiles. The reception lounge is large and low-roofed (with exposed beams), embellished by some beautiful pieces of antique furniture; the walls are covered with a tartan fabric in old yellow and brick red. There is also a beautiful series of old engravings representing the quays of the Seine river. You can compare them with the present-day cityscape that can be seen from one of its eight windows.

Hôtel Observatoire-Luxembourg

107, boulevard Saint-Michel – 75005 Paris
Tel. (0)1 46 34 10 12 – Fax (0)1 46 33 73 86
M. Bonneau
E-mail: sa.sol@wanadoo.fr

Category ★★★ **Rooms** 37 (18 with air-conditioning) with bath or shower, WC, telephone, safe, cable TV. **Price** Single 720-820F / 109,76-125,01€, double 780-935F / 118,91-142,54€, triple 1200F / 182,94€; –15% Mon to Fri (excluding trade fair periods). **Meals** Breakfast 53F / 8,09€. **Credit cards** All major. **Pets** Dogs allowed. **Facilities** Elevator, laundry service. **Parking** 20, rue Soufflot. **How to get there** (Map 10) Bus: 21, 27, 38, 82 and 85 – RER: Luxembourg. **Open** All year.

Lovers of chlorophyll and the wide open spaces will surely appreciate this hotel facing the corner of the Luxembourg gardens, which are open to the public from 7:30 in summer time. Depending on floor and outlook, they can admire all the full greenery of the Luxembourg (room numbers ending with a 6 or 7), the garden of the Institute for the Deaf (room numbers with a 3, 4 or 5), or the generous leafiness of the trees of Boulevard Saint-Michel (all other rooms). Apart from their view, the rooms are pleasantly decorated in cheerful tones with cerused beech wood furniture and coordinated fabrics. All have carefully maintained bathrooms in gray marble. A marble floor is also in the reception area, and the lounge is very welcoming with its corner settee in rainbow colors. The breakfast room is in bistro style but a little cold, although delicately lit by a series of low-power lamps. The welcome is friendly and attentive.

Hôtel du Panthéon

19, place du Panthéon – 75005 Paris
Tel. (0)1 43 54 32 95 – Fax (0)1 43 26 64 65
Mme Moncelli
E-mail: henri4@hotellerie.net

Category ★★★ **Rooms** 34 with air-conditioning, soundproofing, telephone, bath or shower, WC, hairdryer, cable TV and minibar. **Price** Single and double 700-1000F / 106,71-152,45€. **Meals** Breakfast (buffet) 50F / 7,62€, served 7:00-10:30. **Credit cards** All major. **Pets** Dogs not allowed. **Facilities** Elevator, laundry service, room service until 4PM. **Parking** Place du Panthéon, 20, rue Soufflot. **How to get there** (Map 2) Bus: 21, 27, 38, 82, 84, 85 and 89 – Metro: Cardinal-Lemoine – RER: Luxembourg. **Open** All year.

The Hôtel du Panthéon adjoins the Hôtel des Grands Hommes and they are both managed by the same family. The lobby and lounges on the ground floor are vast, airy and very welcoming. The cozy and intimate bedrooms have just been renovated in the style of a large 18th-century house. Thus, a "revisited" Louis XVI style leads the decor: patinated furniture, lined wood trim accompanied by beautiful fabrics. Many refined details make these rooms particularly comfortable and well-done. The bathrooms have benefited from the same attention; one can see all the care given to the finishing touches and to comfort. Most of the rooms have an open view onto the Panthéon. The welcome is friendly, the staff eager to cater to all your needs. An excellent hotel where it is wise to reserve far in advance.

Hôtel Parc Saint-Séverin

22, rue de la Parcheminerie - 75005 Paris
Tel. (0)1 43 54 32 17 - Fax (0)1 43 54 70 71
M. Mulliez
E-mail: hotel.parc.severin@wanadoo.fr

Category ★★★ **Rooms** 27 (18 with air-conditioning) with soundproofing, telephone, bath or shower, satellite TV, hairdryer, minibar and safe. **Price** Single 540F / 82,32€, double 635-1550F / 96,81-236,30€. **Meals** Breakfast (buffet) 55F / 8,38€, served 7:00-11:30. **Credit cards** All major. **Pets** Dogs not allowed. **Facilities** Elevator, landry service. **Parking** Saint-Michel. **How to get there** (Map 2) Bus: 21, 24, 27, 47, 63, 67, 86, 87 and 96 – Metro: Cluny-La Sorbonne and Saint-Michel – RER: Saint-Michel-Notre-Dame. **Open** All year.

At the heart of the Latin Quarter, the Hôtel du Parc Saint-Séverin is on a pedestrian street free of the motor traffic of the Paris center. In this handsome building the large airy spaces have been preserved and the whole effect is very light. The sobriety of the colors and of the contemporary and 1930s furniture in the lounge again augment the sense of space. The same atmosphere is also found in the rooms; bright and often spacious, they are elegant and always agreeably decorated. It is not uncommon to find antique furniture pieces and paintings blending in easily with the more modern elements. If you want a view over the roofs, the Saint-Séverin cloisters and the gardens of the Cluny Museum, choose a room from the *cinquième étage* upwards. Those on the corner of the two upper floors also have terraces, some of them particularly large. The peace and quiet, comfort and smiling service are qualities that make the Parc Saint-Séverin a hotel much sought-after.

Le Relais Saint-Jacques

3, rue de l'Abbé-de-l'Épée – 75005 Paris
Tel. (0)1 53 73 26 00 – Fax (0)1 43 26 17 81
M. Bonneau
E-mail: nevers.luxembourg@wanadoo.fr

Category ★★★★ Rooms 23 with air-conditioning, soundproofing, bath, WC, hairdryer, telephone, minibar, trouser-press, safe, satellite TV – 1 for disabled persons. **Price** Single and double 1170-1400F / 178,37-213,43€ (in low season 970-1190F / 147,88-181,41€), triple 1160-1295F / 176,84-197,42€. **Meals** Breakfast (buffet) 72F / 10,97€, served 7:00-11:00. **Credit cards** All major. **Pets** Dogs not allowed. **Facilities** Elevator, bar, laundry service, room service, airport shuttle up on request. **Parking** Rue Soufflot. **How to get there** (Maps 2 and 10) Bus: 21, 27, 38 and 82 – RER: Luxembourg. **Open** All year.

As confirmed by a commemorative plaque a few meters away affixed to the church of Saint-Jacques-du-Haut-Pas, the Relais Saint-Jacques is on the road taken throughout the centuries by the pilgrims to Saint-Jacques of Compostella in Spain. Like the poet Rainer Maria Rilke, who stayed here for a year, modern-day travelers will also enjoy a very agreeable sojourn. Fully renovated from top to bottom in 1996, the hotel now offers large rooms as cozy as you might like them. They have embroidered hangings and classical decor, Louis XVI– or Directory-style, or even more original furnishings like in the five astonishing "Portuguese rooms". All are comfortable, perfectly equipped and sound-proofed even though there is very little traffic in this very green street which is almost like a square. The rooms are reasonably priced when taking their facilities into account. The breakfast is refined, with a fine reception area and ravishing lounge.It has antique furniture and a corner-bar where one is only too happy to linger.

Les Rives de Notre-Dame

15, quai Saint-Michel
75005 Paris
Tel. (0)1 43 54 81 16 – Fax (0)1 43 26 27 09
M. Degravi and Mlle Grace

Category ★ ★ ★ ★ **Rooms** 9 and 1 suite with air-conditioning, soundproofing, telephone, bath or shower, satellite TV, minibar – 1 for disabled persons. **Price** Single and double 1100, 1550 and 1750F / 167,69, 236,30 and 266,79€, suite 2500F / 381,12€ (2-4 pers.). **Meals** Breakfast 65F / 9,91€, served from 7:00. **Credit cards** All major. **Pets** Small dogs allowed. **Facilities** Elevator, bar, room service. **Parking** Square in front of Notre-Dame and rue Lagrange. **How to get there** (Map 2) Bus: 21, 24, 27, 47, 63, 67, 86, 87 and 96 – Metro and RER: Saint-Michel. **Open** All year.

Between the Place Saint-Michel and Notre-Dame, your windows (except if you stay in the suite on the top floor) will open out onto a real postcard scene: the quays of the Seine with their *bouquinistes* and the banks lower down where the lovers watch the river boats passing by. Excellent soundproofing allows you to take advantage of such a view without suffering from the noise. In each of the ten rooms, a particular decorative effect has been explored via a mixing of motifs and colors. The rooms are spacious with corner lounges where you can find a sofa-bed for an extra person (at no charge). The bathrooms are bright and elegant. On the *premier étage*, three just as charming small rooms are offered for single visitors, but they could also suit a couple. Les Rives de Notre-Dame is a hotel where you will appreciate a smiling welcome and particularly efficient service.

Hôtel Saint-Christophe

17, rue Lacépède – 75005 Paris
Tel. (0)1 43 31 81 54 – Fax (0)1 43 31 12 54
M. Robat
E-mail: hotelstchristophe@compuserve.com

Category ★★★ **Rooms** 31 with bath or shower, WC, telephone, minibar, satellite TV – 1 for disabled persons. **Price** Single 550F / 83,85€, double 680F / 103,67€; in low season (Jan to mid Mar, Jul and Aug, and Nov and Dec, except national holidays) 1 pers. 500F / 76,22€, 2 pers. 550F / 83,85€. **Meals** Breakfast 50F / 7,62€ (at no charge for those staying 3 nights or longer), served 7:00-10:00. **Credit cards** All major. **Pets** Dogs allowed. **Facilities** Elevator, laundry service, room service. **Parking** Rue du Marché des-Patriarches. **How to get there** (Maps 2 and 10) Bus: 47, 67 and 89 – Metro: Place Monge and Cardinal Lemoine – RER and train station: Gare d'Austerlitz. **Open** All year.

The Saint Christophe hotel is a few streets away from the Panthéon and the Jardin des Plantes - the first trees of which can be seen from the lounge. The warm little rooms with their light-colored walls have rustic furniture, curtains matching the *piqué* bedspreads and pleasant bathrooms in beige marble. Those with a number ending with a 2 are our favorites - they are set up in a corner and have two windows - but for a long stay, choose a room with a number ending with a 4 as the alcove framing the bed offers extra storage space. Families will want to reserve adjoining rooms. All are correctly soundproofed, but in summer, if you want to sleep with open windows, be sure to reserve a room giving onto rue de la Clef as they are quieter. For dinner you will find the restaurants of the Contrescarpe district close by, and on the square at no. 1, a plaque indicates the cabaret where Ronsard, Du Bellay and the members of the first *Pléiade* used to meet in the 17th century.

Hôtel Saint-Jacques

35, rue des Écoles
75005 Paris
Tel. (0)1 44 07 45 45 – Fax (0)1 43 25 65 50
M. Rousseau

Categorie ★★ **Rooms** 35 with soundroofing, telephone, satellite TV, 31 with WC, 32 with bath or shower and hairdryer (3 with washstand). **Price** Single 265F and 405-615F / 40,40€ and 61,74-93,76€, double 460-620F / 70,13-94,52€; triple 695F / 105,95€. **Meals** Breakfast 35F / 5,34€, served 7:30-10:30. **Credit cards** All major. **Pets** Dogs not allowed. **Facilities** Elevator, safe and fax. **Parking** Boulevard Saint-Germain. **How to get there** (Map 2) Bus: 24, 47, 63, 86 and 87 – Metro: Maubert-Mutualité. **Open** All year.

"Some people may not like the style of the hotel, but there is not much else that can be held against it" The owner has perfectly summed up what can be said of the Hôtel Saint Jacques, which occupies a beautiful apartment building from the beginning of the century. The inside has not changed much, and in the bedrooms one can find the molded or even painted ceilings, the stucco friezes, the mirror or pier frames that used to decorate lounges and dining rooms. That period seems to have greatly inspired the owner: he has covered the lounges and decorated the bedrooms with *trompe-l'œil* or mural paintings. If this is not your style, you will nevertheless be seduced by the comfort and the spaciousness of the bedrooms (more sober than the common area), very well maintained and with perfect bathrooms. You will find various toiletries and other attentions, such as an information booklet about the district. The corner rooms are our favorites, because you can see the Panthéon from their balconies. A hotel which, when all is said and done, has given itself personality.

Sélect Hôtel

1, place de la Sorbonne - 75005 Paris
Tel. (0)1 46 34 14 80 - Fax (0)1 46 34 51 79
M. Chabrerie
E-mail: select.hotel@wanadoo.fr

Category ★★★ Rooms 68 with air-conditioning and soundproofing, bath or shower, WC, telephone, hairdryer, satellite TV. **Price** Single 550F / 83,85€, double 670-805F / 102,14-122,72€, triple 920F / 140,25€; duplex 1250F / 190,56€. **Meals** Breakfast (buffet) 40F / 6,10€, served 7:00-10:30. **Credit cards** All major. **Pets** Dogs allowed (+30F / 4,57€). **Facilities** Elevator, patio, bar, room service. **Parking** 20, rue Soufflot (at 100m). **How to get there** (Map 2) Bus: 21, 27, 38, 63, 82, 84, 85, 86, 87 and 89 – Metro: Cluny-La Sorbonne – RER: Luxembourg. **Open** All year.

A Mecca for Parisian student life, the Place de la Sorbonne provides a pleasant and lively background to the Select Hôtel. It is a modern hotel, as can be seen from the contemporary graphics of its sign and the row of low-tension lamps in the lobby. Inside, a pyramid-shaped skylight illuminates the stairwell circling around a composition of various plants and leading to the bar and the room where excellent breakfasts are served. In most of the bedrooms, there is sleek, modern, beautifully made furniture. Some rooms have old exposed beams, others have wood panelling as smooth as enamel. Colors harmonize throughout. From the *sixième étage*, the view over the rooftops is magnificent. On the courtyard side, rooms look onto an ochre wall covered with jasmine – a touch of Italy in the heart of Paris. Decorated in blue or orange shades and combining the old and the new, they are completely quiet. The renovated bathrooms are superb. This is a fine hotel animated by an attentive and caring staff.

Hôtel de la Sorbonne

6, rue Victor-Cousin
75005 Paris
Tel. (0)1 43 54 58 08 – Fax (0)1 40 51 05 18
Mme Françoise Testard

Category ★★ **Rooms** 37 with soundproofing, bath or shower, WC, telephone, cable TV. **Price** Single and double 430-500F / 65,55-76,22€; in low season 380-450F / 58,01-68,60€. **Meals** Breakfast 35F / 5,34€, served 7:15-10:30 (free of charge to the reader of this guide for a weekend stay, Sunday night included). **Credit cards** Visa, Eurocard, MasterCard, Amex. **Pets** Dogs allowed. **Facilities** Elevator. **Parking** Rue soufflot. **How to get there** (Map 2) Bus: 21, 27, 38, 82, 84, 85, 89 – Metro: Cluny-La Sorbonne – RER: Luxembourg. **Open** All year.

Rue Victor-Cousin runs into rue Soufflot with the Panthéon on its right. Since 1311, the quarter has been dominated by its student life and so the Hôtel de la Sorbonne, situated just opposite the famous university, has certainly seen many generations of turbulent young people passing under its windows. You go in under the portico and then take the door to the left. The hotel has just changed hands and the long awaited renovation has finally been scheduled. Thus, the reception area will be expanded and a fireplace corner will be added; exotic wood and warm colors will complete the decor. Simple, small and well-cared-for, the rooms have comfortable beds and bathrooms, the latter sometimes rather narrow. Whether giving onto street or courtyard, all are soundproofed with effective double-glazing. Starting in January 2000, they will be refurbished little by little. No large-scale construction work or change of furniture, but here again the plan is to warm up and rejuvenate the decoration by changing the fabrics, carpets and wallpaper. The welcome is nice and natural, quite in the tone of this hotel with more than reasonable prices.

Timhotel Jardin des Plantes

5, rue Linné
75005 Paris
Tel. (0)1 47 07 06 20 – Fax (0)1 47 07 62 74
M. Philippe de La Rochette

Category ★★ **Rooms** 33 with soundproofing, bath or shower, WC, telephone, hairdryer and TV. **Price** Single and double 680F / 103,67€; extra bed 200F / 30,49€. **Meals** Breakfast 49F / 7,48€, served 7:00-11:00. **Credit cards** All major. **Pets** Dogs allowed. **Facilities** Elevator, sauna, terrace, 10 individual safes. **Parking** Rue Censier (at 100m). **How to get there** (Maps 2 and 10) Bus: 67 and 89 – Metro: Jussieu – Train station: Gare d'Austerlitz. **Open** All year.

The hotel's entrance is just opposite the well-known Jardin des Plantes and such proximity plays a considerable role in the establishment's choice of decor. Almost all the rooms give onto the street and the large trees of the park. They have all just been renovated in a variety of yellow shades mingled with bottle greens and dark reds. Without any great fantasy, the whole effect remains attractive and comfortable, with the rooms on the upper floors the most agreeable. The lounge is under the vaults of the basement level, and retains the botanical theme with its collection of prints. For the bar-breakfast lounge wide open onto the street, a more up to date decoration has been chosen, playfully mixing fabrics and colors. Lastly, you should certainly not miss the small communal terrace on the top floor, where, if you wish, you can have your breakfast surrounded by roses and lavender (Room 50 opens straight onto it). This is a very welcoming hotel much appreciated by the professors and researchers of the National Museum of Natural History.

Hôtel des Trois Collèges

16, rue Cujas
75005 Paris
Tel. (0)1 43 54 67 30 – Fax (0)1 46 34 02 99

Category ★★ **Rooms** 44 with soundproofing, bath or shower, WC, telephone, hairdryer, TV. **Price** Single 400-560F / 60,98-85,37€, double 500-700F / 76,22-106,71€, triple 800F / 121,96€. **Meals** Breakfast 45F / 6,86€. Snacks available at lunchtime (around 80F / 12,20€) and tea room. **Credit cards** All major. **Pets** Dogs not allowed. **Parking** 20, rue Soufflot. **How to get there** (Map 2) Bus: 21, 27, 38, 63, 82, 84, 85, 86, 87 and 89 – Metro: Cluny-La Sorbonne and Odéon – RER: Luxembourg and Saint-Michel. **Open** All year.

For centuries this district has been the capital of knowledge and the most famous college of the Montagne Sainte-Geneviève is the Sorbonne, founded in the 13th century. The Sainte-Barbe College is the oldest private establishment in France while the College de France houses the most prestigious teaching chairs. In the shade of such historical buildings is found the small and discreet Hôtel des Trois Collèges. A widespread simplicity reigns throughout the establishment where white dominates, but the rooms lack for no comfort (although the bathrooms show signs of fatigue, with quaint sanitary appliances and slightly flaking paint). The largest rooms have Mansard ceilings with a view over the Sorbonne and Panthéon. On the ground floor there is a charming, light and elegant tea room where you can have your delicious breakfast with home-made jams in peace and quiet, or a light meal later in the day. Next-door a tiny lounge recalls the ancient origins of the place, and you can admire the well once used by the religious order of *Les Frères de Cluny*. A simple hotel, filled with the spirit of the district.

À la Villa des Artistes

9, rue de la Grande-Chaumière
75006 Paris
Tel. 01 43 26 60 86 – Fax 01 43 54 73 70
Mlle Marie Peugeot

Category ★★★ **Rooms** 59 (45 with air-conditioning) with bath or shower, WC, telephone, satellite TV, hairdryer, safe and minibar. **Price** "Standard room" 695-710F / 105,95-108,24€, "club room" 895-910F /136,44-138,73€. **Meals** Breakfast (buffet) included, served 7:00-10:30. **Credit cards** All major. **Pets** Dogs not allowed. **Facilities** Elevator, laundry service, bar, patio. **Parking** At 116, boulevard du Montparnasse (at 50m). **How to get there** (Map 10) Bus: 58, 68, 82, 83 and 91 – Metro: Vavin – RER: Port-Royal – Train station (TGV): Gare Montparnasse. **Open** All year.

Since From the times when Montparnasse was the center of all the trends in the arts, many famous souls have stayed here: Beckett, Fitzgerald, Fujita and Modigliani, who had his studio close by. Today you can see them again in the photos on the bar walls, alongside Kiki, Man Ray, Hemingway and many others. These days the Villa des Artistes still carries on the artistic traditions of the quarter with regular picture exhibitions when painters, friends and clients of the hotel can meet together over a glass at the openings. The lounge is perfect for this kind of event and you will appreciate the comfortable armchairs and sofas and the 1930s spirit of the design. The breakfast room next door looks out on a very attractive patio with tables and deckchairs. The rooms have undergone recent renovation and all are set up with elegant and modern furniture set off by quality fabrics. The lighting has been carefully thought out and the bathrooms are impeccable. This is a quiet place where you are received attentively and with concern for your well-being.

Hôtel de l'Abbaye

10, rue Cassette – 75006 Paris
Tel. (0)1 45 44 38 11 – Fax (0)1 45 48 07 86
M. Lafortune
Web: www.hotel-abbaye.4in.com – E-mail: hotel.abbaye@wanadoo.fr

Category ★★★ **Rooms** 42 and 4 suites (duplex with terrace) with air-conditioning, bath, WC, telephone and TV. **Price** Standard room 1050-1160F / 160,07-176,84€, large room 1580-1650F / 240,87-251,54€, duplex and apart. 2150-2300F / 327,77-350,63€. **Meals** Breakfast included, served 6:00-12:00; snacks available. **Credit cards** Amex, Visa, Eurocard, MasterCard. **Pets** Dogs not allowed. **Facilities** Elevator, garden, bar, room service. **Parking** Place Saint-Sulpice. **How to get there** (Map 1) Bus: 48, 63, 70, 84, 86, 87, 95 and 96 – Metro: Saint-Sulpice and Sèvres-Babylone. **Open** All year.

Preceded by a noble entry court, this elegant hotel in the Saint-Sulpice quarter has all the qualities of a real hotel of charm. Deep sofas and some fine antique furniture around an open fire make an ideal corner for winter days. Next to the lounge, which could be that of a very beautiful Parisian apartment, the high french doors of the bar open onto the patio-garden. Several rooms look out onto this luxuriant and flowery area, and some duplex units have semi-private terraces. The rooms' decor reflects the style of the ground floor: warm, personalized and quite often having antique furniture. To these aesthetic qualities are added an irreproachable comfort and apparently faultless maintenance. This is a hospitable and superb address with the good taste of having preserved full confidentiality.

Hôtel Alliance Saint-Germain-des-Prés

7/11, rue Saint-Benoît - 75006 Paris
Tel. (0)1 42 61 53 53 - Fax (0)1 49 27 09 33
M. Albert Cacciamani
E-mail: alliance.stgermain@wanadoo.fr

Category ★★★★ **Rooms** 113 and 2 junior suites with soundproofing, air-conditioning, bath, WC, telephone, minibar and satellite TV – 4 for disabled persons. **Price** Double 1750-1850F / 266,79-282,03€. **Meals** Breakfast (buffet) 100F / 15,24€, served 6:30-11:00. **Credit cards** All major. **Pets** Dogs allowed. **Facilities** Elevator, laundry service, bar, tea room, safe, Internet facilities **Parking** 169, boulevard Saint-Germain. **How to get there** (Map 1) Bus: 39, 48, 63, 86, 87 and 95 – Metro: Saint-Germain-des-Prés. **Open** All year.

Located just a few steps away from *Le Café Flore* and *Les Deux Magots*, the Hôtel Alliance has just completed its renovation. The reception rooms are divided into several areas (desk, corner lounge, bar, fire-place corner, multimedia area for the guests), all in a superb contemporary cosmopolitan style; dark-brown or beige leather for the armchairs, smooth wood panelling, Japanese style shapes and objects with "ethnic" or 70s references. Two styles dominate the bedrooms: high-tech by Philippe Starck, with curved shapes and subtly spread out patches of vivid colors, or a classical "refined-country"-like style, with Louis XVI inspired pieces of furniture and brocaded wall coverings (rooms with a number ending with a 14 also have four corner windows). The vast breakfast lounge located in the basement is decorated in Courrège-style of pearl gray, pink and light green colors, and all bathed in a surprising effect of natural light. Every morning, a lavish buffet is laid out, and the cook also makes fried eggs and other delicious breakfast treats upon request.

Hôtel d'Angleterre

44, rue Jacob
75006 Paris
Tel. (0)1 42 60 34 72 – Fax (0)1 42 60 16 93
Mme Blouin

Category ★★★ **Rooms** 23 and 3 apartments with soundproofing in street, bath, WC, telephone, hairdryer, cable TV and safe. **Price** Single and double 750-1250F / 114,34-190,56€, suite (with 2 bedrooms) and apart. 1600F / 243,92€ (2 pers.), 1850F / 282,03€ (3-4 pers.). **Meals** Breakfast 60F / 9,15€, served 7:00-12:00. **Credit cards** All major. **Pets** Dogs not allowed. **Facilities** Elevator, garden. **Parking** 169, boulevard Saint-Germain. **How to get there** (Map 1) Bus: 39, 48, 63, 86 and 95 – Metro: Saint-Germain-des-Prés. **Open** All year.

This house has a history; it was here that the independence of the federal republic of the United States was recognized. Today it is a very beautiful hotel with a superb decor of high wainscotted ceilings, polished beams and antique furniture pieces. All the rooms are different, and a good number of them are much larger than those one is used to finding in the quarter. The most beautiful has a huge wall of bare stone that sets off the 17th-century furniture, with a canopied bed of turned wood and some Louis XIII "mutton bone" chairs. You should note that the largest and the quietest give onto the garden but do not expect to find air-conditioning. This is a pity given the real luxury of some rooms. Lastly, the very attentive management will ease your stay in Paris by reserving for you shows, restaurants and so on. A very good address, and you can also have the pleasure in fine weather of eating your breakfast outdoors in the flowery quiet of the patio garden.

L'Atelier Montparnasse

49, rue Vavin – 75006 Paris
Tel. (0)1 46 33 60 00 – Fax (0)1 40 51 04 21
Mme Marie-José Tible
Web: www.ateliermontparnasse.com

Category ★★★ Rooms 17 with soundproofing, bath or shower, WC, telephone, TV, hairdryer, safe, minibar. **Price** Single 700F / 106,71€, double 820F / 125,01€, "Fujita room" (2-3 pers.) 1100F / 167,69€; extra bed 100F / 15,24€. **Meals** Breakfast 50F / 7,62€, served 7:00-11:00. **Credit cards** All major. **Pets** Dogs allowed. **Facilities** Elevator, room service. **Parking** 116, boulevard du Montparnasse. **How to get there** (Map 10) Bus: 58, 68, 82 and 91 – Metro: Notre-Dame-des-Champs and Montparnasse – RER: Port-Royal – Train station (TGV): Gare Montparnasse. **Open** All year.

Very close to La Coupole restaurant, L'Atelier Montparnasse has helped to revive the life of the quarter. The amusing mosaic carpet of the entrance sets the 1930s tone for the very warm decoration of the tiny corner lounge. You will appreciate the elegance of the furniture and the exhibition of paintings that livens up the walls at all times, recreating a link with the *Montparno* tradition. Despite their small size, (apart from the large "Foujita"), the rooms are comfortable and soberly decorated in pink and cream shades. As for the bathrooms, they are astonishing with their molten glass mosaics all reproducing the work of some famous painter representative of the great days of Montparnasse. The energy and know-how of Mme. Tible are found throughout this attractive and hospitable hotel, and she knows well how to make one forget the very smallness of its facilities.

Hôtel Atlantis Saint-Germain-des-Prés

4, rue du Vieux-Colombier – 75006 Paris
Tel. (0)1 45 48 31 81 – Fax (0)1 45 48 35 16
M. Éric Azhar
Web: www.hotelatlantis.com

Category ★★ **Rooms** 27 with soundproofing and air-conditioning, bath or shower, WC, telephone, satellite TV, hairdryer, safe. **Price** Single and double 600-820F / 91,47-125,01€; extra bed 100F / 15,24€. **Meals** Breakfast 40F / 6,10€, served 6:30-10:30. **Credit cards** Visa, Eurocard, MasterCard, Amex. **Pets** Dogs not allowed. **Facilities** Elevator. **Parking** Place Saint-Sulpice. **How to get there** (Map 1) Bus: 39, 48, 63, 70, 86, 87, 95 and 96 – Metro: Saint-Sulpice. **Open** All year.

On the corner of the Place Saint-Sulpice, this fine building is signaled out by its window boxes and carefully maintained interior which has just been renovated. The rooms ending with the number 1 are large and rate among our favorites. Giving onto the street but with air-conditioning and double-glazing, they have a simple but attractive decor. There are bedspreads in white *piqué*, papered walls most often in pale blue, elegant curtains and white lacquered furniture. They have superb white bathrooms enhanced by a frieze in blue tileware. The other rooms are smaller but always well-maintained. Equally successful are those at the back with vast spaces, elegant *Directoire*-style furniture and an unobstructed view on the green and charming courtyards of the other buildings. On the ground floor you will be delighted by the truly charming lounge with its deep leather armchairs and watercolor paintings of Brittany. Breakfast is served close by in the dining room, with the tick-tock of a clock from earlier times.

Au Manoir Saint-Germain-des-Prés

153, boulevard Saint-Germain
75006 Paris
Tel. (0)1 42 22 21 65 - Fax (0)1 45 48 22 25
M. Claude Teil

Category ★★★★ **Rooms** 32 with air-conditioning, soundproofing, telephone, bath or shower, WC, satellite TV, minibar, hairdryer and safe. **Price** Single 950-1200F/144,83-182,94€, double 1100-1456F / 167,69-222,29€; in low season: 1 pers. 853-990F / 130,22-150,92€, 2 pers. 950-1200F / 144,83-182,94€; extra bed 150F / 22,87€. **Meals** Breakfast (buffet) included, served 6:30-10:30. **Credit cards** All major. **Pets** Dogs not allowed. **Facilities** Elevator, laundry service, bar. **Parking** In front of the hotel. **How to get there** (Map 1) Bus: 39, 48, 63, 86, 87 and 95 – Metro: Saint-Germain-des-Prés. **Open** All year.

A neighbor of the famous *Brasserie Lipp* and facing the two ultra-famous cafés, *Le Flore* and *Les Deux Magots*, the Manoir Saint-Germain-des-Prés has one of the best sites in the capital. Recently taken-over and magnificently restored, it should have a lasting and well-earned success. It is impossible not to be charmed by its small lounges with their lime green worked wood with dark set-offs, polished in the old manner, the pale pink silks of the chairs, the genuinely antique furniture pieces, the old gilt moldings of the mirrors and prints. This same timeless refinement, with beautiful *toiles de Jouy* you find in all the rooms, which have also been renovated. The whole effect is handsome, comfortable, perfectly maintained and well-soundproofed. The breakfast is good and the welcome attentive and pleasant.

Hôtel d'Aubusson

33, rue Dauphine - 75006 Paris
Tel. (0)1 43 29 43 43 - Fax (0)1 43 29 12 62
M. Pascal Gimel
Web: www.hoteldaubusson.com

Category ★★★★ **Rooms** 50 with air-conditioning, soundproofing, telephone, bath or shower, WC, hairdryer, satellite TV, minibar and safe – 2 for disabled persons. **Price** "standard" 1200-1450F / 182,94-221,05€, "supérieure" 1550-1850F / 236,30-282,03€, "luxe" (1-2 pers.), duplex and suite (2-4 pers.) 850-2200F / 282,03-335,39€. **Meals** Breakfast (buffet) 110F / 16,77€, served 7:00-12:00. **Credit cards** All major. **Pets** Dogs allowed. **Facilities** Elevator, laundry service, bar, patio, room service (mealtime specials 150-200F / 22,87-30,49€). **Parking** Private, under the hotel (100F / 15,24€ /day). **How to get there** (Map 1) Bus: 24, 27, 58 and 70 – Metro: Odéon, Pont-Neuf. **Open** All year.

The Hôtel d'Aubusson has only been open since November 1996. The entry hall and bar in acajou enhanced by gilded bronze define the spacial layout from which you can walk onto the patio with its noble 17th-century façade, fountain and a few tables for drinks. You can also go directly into the finest room of the hotel, the lounge with high ceiling beams, stone fireplace and Louis XV furniture. With their *Directoir*-style furniture the rooms are beyond criticism in setting comfort and beat all the standards for soundproofing. The carpeting is in perfect harmony with the superb fabrics from the best houses, and while the rooms in the building on the courtyard often add beautiful ceiling beams to their decor, all are very pleasant and have irresistible 1930s-style bathrooms. Breakfast is served on the patio or in a superb dining room just behind the lounge, dominated by a large, green Aubusson in the purest 18th-century-style.

Hôtel Buci Latin

34, rue de Buci - 75006 Paris
Tel. (0)1 43 29 07 20 - Fax (0)1 43 29 67 44
Mme Laurence Raymond
E-mail: hotel@bucilatin.com

Category ★★★ **Rooms** 26 and 1 junior suite (with balcony and whirlpool) with air-conditioning, soundproofing, bath or shower, WC, telephone, cable TV, hairdryer, minibar – 2 for disabled persons. **Price** Single and double 1050-1350F / 160,07-205,81€, duplex 1800F / 274,41€, junior suite 1900F / 289,65€. **Meals** Breakfast included, served from 6:45. **Credit cards** All major. **Facilities** Elevator, laundry service, bar. **Parking** 169, boulevard Saint-Germain. **How to get there** (Map 1) Bus: 39, 48, 58, 63, 70, 86, 87, 95 and 96 – Metro: Mabillon. **Open** All year.

Decorated by an excellent interior decorator, this is probably one of the most beautiful hotels in the neighborhood. Graceful and artistic, its unique decor includes sienna patina on the walls, soft lighting, pale wood furniture embellished with handsome wrought iron, sumptuous bathrooms, cleverly concealed closets and little exotic wardrobes in every bedroom. Even lovelier are the duplex and the suite which has a balcony and whirlpool bathtub; but the least expensive bedrooms (with shower) are just as charming because their layout efficiently compensates for their very small size. Whether your room is on the street or the courtyard, there is no noise problem because the rooms are air-conditioned and the windows double-glazed. Works of young artists are displayed on the doors and in the elevator. Photographs of their works are also exhibited in the lobby, and can be enjoyed from the adjacent lounge. In the basement, there is a charming coffee shop where you will be served breakfast on the house.

Hôtel Le Clément

6, rue Clément - 75006 Paris
Tel. (0)1 43 26 53 60 - Fax (0)1 44 07 06 83
M. and Mme Charrade
E-mail: hclement@worldnet.fr

Category ★★ **Rooms** 31 with air-conditioning, bath or shower, WC, telephone, hairdryer, satellite TV and safe. **Price** Double 560-680F / 85,37-103,67€, triple 780F / 118,91€. **Meals** Breakfast 60F / 9,15€, served 7:00-11:00. **Credit cards** All major. **Pets** Dogs not allowed. **Facilities** Elevator, bar. **Parking** Marché Saint-Germain (in front of the hotel). **How to get there** (Map 1) Bus: 39, 48, 63, 70, 86, 87, 95 and 96 – Metro: Saint-Germain-des-Prés, Mabillon. **Open** All year.

Lovingly maintained by Madame Charrade, this family hotel offers pleasant little rooms at reasonable prices for the district. Next to the elegant reception lounge is the bar (where breakfast is served). Installed in the former restaurant of the hotel, it has retained is Parisian bistro decor. All the rooms can be recommended, with their simple but charming white *piqué* bedspreads, wall coverings coordinated with the curtains, and caned rattan furniture. Rooms 104 and 320 are ideal for families. From the rooms on the upper floors you can see the Saint-Sulpice church emerging over the roofs of the Marché Saint-Germain (except for Rooms 15, 23, 31 and 39, which have no view but are very quiet). From 1482 until 1811, this market was the place where rainbow-colored crowds would buy, sell, attend street shows and drink in the many cabarets. Now everything has quieted down; the bustle is on the side of rue Mabillon and rue de Buci, a few minutes away from the hotel.

Le Clos Médicis

56, rue Monsieur-le-Prince - 75006 Paris
Tel. (0)1 43 29 10 80 - Fax (0)1 43 54 26 90
M. Beherec - M. Méallet
E-mail: clos-médicis@compuserve.com

Category ★★★ **Rooms** 38 with air-conditioning, soundproofing, bath or shower, WC, telephone, cable TV, hairdryer, safe and minibar, (1 avec terrace) – 1 for disabled persons. **Price** "Standard" 790F / 120,43€, "supérieure" 990F / 150,92€, "luxe" and duplex 1090-1200F / 166,17-182,94€, triple 1200F / 182,94€. **Meals** Breakfast 60F / 9,15€, served 7:00-11:00. **Credit cards** All major. **Pets** Dogs allowed (+60F / 9,15€). **Facilities** Elevator, bar, laundry service, room service, patio. **Parking** 20, rue Soufflot. **How to get there** (Map 1) Bus: 21, 27, 38, 58, 82, 84, 85 and 89 – Metro: Odéon – RER: Luxembourg. **Open** All year.

Many hotels in this neighborhood are named after the Medicis Palace, which was built in the Luxembourg Gardens for Marie de Medicis. This one is our favorites. It opens onto a beautiful and inviting reception area and lounge brightened by a cheerful fireplace in winter. With the first fine days of spring, breakfasts are served in the leafy courtyard, which is just off the breakfast room. The bedrooms are calm, very comfortable, with furniture and decoration accessories especially designed for the hotel. They are small but you feel quite at ease there. One has a large private terrace, others are duplex rooms. The walls are a pretty yellow and cream brown and the draperies and bedspreads are coordinated with lovely prints. The total effect is a real accomplishment success. The welcome is youthful and very pleasant.

Crystal Hôtel

24, rue Saint-Benoît – 75006 Paris
Tel. (0)1 45 48 85 14 – Fax (0)1 45 49 16 45
Mme Choukroun - Mme Adda
E-mail: hotel.crystal@wanadoo.fr

Category ★★★ **Rooms** 26 (9 with air-conditioning) with soundproofing, bath or shower, WC, telephone, minibar, safe, satellite TV. **Price** Single 800F / 121,96€, double 900F / 137,20€, "luxe" 1200F / 182,94€, suite (3-4 pers.) 1500F / 228,67€; in low season (Jan to end Mar, mid Jul to end Aug and Nov to Christmas Day, excluding trade fair periods): 1 pers. 650F / 99,09€, 2 pers. 800F / 121,96€, "luxe" 1000F / 152,45€, suite (3-4 pers.) 1200F / 182,94€. **Meals** Breakfast 50F/7,62€, served 7:30-11:00. **Credit cards** All major. **Pets** Dogs allowed. **Facilities** Elevator, laundry service. **Parking** 169, boulevard Saint-Germain. **How to get there** (Map 1) Bus: 39, 48, 63, 70, 86, 87, 95 and 96 – Metro: Saint-Germain-des-Prés. **Open** All year.

At the end of the 17th century the "road of the cows" that ran alongside the moats of the Saint-Germain Abbey was renamed the Saint-Benoît. In the 1950s its bistros were frequented by Juliette Gréco and Boris Vian and they were a major feature of this quarter. The entrance of the Crystal Hôtel does not seem to have changed since that era: framed by two lanterns, it leads into a very inviting British lounge with its old Chesterfields and Chippendale armchairs. You find this classical and comfortable charm again in the very cozy rooms. Often large, they have a pleasant decor with wall-hangings and bedspreads happily matched, while the antique or *style* furniture adds a touch of character. The brand new bathrooms are absolutely perfect. Some give onto the street but efficient soundproofing (and air-conditioning in some rooms) ensures a necessary quiet. An excellent breakfast is served under the barrel vaults of a friendly little dining room in the cellar.

Hôtel du Danemark

21, rue Vavin
75006 Paris
Tel. (0)1 43 26 93 78 – Fax (0)1 46 34 66 06
M. Nurit

Category ★★★ **Rooms** 15 with soundproofing, bath, WC, telephone, satellite TV, hairdryer and minibar. **Price** Single 620F / 94,52€, 790F / 120,43€ (with jacuzzi), double 790F / 120,43€, 890F / 135,68€ (with jacuzzi). In Aug 490F / 74,70€ (without jacuzzi). **Meals** Breakfast 55F / 8,38€. **Credit cards** All major. **Pets** Dogs allowed. **Facilities** Elevator. **Parking** 116, boulevard du Montparnasse. **How to get there** (Map 10) Bus: 58, 68, 82, 83 and 91 – Metro: Vavin and Notre-Dame-des-Champs – RER: Port-Royal – Train station (TGV): Gare Montparnasse. **Open** All year.

The Hôtel du Danemark faces the unusual "Sporting House built in tiers" (*Maison à Gradins Sportive*) built in 1912 by Henri Sauvage. Some rooms overlook this modern architectural masterpiece. It may be due to this influence, or to recall the Danish taste for design, that the management has opted for a modern decor. The reception area and corner lounges have preserved their stone walls, but are in bright and very contrasting colors. We somewhat regret that the same was not done in the bedrooms whose decoration seems almost dull by comparison. They are few in number, well-soundproofed and comfortable despite their small size. Those with a jacuzzi are more spacious and those on the top floor are pleasantly large. A good little hotel near to the Luxembourg Gardens and the large *brasseries* of Montparnasse. The welcome is friendly and receptive to your needs.

Hôtel du Danube

58, rue Jacob
75006 Paris
Tel. (0)1 42 60 34 70 - Fax (0)1 42 60 81 18

Category ★★★ **Rooms** 40 with bath or shower, WC, telephone, cable TV. **Price** Double 620-920F / 94,52-140,25€, suite 1200F / 182,94€ (2-4 pers.). **Meals** Breakfast 55F / 8,38€, served 7:15-10:45. **Credit cards** Visa, Eurocard, MasterCard, Amex. **Pets** Dogs allowed (+30F / 4,57€). **Facilities** Elevator, patio. **Parking** Boulevard Saint-Germain-des-Prés. **How to get there** (Map 1) Bus: 39, 48, 63, 95 – Metro: Saint-Germain-des-Prés. **Open** All year.

This beautiful Napoleon III building rates among the most charming hotels in Paris; behind its discrete oak window you can glimpse the antique furniture, bronze lamps and sofas of a lounge with floral chintz wall fabrics. Decorated in the same spirit, the delightful bedrooms are distributed between two buildings. Those overlooking the courtyard are very quiet and in various sizes; some are arranged in suites, others, tiny but adorable, provide excellent quality for the price. On the street side, they often have two high windows and a lounge corner with a mahogany pedestal table and elegant wing chairs. These are of a very rare size for that district, but funnily not yet equipped with double-glazing (but considering their roominess, their prices are the lowest in the neighborhood). The good breakfasts are served in a room with pale, smooth, wood panelling on which small Chinese porcelains pieces are displayed. It opens onto a patio where tables are set out in good weather. A hotel of rare and enchanting charm. Here it is better to book well in advance.

Hôtel Dauphine Saint-Germain

36, rue Dauphine – 75006 Paris
Tel. (0)1 43 26 74 34 – Fax (0)1 43 26 49 09
M. Noël Janvier
Web: www.dauphinestgermain.com – E-mail: dauphine@cybercable.fr

Category ★★★ **Rooms** 29 and 1 suite with air-conditioning, soundproofing, bath or shower, WC, telephone, outlet for fax, cable TV, radio, hairdryer and safe. **Price** Single and double 930F / 141,78€, suite 1155F / 176,08€ (1-2 pers.), 1355F / 206,57€ (3-4 pers.). **Meals** Breakfast (american buffet) 75F / 11,43€, served 7:00-12:00. **Credit cards** All major. **Pets** Dogs allowed. **Facilities** Elevator, laundry service, bar, tea room, baby-sitting, room service. **Parking** 27, rue Mazarine. **How to get there** (Map 1) Bus: 24, 27, 58 and 70 – Metro: Odéon, Pont-Neuf – RER: Saint-Michel-Notre-Dame. **Open** All year.

Installed in a building from the 17th century, the Dauphine Saint-Germain is a beautiful hotel, both classical and cozy. It was totally refurbished in 1996, yet it has retained much of its character: superb beamed ceilings in the bedrooms, or the stone vaulting and walls on the ground floor. Having crossed an entry hall lined in pale oak, you come to a very attractive little bar and tearoom. This room is very light and gives straight onto the outside, and is one of the delights of the hotel. In the mornings the breakfast buffet is set out here, and later on guests may sit and read their newspapers or just watch the street as it starts to come alive. The rooms are pleasant, comfortable and very classic (those with numbers ending in a 5 are a bit small); the baths are impeccable. This is really a fine Parisian address where an excellent welcome is reserved for you.

Hôtel Delavigne

1, rue Casimir-Delavigne - 75006 Paris
Tel. (0)1 43 29 31 50 - Fax (0)1 43 29 78 56
M. Fraïoli
Web: www.hoteldelavigne.com - E-mail: resa@hoteldelavigne.com

Category ★★★ **Rooms** 34 with bath or shower, WC, telephone, safe, satellite TV. **Price** Single 560-640F / 85,37-97,57€, double 640-720F / 77,75-89,94€, triple 840F / 128,06€; in mid Jul to end Aug: 1 pers. 510-590F / 77,75-89,94€, 2 pers. 590-620F / 89,94-94,52€, 3 pers. 740F / 112,81€. **Meals** Breakfast 60F / 9,15€, served from 7:30. **Credit cards** Visa, Eurocard, MasterCard. **Pets** Dogs not allowed. **Facilities** Elevator, bar. **Parking** Rue de l'École de Médecine. **How to get there** (Map 1) Bus: 21, 27, 38, 58, 63, 82, 84, 85, 86, 87 and 89 – Metro: Odéon – RER: Luxembourg. **Open** All year.

Quietly located right in the center of the Saint-Germain/ Saint-Michel/Luxembourg triangle, the Hôtel Delavigne offers pretty rooms with walls covered with Japanese wickerwork enhanced by a small frieze or well-draped in fabrics, with elegant bedspreads made of raw cotton (or sometimes printed), and always with a small picture. The furniture is extremely varied; in some rooms you will find colored cane types, in others interesting headboards in wood or wrought iron, while again in others - but less often - some elegant antique pieces. Room sizes vary but you should note that those on the corner are attractively sized. The bathrooms are a little outdated but still provide all the comforts. A pretty series of prints of Paris monuments add interest to the corridors, and a very attractive corner lounge is on the ground floor. This is a friendly hotel where the small details such as a bottle of mineral water and sweets in every room give you the pleasant impression of having been expected.

Hôtel des Deux Continents

25, rue Jacob
75006 Paris
Tel. (0)1 43 26 72 46 – Fax (0)1 43 25 67 80
M. Henneveux

Category ★ ★ ★ **Rooms** 41 (10 with air-conditioning) with bath or shower, WC, telephone, hairdryer, satellite TV. **Price** Single 795F / 121,20€, double 865-915F / 131,87-139,49€, triple 1120F / 170,74€. **Meals** Breakfast 60 and 65F / 9,15 and 9,91€, served until 11:00. **Credit cards** Visa, Eurocard, MasterCard. **Facilities** Elevator, laundry service. **Parking** 169, boulevard Saint-Germain. **How to get there** (Map 1) Bus: 39, 48, 63, 86, 87, 95 and 96 – Metro: Saint-Germain-des-Prés, Mabillon. **Open** All year.

The "two continents" means Europe and the New World, the latter is illustrated by a large fresco of 19th-century New York on a wall in the breakfast room. With its thick green carpet, wall upholstery and paintings, the lounge next to it truly expresses a muffled atmosphere of opulence that can be found again in the bedrooms which are divided into three buildings. If the noise of the street doesn't bother you, ask for a room in front, as these are the largest or one in the second building (slightly less spacious, but quieter). The smallest rooms are in the third building are just as charming, with the additional advantages of air-conditioning and silence. All the rooms are lined with very elegant wall fabrics and coordinated drapes (from the renowned designer shops in the neighborhood) and have classical or patinated furniture (as in Provence). Comfort and maintenance are perfect everywhere, including in the light-colored marble bathrooms. Friendly service from a staff always at your disposal.

Hôtel Ferrandi

92, rue du Cherche-Midi – 75006 Paris
Tel. (0)1 42 22 97 40 – Fax (0)1 45 44 89 97
Mme Lafond
E-mail: hotel.ferrandi@wanadoo.fr

Category ★★★ Rooms 41 and 1 suite with air-conditioning, soundproofing, bath or shower, WC, telephone, satellite TV, hairdryer. **Price** Single and double 620-1280F / 94,52-195,13€, suite 1500F / 228,67€ –Special rates in low season on request. **Meals** Breakfast 45-65F / 6,86-9,91€; snacks available on request. **Credit cards** All major. **Pets** Dogs allowed. **Parking** Garage at hotel (140F / 21,34€ /day) and opposite the *Bon Marché* department store. **How to get there** (Map 1) Bus: 28, 39, 48, 70, 82, 89, 92, 94, 95 and 96 – Metro: Saint-Placide, Vaneau. **Open** All year.

The Hôtel Ferrandi is a classic of the quarter, just midway between Montparnasse and Saint-Germain-des-Prés. The reception areas are vast and fitted-out in the Restoration-style, with mahogany furniture, wide draped fabrics and numerous small corner lounges. Their size and style are worthy of a grand luxury hotel and are a major asset of this house. The rooms look out onto the street side, but for this reason all have been air-conditioned and have effective double-glazing. They are often spacious and individually decorated. This makes for a *bourgeois* and cosseted whole, with very pretty wallpapers (sometimes in *toile de Jouy* fabrics) in the recently renovated rooms. The bathrooms that go with them are impeccable, the suites are most attractive. The Hôtel Ferrandi directly faces the Hôtel de Montmorency now housing the works of Ernest Hébert, which thus provides an opportunity to discover this French artist much in fashion in the 19th century.

Hôtel de Fleurie

32, rue Grégoire-de-Tours – 75006 Paris
Tel. (0)1 53 73 70 00 and (0)1 53 73 70 10 – Fax (0)1 53 73 70 20
Famille Marolleau
Web: www.hotel-de-fleurie.tm.fr – E-mail: bonjour@hotel-de-fleurie.tm.fr

Category ★★★ **Rooms** 29 with air-conditioning, soundproofing, bath or shower, WC, telephone, outlet for modem, satellite TV, hairdryer, safe, minibar. **Price** Single 800-1000F / 121,96-152,45€, double 1000F / 152,45€, "luxe room" 1350F / 205,81€, family room (3-4 pers.) 1800F / 274,41€; in low season (from end Jan to mid Feb, end Jul to end Aug and in Dec): double 900F / 137,20€, familyroom 1700F / 259,16€. **Meals** Breakfast (buffet) 50F / 7,62€. Snacks available. **Credit cards** All major. **Pets** Dogs not allowed. **Facilities** Elevator, laundry service. **Parking** Marché Saint-Germain. **How to get there** (Map 1) Bus: 58, 63, 70, 86, 87 and 96 – Metro: Odéon – RER: Saint-Michel. **Open** All year.

At a few paces from the Odéon crossroads and on both sides of the boulevard Saint-Germain, the small rue Grégoire-de-Tours benefits from a very quiet and central location. The white façade of the Hôtel de Fleurie, with a small niche on each story to shelter a small statuette, attracts the eye immediately. Light tones are found in the interior, and the white stones and certain elements from the very beautiful architecture have been preserved to recreate an 18th-century atmosphere. The wood pieces, pictures and other objects mix well with the cane or tapestried chairs and the furniture in the lounge and the breakfast room. The same softness is found in the rooms, which are not large; those ending with a 4 are bigger. They are classically decorated with both care and taste and have comfortable bathrooms. Run by a hospitable and highly motivated family, this hotel has managed to create a homey atmosphere but with service that is all attention and energy.

Hôtel du Globe and des 4 Vents

15, rue des Quatre-Vents
75006 Paris
Tel. (0)1 46 33 62 69 and (0)1 43 26 35 50 - Fax (0)1 46 33 17 29
Mme Simone Ressier

Category ★★ **Rooms** 15 with soundproofing, bath or shower, WC, telephone, TV. **Price** Single with washstand 300F / 45,73€, double 410-595F / 62,50-90,71€. **Meals** Breakfast 45F / 6,86€, served 7:00-11:00. **Credit cards** Visa, Eurocard, MasterCard. **Pets** Dogs allowed. **Parking** Place Saint-Sulpice. **How to get there** (Map 1) Bus: 63, 70, 86, 87 and 96 – Metro: Odéon – RER: Saint-Michel. **Closed** Aug 5 – 31.

One finds it hard to believe that there are still small hotels right in the heart of Paris that offer real quality for some FRF 500 (76,22€) per room. This is the case with the Globe, which, as well as being economical, also offers the luxury of being entirely filled with antique furniture. Situated on a narrow street among venerable houses with their superb ironwork, the hotel is happy to remain hidden away. To the right of the entrance area is a tiny room with two magnificent Louis XV wing chairs enhanced in green, an 18th-century mirror in gilded wood, a cupboard and a small fountain. You climb a narrow staircase to reach the loggia, which serves as reception area. Alongside and upstairs are the cute little rooms, none the same as its neighbor. Certainly you find wooden beams everywhere, and very often some beautiful 18th-century wardrobe doors serving as headboards. The rest of the decoration is varied: fabric wall drapes, amusing prints, an old cupboard or stately armchair, lace bedspreads and other objects. There is a lot of personality with a touch of exuberance and of the Bohemian, and this is a rare type of hotel to be discovered, but only by reserving well in advance.

Grand Hôtel des Balcons

3, rue Casimir-Delavigne – 75006 Paris
Tel. (0)1 46 34 78 50 – Fax (0)1 46 34 06 27
M. and Mme Corroyer
Web: www.balcons.com

Category ★★ **Rooms** 55 with soundproofing, bath or shower, WC, telephone, satellite TV. **Price** Single 425-540F / 64,79-82,32€, double 505-800F / 76,99-121,96€, triple 950F / 144,83€ (free for children under 10 years). **Meals** Breakfast (buffet) 55F / 8,38€, served 7:30-10:00 (free of charge on your birthday). **Credit cards** Visa, Eurocard, MasterCard. **Pets** Dogs allowed. **Facilities** Elevator. **Parking** Rue de l'École de Médecine. **How to get there** (Map 1) Bus: 21, 27, 38, 63, 82, 84, 85, 86, 87 and 89 – Metro: Odéon – RER: Luxembourg. **Open** All year.

Quietly situated at a couple of paces from the Luxembourg in a small street linking the Place de l'Odéon to the more lively districts of the boulevards Saint-Germain and Saint-Michel, the hotel proudly displays its beautiful façade and its rows of small flowered balconies. The reception rooms have kept their *art nouveau* character which gives the hotel its originality: a very pretty breakfast room in bistro style with its chairs in the convoluted forms of the period, a beautiful reception area, a corner-lounge. All is embellished with green plants, 1900s carved wood and stained glass pieces. The rooms are more colorful, and despite their rather standardized format, one feels at home in them. They vary in size and some are perfect for families. They have attractive little bathrooms and all is generally very well maintained with frequent renovations. The bill still remains reasonable especially when taking the quality of the breakfast and its unlimited self-service style into account. A small and charming family-style hotel where you will find friendly hospitality.

Grand Hôtel de l'Univers

6, rue Grégoire-de-Tours
75006 Paris
Tel. (0)1 43 29 37 00 – Fax (0)1 40 51 06 45
M. Nouvel

Category ★★★ Rooms 34 with air-conditioning, soundproofing, bath, WC, telephone, satellite TV, hairdryer, safe, minibar. **Price** Single 850F / 129,58€, double 880-980F / 134,16-149,40€; in Aug: –10%. **Meals** Breakfast continental 40F / 6,10€, buffet 60F / 9,15€, served 7:30-11:00. **Credit cards** All major. **Pets** Dogs allowed. **Facilities** Elevator, laundry service, bar, room service. **Parking** Rue Mazarine, rue de l'École de Médecine. **How to get there** (Map 1) Bus: 58, 63, 70, 86, 87 and 96 – Metro: Odéon – RER: Saint-Michel. **Open** All year.

Tradition goes back to the 15th century for the origins of this building in one of the most charming corners of Saint-Germain-des-Prés, and so it is no surprise that a classical atmosphere has been chosen to decorate the Grand Hôtel de l'Univers. The bare stonework and ceiling beams found in a good number of the rooms are in total harmony. The reception area thus displays beautiful stone facing, but its classical and slightly dull decoration, notably copies in an 18th century-style (comfortable but somewhat over-ornate), could be improved. The bar corner behind is more cheerful, with light oak woodwork and well-balanced lighting. As for the bedrooms, recent renovation has made them truly attractive: carpeting as elegant as it is soft, beautiful coordinated fabrics for both curtains and bedspreads. This bright, comfortable and inviting effect is found also in the bathrooms with shining chrome and green marble. Back to more rustic times when breakfast is served in a vaulted room in the cellar with a Louis XIII decor. Your welcome will be friendly.

Hôtel-Jardin Le Bréa

14, rue Bréa
75006 Paris
Tel. (0)1 43 25 44 41 – Fax (0)1 44 07 19 25
Mme Faïza Elguermaï

Category ★★★ **Rooms** 23 with air-conditioning, soundproofing, telephone, bath or shower, WC, satellite TV, radio, safe, 4 with minibar. **Price** Single 700F / 106,71€, double 770-900F / 117,39-137,20€, triple 900F / 137,20€; extra bed 100F / 15,24€ – Special rates in low season –10 % or 20 %. **Meals** Breakfast 55F / 8,38€, served 7:30-10:30. **Credit cards** All major. **Pets** Dogs not allowed. **Facilities** Elevator, laundry service, bar. **Parking** Montparnasse, Raspail. **How to get there** (Map 10) Bus: 58, 68, 82 and 91 – Metro: Vavin, Notre-Dame-des-Champs – RER: Port-Royal. **Open** All year.

The brand-new Hôtel-Jardin Le Bréa is ideally placed for those wanting to stay in the heart of Montparnasse and enjoy all the life of this quarter, with a visit to the Luxembourg Gardens. The hotel has just been fully renovated with Jean-Philippe called on to do the decoration. He has created a cosseted and warm atmosphere in an up-to-date style. The South inspired the garden layout now converted into a winter garden, along with the lounge and the breakfast room, all now particularly attractive. The pretty rooms are split between two small buildings, one giving onto a quiet street, the other onto the interior courtyard, and the largest rooms are in the latter. Everywhere the colors are warm, the fabrics heavy and nothing is lacking for comfort. The white bathrooms enhanced with russet marble have received the same care. The Hôtel-Jardin Le Bréa is now a member of that new generation of hotels which are all highly recommendable.

Left Bank Saint-Germain Hôtel

9, rue de l'Ancienne-Comédie
75006 Paris
Tel. (0)1 43 54 01 70 – Fax (0)1 43 26 17 14
M. Claude Teil

Category ★★★ **Rooms** 30 and 1 suite with air-conditioning, soundproofing, bath, WC, telephone, cable TV, outlet for modem, safe, hairdryer, minibar. **Price** Single 1082F / 165,19€, double 1351F / 206,25€; in low season (Nov to Mar 14 excluding trade fair periods, and Jul to Aug) 853F / 130,22€ (1 pers.), 984F / 150,22€ (2 pers.), suite (2 pers.) 1800F / 274,41€; extra bed 100F / 15,24€. **Meals** Breakfast (buffet) included. **Credit cards** All major. **Pets** Dogs not allowed. **Facilities** Elevator, laundry service. **Parking** Rue de l'Ecole de Médecine and 27, rue Mazarine. **How to get there** (Map 1) Bus: 58, 63, 70, 86, 87 and 96 – Metro: Odéon – RER: Saint-Michel. **Open** All year.

The Left Bank is in the heart of Saint-Germain-des-Prés, a neighbor of the *Procope* café with all its memories of the revolutionaries, the *Encyclopédistes* and the romantic movement. The small reception area opens onto a pretty lounge that already sets the tone of the house. Indeed various carved wood pieces in oak and walnut were made for the hotel and they well match the few antique furniture pieces and Aubusson tapestries. The same solid walnut-style furniture is in the bedrooms, recently renovated with their walls hung with silk damasks or *toile de Jouy* (our favorites), coordinated with double curtains. All adds to the warm and very comfortable ambiance of the hotel. Room sizes vary and those with a number ending in a 4 or 6 are the largest. From the courtyard rooms of the upper floors, you can get a glimpse of Notre-Dame, All have beautiful bathrooms where nothing has been forgotten. Breakfasts are good and copious.

Hôtel Libertel Prince de Condé

39, rue de Seine
75006 Paris
Tel. (0)1 43 26 71 56 – Fax (0)1 46 34 27 95
M. Philippe Roye

Category ★★★ **Rooms** 12 with air-conditioning, soundproofing, telephone, bath, WC, hairdryer, minibar, safe, cable TV to 1 for disabled persons. **Price** Single 1016,73F / 155€, double 1082,33F / 165€, suite 1849,79F / 282€. **Meals** Breakfast (buffet) 78,71F / 12€, served 7:30-10:30. **Credit cards** All major. **Pets** Dogs allowed. **Facilities** Elevator, laundry service, room service. **Parking** Rue Mazarine. **How to get there** (Map 1) Bus: 24, 27, 58 and 70 – Metro: Odéon. **Open** All year.

With a very impressive sense for detail, the interior decor of this small hotel is based on a classical style, half Napoleon III and half English, with the furniture pieces, wall drapings and other materials all top quality. Each room enjoys the same level of quality, and the sound-proofing is excellent both internally and externally. Sizes are always adequate and satisfactory but with some advantage to rooms with numbers ending with a 2. We must also stress the excellent price charged for the suite. The pleasant breakfast room is well-designed bringing together two small rooms. It lets you overlook the rather austere and venerable vaulted basement, thanks to its range of small sofas and low armchairs in brightly colored fabrics, always arranged around a low table. There are only twelve rooms in this small hotel in one of the most charming districts of the capital, which is the real guarantee of genuine privacy and an attentive welcome.

Hôtel Libertel Prince de Conti

8, rue Guénégaud
75006 Paris
Tel. (0)1 44 07 30 40 – Fax (0)1 44 07 36 34
M. Philippe Roye

Category ★★★ **Rooms** 26 with air-conditioning, soundproofing, bath or shower, WC, telephone, hairdryer, cable TV, safe, minibar. **Price** Single 1016,73F / 155€, double 1082,33F / 165€, suite and duplex 1554,62F/ 237€. **Meals** Breakfast (buffet) 78,71F/ 12€, served 7:00-10:30. **Credit cards** All major. **Pets** Dogs allowed. **Facilities** Elevator, laundry service, room service. **Parking** Rue Mazarine. **How to get there** (Map 1) Bus: 24, 27, 58 and 70 – Metro: Odéon and Pont-Neuf – RER: Saint-Michel. **Open** All year.

A few meters from the Seine and the *bouquinistes*, and in the heart of the art gallery quarter of Saint-Germain-des-Prés, the Hôtel Prince de Conti is lodged in an 18th-century building of the rue Guénégaud. Renovation of the house has created twenty-six rooms, but it should be said straight away that they are not always large while adding that they are truly ravishing. The choice of the various coordinated colors is superb; there is quality furniture and the details are always carefully handled so that you really feel at home. On the comfort side, nothing is lacking and all the rooms are double-glazed and air-conditioned with pretty, functional and well-equipped bathrooms. The duplex suites are also all charming and much larger, with a lounge and a room on a higher floor. You should also note one huge room (no. 1) and two singles giving onto the ground floor's flowery courtyard. There is a roomy and very attractive area in the cellar with its lounge, bar and breakfast corner. Here is a very British and refined atmosphere with professional and friendly service.

Hôtel Louis II

2, rue Saint-Sulpice - 75006 Paris
Tel. (0)1 46 33 13 80 - Fax (0)1 46 33 17 29
M. François Meynant
E-mail: louis2@club-internet.fr

Category ★★★ **Rooms** 22 with soundproofing, bath or shower, WC, TV, minibar, hairdryer. **Price** Single or double 580-890F / 88,42-135,68€, triple 1090F / 166,17€. **Meals** Breakfast 59F / 9€. **Credit cards** All major. **Pets** Dogs allowed. **Facilities** Elevator. **Parking** Saint-Sulpice and École de Médecine. **How to get there** (Map 1) Bus: 58, 63, 70, 86, 87 and 96 – Metro: Odéon, Saint-Michel – RER: Saint-Michel. **Open** All year.

Between Place Saint-Sulpice and the Odeon, this is a cozy, soothing and comfortable hotel. As soon as you enter, it feels like a private house, especially when the beautiful 18th- and 19th-century provincial furniture in the lounge catches your eye. A very pleasant decor which everyone can enjoy, since this is also where breakfast is served (excellent Viennese pastries, preserves made in the traditional way and fresh toasted bread whose aroma rises up the stairs every morning). Set around narrow landings, all the bedrooms overlook the street (the absence of air-conditioning is quite perceptible in summer). They are usually small (apart from two beautiful suites on the top floor) but full of warmth, with floral wall paper and a beautiful beamed ceiling. There are some with amusing *trompe-l'œil* effects. The result is sometimes a bit over the top, but the bedspreads in *Le Puy* lace and mattresses in real wool have a charming grandmotherly feel, reinforced by some antique or *style* furniture skillfully integrated into the decor. A place of many contrasts but undeniable charm.

Hôtel Luxembourg

4, rue de Vaugirard - 75006 Paris
Tel. (0)1 43 25 35 90 - Fax (0)1 43 26 60 84
M. and Mme J. Mandin
Web: hotel-luxembourg.com - E-mail: luxhotel@luxembourg.grolier.fr

Category ★★★ **Rooms** 33 with bath or shower, WC, telephone, safe, satellite TV, minibar, fan, hairdryer. **Price** Single 781-879F / 119,23-134,19€, double 892-971F / 136,18-148,24€ – Special rates all year (weekends, 2 nights, stays 5 nights or longer, special rates for families). **Meals** Breakfast (buffet) including, served 7:00-10:30. **Credit cards** All major. **Pets** Small dogs allowed. **Facilities** Elevator, laundry service, bar, patio. **Parking** Rue Soufflot. **How to get there** (Map 1) Bus: 21, 27, 38, 58, 82, 84, 85 and 89 – Metro: Odéon – RER: Luxembourg. **Open** All year.

The building formerly served to lodge the post-horse riders of Louis XIV but has today become one of the prettiest hotels in the Luxembourg - Odéon perimeter. The tone is set right from the entry: elegant fabrics with their warm colors and furniture in the 18th-century-style form the corner lounges, and the whole opens onto a ravishing flowered patio where one can have a drink near a small tinkling fountain. The same care and comfort are found in the rooms; of a good size with the smaller units available as singles, they have prettily patinated furniture, elegant armchairs, headboards in the shape of antique pediments and the same taste in beautiful fabrics. About half of them look onto the patio, while the others have understandably been double-glazed to keep out the street noise. As is often the case in Paris, the breakfast-brunch is served in a vaulted room in the cellar. A refined hotel well-located, where people are always attentive to your well-being.

Hôtel du Lys

23, rue Serpente
75006 Paris
Tel. (0)1 43 26 97 57 - Fax (0)1 44 07 34 90
Mme Decharne

Category ★★ **Rooms** 22 with bath or shower, WC, telephone, satellite TV, hairdryer, safe. **Price** Single 400-520F / 60,98-79,27€, double 550F / 83,85€, triple 680F / 103,67€. **Meals** Breakfast included. **Credit cards** Visa and MasterCard. **Pets** Dogs allowed. **Parking** Rue de l'École de Médecine. **How to get there** (Map 2) Bus: 21, 27, 38, 63, 85, 86, 87 and 96 – Metro: Saint-Michel, Odéon – RER: Saint-Michel. **Open** All year.

Right in the Latin Quarter, this small hotel lets you have a room at quite an unexpected price in a beautiful town house from the 17th-century, still rich in memories from that era. This explains the rather varied nature of the rooms and the wooden staircase, as old as the place, is worth giving your legs a workout. Some rooms are no bigger than a pocket handkerchief (numbers 5 and 10) while others are more generous in size (8, 11, 13, 18, etc). There are wooden beamed ceilings and some walls at sharp angles. Much charm can be found in the decoration chosen by Mme Decharne, with wallpaper and fabrics in real harmony, small antique furniture pieces here and there, sometimes a pretty pair of prints, and so on. On the sanitation side, the bathrooms have been renovated. Each morning the entry hall is transformed into a breakfast room. For lack of space, many breakfasts are also served in the rooms. You get a warm welcome, with a clientele often of artists and intellectuals, in the general tone of the authentic Saint-Germain-des-Prés quarter.

Hôtel Madison

143, boulevard Saint-Germain - 75006 Paris
Tel. (0)1 40 51 60 00 - Fax (0)1 40 51 60 01
Mme Maryse Burkard
Web: www.hotel-madison.com - E-mail: resa@hotel-madison.com

Category ★★★ **Rooms** 53 and 1 apart with air-conditioning, soundproofing, telephone, bath or shower, WC, satellite TV, minibar, hairdryer, safe. **Price** Single 800-1000F / 121,96-152,45€, double 1110-2250F / 169,22-343,01€ – Special rates in Jan, Feb and Aug. **Meals** Breakfast (buffet) included, served 6:30-11:00. **Credit cards** All major. **Pets** Dogs allowed. **Facilities** Elevator. **Parking** Saint-Germain, Saint Sulpice. **How to get there** (Map 1) Bus: 39, 48, 63, 86, 87 and 95 – Metro: Saint-Germain-des-Prés. **Open** All year.

This is the hotel Albert Camus opted for when visiting Paris and where he finished the manuscript of his novel "The Stranger". Set slightly back from the boulevard on a little square with its trees, it directly faces the church of Saint-Germain-des-Prés. You can choose a room with this view, while the higher you are, the more the view widens over the roofs of the area. The rooms are large, classical and irresistibly elegant, often with antique furniture. You will find the same comfort throughout: beautiful fabrics from *Chez Lelièvre*, deep printed carpeting, large cupboards with drawers in the English style, bathrooms with Italian tiles. All the corridors have received the same care. The lounge is magnificent, in 18th-century style: wood carvings, Aubusson greenery, elegant wing chairs. The breakfast room (buffet-brunch formula) is just as lovely, with its studded floor and its hearth which is ablaze from 6 AM until midnight as of the first signs of wintry weather. This is a superb hotel offering an attentive and good-humored welcome.

Hôtel des Marronniers

21, rue Jacob
75006 Paris
Tel. (0)1 43 25 30 60 – Fax (0)1 40 46 83 56
M. Henneveux

Category ★★★ **Rooms** 37 with air-conditioning, bath or shower, WC, satellite TV. **Price** Single 620F / 94,52€, double 815-1120F / 124,25-170,74€, triple 1220F / 185,99€. **Meals** Breakfast 60 and 65F / 9,15 and 9,91€, served 7:30-11:00. **Credit cards** Visa, Eurocard, MasterCard. **Pets** Dogs not allowed. **Facilities** Elevator, safe at reception, garden. **Parking** 169, boulevard Saint-Germain and on rue Mazarine. **How to get there** (Map 1) Bus: 39, 48, 58, 63, 70, 86, 87, 95 and 96 – Metro: Saint-Germain-des-Prés. **Open** All year.

The rue Jacob conceals an incalculable number of tapestry dealers, decorators, antique sellers and the Hôtel Les Marronniers, which seems most content among such neighbors. This very pretty address also offers the luxury of a genuine little garden right in the center of Paris, and has managed a most happy interior transformation. There is first the small but warm entry area with its warm tones and a few antique pieces. Then follows the veranda in Napoleon III–style, used as a tearoom and also the breakfast room, with the whole having a rather "Empress Eugénie" character with wrought iron garden furniture against a background of flowery carpeting and billowing curtains. Lastly, the rooms and their bathrooms are all recently renovated and well-equipped. From the *troisième étage*, those with a number ending with a 1 or 2 look onto the garden, while those on the *cinquième* and *sixième étages* look onto the courtyard, and have a pretty view over the roofs of the district. The welcome is cheerful.

Millésime Hôtel

15, rue Jacob
75006 Paris
Tel. (0)1 44 07 97 97 – Fax (0)1 46 34 55 97
Laurence Leclercq

Category ★★★ **Rooms** 21 air-conditioning, soundproofing, telephone, bath, WC, hairdryer, satellite TV, minibar, safe – 1 for disabled persons. **Price** Single 900F / 137,20€, double 1000-1050F / 152,45-160,07€, "Millésime room" 1150F / 175,32€. **Meals** Breakfast 55 and 60F / 8,38 and 9,15€, served 7:00-12:00. **Credit cards** Visa, Eurocard, MasterCard, Amex. **Pets** Small dogs allowed. **Facilities** Elevator, laundry service. **Parking** 169, boulevard Saint-Germain. **How to get there** (Map 1) Bus: 39, 48, 58, 63, 70, 86, 87, 95 and 96 – Metro: Saint-Germain-des-Prés and Mabillon. **Open** All year.

From the outside you can see the small welcome lounge of the Millésime, the foretaste of a classical style and fashion well-matching the tone of this street so rich in boutiques and antique shops. Like us, you will delight to cross the threshold with its light wood tones and orange-ocre colorings seen from the front, and will soon note that the rest of the hotel does not disappoint your first impressions. The rooms are large and have comfortable beds standing against Directory-style pediments and covered with rich mixed *piqué* fabrics matching the dominant colorway. The walls are covered in beige tones topped with a frieze, and you find a half-moon picture in each one, the reproduction of an Italian villa. The bathrooms are elegant, with white with grey touches, smart chromed taps which are new editions of older fixtures. You should note the *Millésime* room with its double sloped ceiling and very pretty view. Breakfasts are served in the vast cellar in a huge room centered around an impressive pillar dating from the Middle Ages. This is one of the most successful renovations in this quarter.

Hôtel Normandie Mayet

3, rue Mayet
75006 Paris
Tel. (0)1 47 83 21 35 – Fax (0)1 40 65 95 78
M. Atmoun

Category ★ ★ ★ Rooms 23 with bath or shower, WC, telephone, hairdryer, safe and satellite TV. **Price** Single 450F / 68,60€ (420F / 64,12€ for readers of this guide), double 650F / 99,09€ (550F / 83,85€ for readers of this guide); in low season: 1 pers. 400F / 60,98€, 2 pers. 490F / 74,70€. **Meals** Breakfast 36F / 5,49€, served 7:30-10:00. **Credit cards** All major. **Pets** Dogs allowed. **Facilities** Elevator, bar. **Parking** Montparnasse. **How to get there** (Map 1) Metro: Duroc – Bus: 39, 70, 82, 87, 89 and 92. **Open** All year.

Close to the lively area but in total quiet, the small rue Mayet is an ideal spot for relaxation without isolation. To decorate the reception area of this discreet little hotel, Italian artists came to complete the foliated frescoes as well as the peacocks decorating the walls and the superb assembly of worked woods linking the bar to the reception areas. The ground floor has recently been enlarged and now you can enjoy a pleasant lounge corner whose decoration is Orient-inspired. The small rooms, well-maintained, are simpler, with all the necessary comforts, yellow walls and floral fabrics. We recommend those on the street side which are slightly larger (those with a number ending with a 2 have three windows, one of which is in the bathroom); on the courtyard side they face a blank wall and should only should only be taken in an emergency. There is no restaurant, but La Cadolle is just next door and it will surely be an excellent discovery.

Hôtel Novanox

155, boulevard du Montparnasse
75006 Paris
Tel. (0)1 46 33 63 60 - Fax (0)1 43 26 61 72
M. Bertrand Plasmans

Category ★★★ **Rooms** 27 with soundproofing, telephone, bath or shower, WC, minibar, hairdryer, safe. **Price** Single 550-750F / 83,85-114,34€, double 580-750F / 88,42-114,34€; from mid Jul to end Aug: 1 pers. 490F / 74,70€, 2 pers. 550F / 83,85€. **Meals** Breakfast 50F / 7,62€, served 7:00-12:00; snacks available. **Credit cards** All major. **Pets** Dogs allowed. **Facilities** Elevator, bar, terrace. **Parking** Montparnasse, Raspail. **How to get there** (Map 10) Bus: 38, 83, 91 — Metro: Vavin, Raspail — RER: Port-Royal. **Open** All year.

Hidden by a small hedge behind which several teak chairs and tables are set out, the Novanox strikes you with its originality. Designer fabrics and pale-wood furniture especially designed for the hotel create a contemporary atmosphere that is both sophisticated and pleasant. With their smart desk-dressing tables, elegant wardrobes, and handsomely upholstered chairs, the bedrooms are individually furnished. The bathrooms are well-equipped but they are much less remarkable. If you're concerned about noise from the boulevard (despite the double-glazed windows), ask for a room on the rue Notre-Dame-des-Champs side. Breakfast is served in the lounge-bar. There's a vast choice of famous, late-night restaurants and *brasseries* here in Montparnasse.

Hôtel de l'Odéon

13, rue Saint-Sulpice – 75006 Paris
Tel. (0)1 43 25 70 11 – Fax (0)1 43 29 97 34
M. and Mme Pilfert
Web: www.hoteldelodeon.com – E-mail: hotelodeon@wanadoo.fr

Category ★ ★ ★ **Rooms** 30 with air-conditioning, soundproofing on the street side, bath or shower, WC, telephone, cable TV, outlet for Fax, hairdryer, safe. **Price** Depending on the season (high season: May, June, Sep and Oct) Single 740-1000F / 112,81-152,45€, double 880-1000F / 134,16-152,45€, "supérieures" 1150-1270F / 175,32-193,61€, "luxes" 1300-1420F / 198,18-216,48€, 3-4 pers. 1350-1690F / 205,81-257,64€. **Meals** Breakfast 60F / 9,15€, (free in high season). **Credit cards** All major. **Pets** Dogs allowed. **Facilities** Elevator, patio, bar. **Parking** Place Saint-Sulpice. **How to get there** (Map 1) Bus: 58, 63, 70, 86, 87 and 96 – Metro: Odéon – RER: Saint-Michel. **Open** All year.

In this ideally located 16th-century building, all the styles have been happily mingled with the Louis-Philippe winged chairs and pedestal tables of the tiny lounge alongside a church pew, a few Oriental carpets, flowered English carpeting and so on. If you add in a telephone box that seems to have come directly from Trafalgar Square in London, some splendid old stained glass pieces delicately lightened, then you create a particularly warm atmosphere quite able to make you overlook the smallness of the place and some of the rooms. With these, originality has also been shown and there is not one that resembles another. Some are *haute-époque* with a canopied bed, others are romantic style with a copper bedstead or twinned Sicilian beds of painted wrought iron with mother-of-pearl effects. Yet others offer integrated painted and polished furniture in the old style. All have a small corner area for writing or just relaxation. This is an astonishing place with the decor applied so that you forget you are even in a hotel.

Hôtel La Perle

14, rue des Canettes – 75006 Paris
Tel. (0)1 43 29 10 10 – Fax (0)1 46 34 51 04
Mme Spowe – M. Laterner
Web: www.hotellaperle.com – E-mail: booking@hotellaperle.com

Category ★★★ **Rooms** 38 with air-conditioning, soundproofing, bath or shower (some with whirlpool), WC, telephone (some with fax), minibar, safe, hairdryer, satellite TV – 2 for disabled persons. **Price** Single 900F / 137,20€, double 950-1400F / 144,83-213,43€. **Meals** Breakfast (buffet) 85F / 12,95€, served from 7:00. **Credit cards** All major. **Pets** Dogs allowed. **Facilities** Elevator, laundry service, bar, patio. **Parking** Saint-Germain and Saint-Sulpice. **How to get there** (Map 1) Bus: 58, 63, 70, 86, 87 and 96 – Metro: Saint-Germain-des-Prés, Saint-Sulpice, Mabillon. **Open** All year.

Lively with its many small restaurants, the narrow rue des Canettes dates back to the 13th century and is one of the most picturesque streets of the Left Bank. La Perle recently opened in an 18th-century house here, which is adorned in a beautiful combination of contemporary and classic styles. Old beams, pillars, and exposed-stone walls are used to handsome advantage in the reception areas. There is a pleasant bar that is designed somewhat like a boat, with exotic wood panelling and copper portholes. Adjacent to it is the bright breakfast room, which is in the old, almost entirely glassed-in interior courtyard. The comfortable, immaculately kept bedrooms, whose predominant colors vary with each floor, are air-conditioned and sound-proofed with effective double-glazing. They have beautiful beamed ceilings, but the decor, although tasteful, is somewhat conventional.

Hôtel Le Régent

61, rue Dauphine – 75006 Paris
Tel. (0)1 46 34 59 80 – Fax (0)1 40 51 05 07
Mme Danièle Martin
E-mail: hotel.leregent@wanadoo.fr

Category ★★★ **Rooms** 25 with air-conditioning, soundproofing, bath or shower, WC, telephone, satellite TV, radio, hairdryer, safe and minibar. **Price** Single and double 750-1100F / 114,34-167,69€ – Special rates in low season. **Meals** Breakfast 60F / 9,15€, served 7:00-11:00. **Credit cards** All major. **Pets** Dogs not allowed. **Facilities** Elevator, laundry service. **Parking** 27, rue Mazarine. **How to get there** (Map 1) Bus: 24, 27, 58, 63, 70, 86, 87 and 96 – Metro: Odéon – RER: Saint-Michel. **Open** All year.

Fully renovated, the Hôtel le Régent is in an old 18th-century building between the Boulevard Saint-Germain and the quays of the Seine. In the entry hall a wall mirror reflects the painted beams and ancient stonework of the house, and the classical lounge continues in a similar style. The rooms are a success due to a very beautiful harmony of coral, cream or lime-green shades and materials, with more contrasted colors on the top floor and superb enamel faience in the bathrooms. All are light, furnished with elegance, extremely comfortable and in perfect taste. Converted into the breakfast room, the vaulted cellar is very warm but there is some risk of crowding when the hotel is full, and it may be better to have breakfast in your own room. The hotel owners also own the legendary *Café des Deux Magots* where you can enjoy your meals at leisure.

Regent's Hôtel

44, rue Madame
75006 Paris
Tel. (0)1 45 48 02 81 – Fax (0)1 45 44 85 73
Juliette and Alexis Aymard

Category ★★ **Rooms** 34 with soundproofing (3 with terrace) with bath or shower, WC, telephone and satellite TV – 1 for disabled persons. **Price** Single 450F / 68,60€, double 500-600F / 76,22-91,47€, triple 700F / 106,71€. **Meals** Breakfast 40F / 6,10€, served 7:00-11:00. **Credit Cards** Visa, Eurocard, MasterCard, Amex. **Pets** Dogs allowed. **Facilities** Elevator, patio, drinks machine. **Parking** Saint-Sulpice. **How to get there** (Map 1) Bus: 48, 58, 83, 84, 89, 95 and 96 – Metro: Saint-Sulpice and Rennes. **Open** All year.

Located in a quiet spot between Saint-Sulpice and Montparnasse, the Regent's Hôtel has just been renovated. The rooms are simply and tastefully decorated, with yellow and blue tones dominating (numbers 11, 21 and 31 are a bit small and therefore better for singles). Reserve the upper floors rooms in priority; they are larger and better laid-out, with beautiful furniture especially designed for the hotel (the bathrooms are also better). In summertime, the rooms most in demand are numbers 51, 52 and 57 because of their well-furnished terraces, but families might prefer the small house in the flowered courtyard, that has been turned into a suite. Breakfast can be served on this patio, but when the weather is not warm enough, you can still enjoy its greenery from the large dining-room windows. A pleasant establishment, along the lines of those small hotels redecorated in keeping with today's style.

Hôtel Relais Christine

3, rue Christine - 75006 Paris
Tel. (0)1 40 51 60 80 - Fax (0)1 40 51 60 81
M. Yves Monnin
Web: www.relais-christine.com - E-mail: relaisch@club-internet.fr

Category ★★★★ **Rooms** 35 and 16 duplexes, with air-conditioning, soundproofing, bath, WC, telephone (fax with extra charge), cable TV, hairdryer, safe and minibar. **Price** Single 1850F / 282,03€, double 1950F / 297,28€ (from Jul 15 to end Aug 1900F/ 289,65€ with breakfast (buffet) and a museum-pass for 1 day), room with lounge 2600F / 396,37€, duplex 2450-4000F / 373,50-610,68€. **Meals** Breakfast 110F / 16,77€, buffet 135F / 20,58€, served at any time. Snacks available. **Credit cards** All major. **Pets** Dogs allowed. **Facilities** Elevator, laundry service, bar, garden, room service. **Parking** Free private parking. **How to get there** (Map 1) Bus: 24, 27, 58, 63, 70, 86, 87 and 96 – Metro: Odéon, Saint-Michel – RER: Saint-Michel. **Open** All year.

This hotel from the early 17th century occupies a part of the former Augustins Convent and is reached via a paved green courtyard. The interior has nothing nun-like about it, quite the contrary. A full range of warm colors has been chosen for the decoration, whether in the wainscotted lounge with its pretty collection of antique furniture pieces and portraits, or in the very pleasant rooms, with some facing onto a real leafy garden. Small or somewhat larger, all are extremely comfortable and decorated in a classical and bright style. You should also note the duplexes, much appreciated by families and perfect for longer stays if the means allow. The breakfast room is in a superb vaulted room set around an imposing central pillar. This was the former kitchen area dating from the early 13th century whose fireplace and well can still be seen. Offering a very attentive, discreet and efficient welcome, the Relais Christine has become a classic among the Parisian hotels of charm.

Le Relais Médicis

23, rue Racine
75006 Paris
Tel. (0)1 43 26 00 60 - Fax (0)1 40 46 83 39
M. Chérel

Category ★★★ **Rooms** 16 with air-conditioning, soundproofing, bath, WC, telephone, cable TV, hairdryer, safe, minibar. **Price** Single 990-1230F / 150,92-187,51€, double 1100-1595F / 167,69-243,16€. **Meals** Breakfast included, served 7:00-12:00. **Credit cards** All major. **Pets** Dogs not allowed. **Facilities** Laundry service. **Parking** Rue de l'Ecole de Médecine. **How to get there** (Map 1) Bus: 58, 63, 70, 84, 86, 87, 89 and 96 – Metro: Odéon – RER: Luxembourg. **Open** All year.

The Relais Médicis appropriately defines itself as a hotel with the colors of Provence and the scent of Italy. There is truly a warm and sunny atmosphere inside. Waxed beamed ceilings, antique furniture in all styles, old photos in sepia tones, small impressionist paintings and amusing chromos give character to the reception rooms downstairs. These are set up in a U-shape around a neatly tended little garden with chirping birds. These are fed regularly so that they come back and enliven the place. The bedrooms are cheerful, very comfortable and pleasantly furnished, the bathrooms do not pale by comparison. The largest rooms overlook the street but all can be recommended. The breakfast room has embellishments in *barbotine* and checked table cloths. This hotel has been conceived as a place that you will look forward to coming back to in the evening.

Le Relais Saint-Germain

9, carrefour de l'Odéon
75006 Paris
Tel. (0)1 43 29 12 05 - Fax (0)1 46 33 45 30
M. Laipsker

Category ★ ★ ★ ★ **Rooms** 22 with air-conditioning, soundproofing, bath, WC, telephone, cable TV, hairdryer, safe, minibar. **Price** Single 1290F / 196,66€, double 1600-1850F / 243,92-282,03€, suite 2100F / 320,14€, duplex (4-5 pers.) 3300F / 503,08€. **Meals** Breakfast included; snacks available. **Credit cards** All major. **Pets** Dogs allowed. **Facilities** Laundry service, room service. **Parking** Rue de l'Ecole de Médecine. **How to get there** (Map 1) Bus: 58, 63, 70, 86, 87 and 96 – Metro: Odéon – RER: Saint-Michel. **Open** All year.

Pleasantly situated, this small and charming luxury hotel wants for nothing in comparison with the very largest types, and the tone is set right from the reception area and neighboring lounge. Some beautiful 18th-century paintings in the style of Joseph Vernet set off a Louis XIV commode, various refined objects and shimmering fabrics, and we are here very far removed from some anonymous and standardized hotel. The exception proves the rule but the Relais Saint-Germain has only twenty-two rooms, all very perfectly done, thanks to the owners' taste and sense of comfort. Spacious or more cozy, with antique furniture pieces of a flare and luxury that might surprise; they have beautiful printed or striped fabrics blending with the dominant color. The suites are superb and their prices seem entirely justified. There are open views from everywhere with the hotel giving onto the very typical Place de l'Odéon. The welcome and service are naturally faultless.

Hôtel Relais Saint-Sulpice

3, rue Garancière
75006 Paris
Tel. (0)1 46 33 99 00 - Fax (0)1 46 33 00 10
Mme Touber

Category ★★★ **Rooms** 26 with air-conditioning, soundproofing, bath, WC, telephone, satellite TV, hairdryer, minibar, safe – 2 for disabled persons. **Price** Single and double 950-1150F / 144,83-175,32€; extra bed 100F / 15,24€. **Meals** Breakfast (buffet) 50F / 7,62€, served 7:00-11:00. **Credit cards** All major. **Pets** Elevator, bar, laundry service. **Parking** In the hotel (150F / 22,87€ /day) and Place Saint-Sulpice. **How to get there** (Map 1) Bus: 58, 63, 70, 86, 87 and 96 – Metro: Saint-Sulpice, Mabillon. **Open** All year.

Very much in fashion, the Saint-Sulpice district is attracting more and more clothing boutiques and luxurious renovation. With the opening of the Relais Saint-Sulpice, the hotel business has not lagged behind in this trend and we are sure that this new hotel will soon find its clientele. The entry area is in the form of a lounge-library. The rooms are often small but made extremely comfortable with superb beds made irresistible by generous quilts and four pillows. The bathrooms are ravishing: the whole effect testifies to a real concern for details both in the quality of materials and forms and colors, very representative of modern trends. Taken over by a large greenhouse full of plants and flowers, the central courtyard which you can look at but not enter, lights a vast dining room in the basement. Breakfast is served in a winter garden atmosphere, with teak and wrought iron furniture, warmed by the dominant colors of yellow-orange and elegant prints. This is a fine and welcoming hotel.

Relais Hôtel du Vieux-Paris

9, rue Gît-le-Cœur - 75006 Paris
Tel. (0)1 44 32 15 90 - Fax (0)1 43 26 00 15
Mme Claude Odillard
Web: www.sollers.fr/rhvp - E-mail: vieuxparis@sollers.fr

Category ★★★★ **Rooms** 13 and 7 suites with air-conditioning, soundproofing, bath (whirlpool in suites), WC, telephone, cable TV, outlet for fax, safe, hairdryer and minibar. **Price** Single and double 1090-1470F / 166,17-224,10€, suite 1650-1800F / 251,54-274,41€. **Meals** Breakfast 80F / 12,20€, served 8:00-11:30; snacks available. **Credit cards** All major. **Pets** Dogs not allowed. **Facilities** Elevator, laundry service. **Parking** Place Saint-André-des-Arts. **How to get there** (Map 2) Bus: 21, 24, 27, 38, 85 and 96. Metro and RER: Saint-Michel. **Open** All year.

This is the very heart of the old Paris with Notre-Dame and the flower market. The building dates from 1480 and has conserved numerous traces of its past, such as the huge stone pillar in the small yellow dining room, bays and ceilings *á la francaise* and amusing volumes. In short, the place is not lacking in style. Mme Odillard has decorated it with as much attention to detail as if it were her own home: very fine coordinated fabrics, always well-designed furniture, even a little bell on the door of each room. A lot of comfort despite somewhat small proportions, a charming *bijou* style, along with beautiful bathrooms with heating lamps and bathrobes (there are jacuzzis in the suites). Breakfasts are refined including freshly squeezed orange juice and fresh tea. The welcome is very attentive and aimiable – one of the reasons why this hotel has been and keeps on receiving so many famous artists and writers.

Résidence des Arts

14, rue Gît-le-Cœur - 75006 Paris
Tel. (0)1 55 42 71 11 - Fax (0)1 55 42 71 00
M. Robert Chevance
Web: www.residence-des-arts.com - E-mail: rdesarts@aol.com

Rooms 5 and 6 suites with air-conditioning and soundproofing, with bath or shower, WC, hairdryer, telephone, satellite TV, safe, minibar and kitchenette. **Price** Rooms (1-2 pers.) 950F / 144,83€, suite (2-4 pers.) 1500-1800F / 228,67-274,41€, apart. (4-6 pers.) 2300F / 350,63€; from mid Nov to Mar: Rooms (1-2 pers.) 750F / 114,34€, suite (2-4 pers.) 1200-1500F / 182,94-228,67€, apart. (4-6 pers.) 1900F / 289,65€. **Meals** Breakfast 50F / 7,62€, served 8:00-10:00. **Credit cards** Visa, Eurocard, MasterCard, Amex. **Pets** Dogs not allowed. **Facilities** Elevator, laundry service, bar, room service. **Restaurant** Mealtime specials 89 and 130F / 13,58 and 19,82€. **Parking** Saint-Michel. **How to get there** (Map 2) Bus: All to Saint-Michel – Metro and RER: Saint-Michel. **Open** All year.

In the very heart of the Quartier Latin, behind the Place Saint Michel, this small residence hotel is on a narrow street punctuated by the sometimes tilted façades of very ancient houses. The inside has been integrally renovated. At first sight, it gives a false impression of being cramped. The reception area is indeed quite small, but this is not at all the case with the bedrooms, which have have a skillfully installed kitchenette and are perfectly suitable for long stays. The same characteristics are found in the suites, where a lounge area can provide extra sleeping space. The whole decor is warm and cheerful: thick carpeting, beautiful fabrics in sunny tones, old paintings or engravings and charming retro furniture from the Hotel Meurice. Beamed ceilings on the lower levels, sun in the upper ones. The last floor is reserved to one large apartment. An real fine address, which is as well-maintained as it is comfortable.

Hôtel de Saint-Germain

50, rue du Four – 75006 Paris
Tel. (0)1 45 48 91 64 – Fax (0)1 45 48 46 22
M. Lassalle
Web: hotel-saint-germain.com – E-mail hotel.de.st.germain@wanadoo.fr

Category ★★ Rooms 30 with bath or shower, WC, telephone, satellite TV, minibar, safe (+10F/1,52€ /day), 25 with hairdryer. **Price** Single 590-700F / 89,94-106,71€, double 705F / 107,48€ – Special rates in low season (Jan to end Feb, mid Jul to end Aug and mid Nov to end Dec, except national holidays, trade fair periods): 1 pers. 420-525F / 64,12-80,04€, 2 pers. 530F / 80,80€; extra bed +125F / 19,06€ (free for children under 12 year). **Meals** Breakfast continental 45F / 6,86€, englisch 60F / 9,15€, served 7:00-11:00. **Credit cards** All major. **Pets** Dogs not allowed. **Facilities** Elevator, laundry service. **Parking** Opposite the *Bon Marché* department store. **How to get there** (Map 1) Bus: 39, 48, 63, 70, 83, 84, 87, 94, 95 and 96 – Metro: Saint-Sulpice, Sèvres-Babylone. **Open** All year.

A mini-reception area with a lounge corner, flowers, a small desk, and all is in place. At the Hôtel de Saint-Germain, space is in short supply but it has been made welcoming and warm. Although the rooms are also not very large, their English pine furniture with a small desk or cupboard fit them perfectly. Depending on the floor, some have been kept in natural wood, while others have had their furniture changed into green, blue or red. The result is quite cheerful, and the are bright pocket-sized bathrooms have all the comforts. Those with a number ending in a 5 are slightly larger, while those with a 1 are at the back and quiet, but a bit dark. Number 11 also enjoys a tiny little courtyard with a table and chairs. However most of them give onto the street with a lot of activity and, despite the double-glazing, there is never complete silence, especially on the lower floors. A small hotel, whose prices are mostly interesting in low season.

Hôtel Saint-Germain-des-Prés

36, rue Bonaparte - 75006 Paris
Tel. (0)1 43 26 00 19 - Fax (0)1 43 25 74 39
M. Nouvel
E-mail: hotel-saint-germain-des-prés@wanadoo.fr

Category ★★★ **Rooms** 28 and 2 suites with air-conditioning and soundproofing, bath or shower, WC, telephone, TV, minibar, safe, hairdryer. **Price** Single 780-990F / 118,91-150,92€, double 940-1350F / 143,30-205,81€, suite 1700F / 259,16€ (2 pers.) — In Aug: −10%. **Meals** Breakfast 50F / 7,62€, served 7:30-10:30. **Credit cards** Visa, Eurocard, MasterCard, Amex. **Pets** Small dogs allowed. **Facilities** Elevator, laundry service. **Parking** Saint-Germain-des-Prés. **How to get there** (Map 1) Bus: 39, 48, 63, 86, 87 and 95 — Metro: Saint-Germain-des-Prés. **Open** All year.

Two steps off the Place Saint-Germain-des-Prés, this hotel reflects the beauty and sophistication of the famous neighborhood for which it is named. The handsome, antique oak doorway, set slightly back from the street, opens into a lobby in a nicely theatrical decor: noble marble walls in *trompe-l'œil*, *Haute Epoque* furniture, an Aubusson tapestry and antiques. In the lounge, with its immense glass wall and floral fresco, you can have breakfast or a drink. The renovated bedrooms are often small, but charming, with exposed beams and classic decor. The largest have beautiful antique or waxed oak furniture. Although there is double-glazing and air-conditioning. Still, the rue Bonaparte is very busy, so it's best to ask for a room overlooking the courtyard. The reception and service are particularly cheerful.

Hôtel Le Saint-Grégoire

43, rue de l'Abbé-Grégoire - 75006 Paris
Tel. (0)1 45 48 23 23 - Fax (0)1 45 48 33 95
Mme Agaud - M. Bouvier - M. de Bené
Web: www.hotelsaintgregoire.com - E-mail: hotel@saintgregoire.com

Category ★★★ Rooms 20 with air-conditioning, soundproofing, bath (1 with shower), WC, telephone, satellite TV, hairdryer. **Price** Double 690-1090F/ 105,19-166,17€, suites and rooms with terrace 1390-1490F / 211,90-227,15€; extra bed 100F / 15,24€. **Meals** Breakfast 60F / 9,15€; snacks available. **Credit cards** All major. **Pets** Small dogs allowed (+70F /10,67€). **Facilities** Elevator. **Parking** Rue de l'Abbé-Grégoire, rue de Rennes. **How to get there** (Map 1) Bus: 48, 89, 94, 95 and 96 – Metro: Saint-Placide, Rennes. **Open** All year.

Midway between Montparnasse and Saint-Germain, the Saint-Grégoire is in a small 18th-century building whose intimate decor is both chic and successfully done. In the lounge there is often an open fire burning and play has been made with a range of warm colors subtly marrying orange and plum tones. The rooms ally the delicacy of yellow or pink walls with beautiful wall-hangings. Elegant and well-arranged they out, they are large (more or less so), and always personalized by attractive furniture pieces and little "kilims", to form a really comfortable overall ambiance. The very functional bathrooms meet the same standard. Some rooms even have a flowery terrace where breakfast can be served and fine weather can be appreciated. An attractive hotel where you will enjoy an attentive and smiling welcome.

Hôtel Saint-Paul - Rive Gauche

43, rue Monsieur-le-Prince - 75006 Paris
Tel. (0)1 43 26 98 64 - Fax (0)1 46 34 58 60
Mlle Marianne Hawkins
E-mail: hotel.saint.paul@wanadoo.fr

Category ★★★ **Rooms** 30 (8 with air-conditioning) and 1 duplex (4 pers.) with bath or shower, WC, telephone, satellite TV, minibar, safe, hairdryer. **Price** Single 620-820F / 94,52-125,01€, double 720-1020F / 109,76-155,50€, duplex (4 pers.) 1320F / 201,23€; extra bed +180F / 27,44€. **Meals** Breakfast 55F / 8,38€, served 7:00-11:00. **Credit cards** All major. **Pets** Dogs allowed. **Facilities** Elevator, room service. **Parking** Rue Soufflot, rue de l'École de Médecine. **How to get there** (Map 1) Bus: 21, 27, 38, 58, 63, 82, 84, 85, 86, 87, 89 and 96 – Metro: Odéon – RER: Luxembourg. **Open** All year.

Marianne Hawkins takes care of her hotel as it if were her home; it should be said that this hotel has belonged to the same family for four generations, and they still greet you with the same pleasure. Many rooms have a pretty flower box in the window, and if you're lucky enough to be in the rear of the hotel, you'll have a lovely view of a large tree in the tiny patio near the reception area. The bedrooms, which are often larger on the street side, have beautiful beamed ceilings, oak doors and closets. They are furnished with marble baths. Their decoration gives prominence to two distinct styles: *Haute Epoque* for some rooms, and more colorful and up-to-date for others (our favorites). Breakfast is served in a 17th-century barrel-vaulted cellar with a well. There, while you taste the delicious Viennese pastries, you are likely to be greeted by Spoutnik, the house cat. You might also find him snoozing on the sofa in the lovely small lounge.

Hôtel Sainte-Beuve

9, rue Sainte-Beuve
75006 Paris
Tel. (0)1 45 48 20 07 - Fax (0)1 45 48 67 52
M. Jean-Pierre Egurréguy

Category ★★★ **Rooms** 22 with air-conditioning, bath, WC, telephone, satellite TV, safe, minibar. **Price** Single and double 760-1400F / 115,86-213,43€, suite 1700F / 259,16€, apartment 1810F / 275,93€. **Meals** Breakfast 80F / 12,20€, served from 7:00; snacks available. **Credit cards** All major. **Pets** Dogs not allowed. **Facilities** Elevator, bar. **Parking** 116, boulevard du Montparnasse. **How to get there** (Maps 1 and 10) Bus: 58, 68, 82, 83 and 91 – Metro: Vavin, Notre-Dame-des-Champs – RER: Port-Royal. **Open** All year.

The Sainte-Beuve is a model hotel of charm, decorated by the Paris workshop of David Hicks, and you find here all the touches of the master with its unfussy and comfortable luxury. All is very refined via a subtle harmony of colors and materials animating the new architecture of the lounge. Fully renovated in 1996, comfortable sofas and armchairs have been set up facing the fireplace, with a fire lit as soon as the weather turns cold. Everything has been refurbished in the bright and spacious rooms, done in a delicate celadon green with the ivory walls showing off the fine antique furniture, prints, superb wall curtains alongside the small *bonne-femme* taffeta curtains, and all those charming details that make the Sainte-Beuve such a refined establishment. The bathrooms are beautiful and sober. Breakfasts are particularly well prepared and delicious. Both service and attention are irreproachable and can only confirm that this really is a very fine hotel.

Hôtel des Saints-Pères

65, rue des Saints–Pères - 75006 Paris
Tel. (0)1 45 44 50 00 - Fax (0)1 45 44 90 83
Mme Salmon
E-mail: hotelsts.peres@wanadoo.fr

Category ★★★ **Rooms** 39 and 3 suites with air-conditioning, soundproofing, bath or shower, WC, telephone, satellite TV, safe, minibar. **Price** Single and double 550-1750F / 83,85-266,79€, suite 1750F / 266,79€. **Meals** Breakfast 70F / 10,67€, served 7:15-11:30; snacks available. **Credit cards** Amex, Visa, Eurocard, MasterCard. **Pets** Dogs not allowed. **Facilities** Elevator, patio, bar. **Parking** 169, boulevard Saint-Germain. **How to get there** (Map 1) Bus: 39, 48, 63, 68, 70, 83, 84, 87, 94 and 95 – Metro: Saint-Germain-des-Prés, Sèvres-Babylone. **Open** All year.

Built in the 17th-century by an architect of Louis XIV, the Hôtel des Saints-Pères is one of our favorites in Paris. Very cool and airy, its interior layout is set around a flowery and peaceful patio onto which most of the rooms look out on. It leads to a warm lounge with comfortable leather furniture, a bar and dining room. Comfortable, quiet and very well-equipped, all the rooms are decorated with antique furniture pieces, often in acajou, all matching with the prints or pictures from the 18th and 19th centuries, the chintz of the curtains, the colored carpeting and so on. A unique room and worthy of the major palaces, the so-called "Frescoes Room", with its magnificent allegorical ceiling, boasts all the splendors of the *Grand Siècle* in tones of deepest blue. On fine days a few tables are set out on the patio, and it is a real pleasure to start your day with a fresh-air breakfast surrounded by the small shrubs and flowers.

Hôtel de Seine

52, rue de Seine
75006 Paris
Tel. (0)1 46 34 22 80 – Fax (0)1 46 34 04 74
M. Henneveux

Category ★★★ **Rooms** 30 with soundproofing, bath, WC, hairdryer, telephone, satellite TV, safe. **Price** Single 755F / 115,10€, double 900-970F / 137,20-147,88€, triple 1150F / 175,32€. **Meals** Breakfast 60 and 65F / 9,15 and 9,91€, served 7:00-11:00. **Credit cards** Visa, Eurocard, MasterCard. **Pets** Dogs not allowed. **Facilities** Elevator. **Parking** 27, rue Mazarine. **How to get there** (Map 1) Bus: 39, 48, 58, 63, 70, 86, 87, 95 and 96 – Metro: Mabillon, Saint-Germain-des-Prés – RER: Saint-Michel. **Open** All year.

The Hôtel de Seine occupies a choice location, at the angle of the rue Jacob and rue de Seine. Famous for its art galleries, the latter links the Odéon district to the Institut de France, which is only separated from the Louvre by the charming Pont des Arts, the pedestrian bridge over the Seine - so you have some pleasant walks to look forward to. You will like the provincial charm of the lounge open on the street. Its panelling and wooden fireplace are brightened by a copy of a tapestry with a leafy motif. The rooms are comfortable and just as pleasantly decorated with provincial fabrics and polished painted furniture. The marbled bathrooms are also well-equipped. You should note there is one ground floor bedroom with a bathroom in duplex, that gives directly onto the lounge. One small remark however: the price increase for the twin rooms seems somewhat excessive (but they are recommendable all the same). Both service and welcome are lively.

Hôtel Sèvres-Azur

22, rue de l'Abbé-Grégoire - 75006 Paris
Tel. (0)1 45 48 84 07 - Fax (0)1 42 84 01 55
M. and Mme Baguès
Web: www.hotelsevresazur.com - E-mail: sevres.azur@wanadoo.fr

Category ★★ **Rooms** 31 with soundproofing, bath or shower, telephone, satellite TV, hairdryer – 1 for disabled persons. **Price** Single and double 440-520F / 67,08-79,27€, triple 620F / 94,52€; extra bed 90F / 13,72€. **Meals** Breakfast 40F / 6,10€, served 7:15-10:00. **Credit cards** All major. **Pets** Dogs allowed. **Facilities** Elevator. **Parking** Boucicaut, rue de Sévres opposite the *Bon Marché* department store. **How to get there** (Map 1) Bus: 39, 63, 68, 70, 83, 84, 87 and 94 – Metro: Sèvres-Babylone, Saint-Placide. **Open** All year.

Very well-set in the triangle between Montparnasse, Saint-Germain-des-Prés, and Le Bon Marché, the rue de l'Abbé-Grégoire is one of the quieter streets where the Hôtel Sèvres-Azur is found. The rooms have been renovated and they are comfortable and very attractive: egg-shell walls, elegant curtains, assorted bedspreads and divan bases, all mixing the warm shades of yellow and raspberry. The furniture is in light cerused wood, but whenever possible the bedsteads in copper or wrought iron, now once again sought after by the antique dealers, have been conserved. Whether facing street or courtyard, the rooms are highly recommended. Their bathrooms are impeccable. The ground floor is shared by the reception area, a lounge with its black leather sofas and the breakfast room which also serves as bar. All give onto a tiny little patio all in green with its small bench seat. One has a real "affair of the heart" with this small hotel offering some of the best value for the money in Paris, along with one of the friendliest of welcomes.

Victoria Palace Hôtel

6, rue Blaise-Desgoffe - 75006 Paris
Tel. (0)1 45 49 70 00 - Fax (0)1 45 49 23 75
M. Philippe Venet
E-mail: victoria@club-internet.fr

Category ★★★★ **Rooms** 33, 30 junior suites and 2 apart. with air-conditioning and soundproofing with bath, WC, hairdryer, telephone, cable TV, safe and minibar – 3 for disabled persons. **Price** Single and double 1700F / 259,16€, junior suite (1-2 pers.) 2200F / 335,39€, apart. (1-2 pers.) 3800F / 580,15€; extra bed 300F / 45,73€ (free until 12 year). **Meals** Breakfast (buffet) 95F / 14,48€, served 7:00-10:30. **Credit cards** All major. **Pets** Dogs allowed. **Facilities** Elevator, bar, laundry service, patio, room service. **Parking** In hotel (150F / 22,87€ /day). **How to get there** (Map 1). Bus: All to Montparnasse – Metro: Saint-Placide. **Open** All year.

The rarity of palaces on the left bank makes the brilliant renovation of the Victoria even more attractive. You certainly need a large budget to stay in this superb establishment, but once here you will not regret your choice. Everything has obviously been arranged to enchant you. The atmosphere of the reception lounges and the bar is identifiably Victorian. Close-woven velvet, Persian fabrics, printed carpets, waxed furniture and Chinese procelaine recreate a chic and soothing world that has a totally authentic feel. The same care for detail can be found in the bedrooms and suites, which often have very elegant furniture in a Louis XVI or *Directoire*-style: fabrics with classic motifs and cheerful tones, sanguine drawings, extremely well-chosen and of irreproachable comfort. All the standard rooms have a nice size, those ending with a number 13 being the largest. A magnificent, classic address at competitive prices.

La Villa

29, rue Jacob
75006 Paris
Tel. (0)1 43 26 60 00 – Fax (0)1 46 34 63 63
M. Leclercq

Category ★★★★ **Rooms** 32 with air-conditioning, soundproofing, bath or shower, WC, telephone, minibar, safe, satellite TV. **Price** Single and double 900-1800F / 137,20-274,41€, suite 2000-3000F / 304,90-457,35€. **Meals** Breakfast 80F / 12,20€, served 7:00-12:00; snacks available: salmon, foie gras, ham, fruits. **Credit cards** Visa, Eurocard, MasterCard, Amex. **Pets** Dogs not allowed. **Facilities** Elevator, bar. **Parking** 169, boulevard Saint-Germain. **How to get there** (Map 1) Bus: 39, 48, 63, 86, 87, 95 and 96 – Metro: Saint-Germain-des-Prés. **Open** All year.

Ever since its creation, La Villa has aimed at being a unique and totally contemporary hotel. The reception area is sober and spare, brightened with a large Japanese-inspired floral spray. The room numbers are shown in lighted figures on each door. Once inside, a feeling of serenity comes over the traveler. Two styles characterize the bedrooms. For some, furniture with sleek lines and often upholstered with colored leather; extra-wide beds surmounted by low-tension lamps in the ceiling. Just as contemporary in their choice of warm materials and colors, the others play on a less original but more universal theme. They all have sublime bathrooms whose dark-gray marble reflects the chrome basins, silver mirrors, and opaque, frosted-glass shelves. Breakfasts are served in a modern bar of streamlined decor, very much in the style of the 80s. The welcome is pleasant.

Hôtel Académie

32, rue des Saints-Pères - 75007 Paris
Tel. (0)1 45 49 80 00 - Fax (0)1 45 49 80 10
M. Chekroun
Web: www.academiehotel.com - E-mail: aaacademie@aol.com

Category ★★★ **Rooms** 28 and 6 junior suites with soundproofing, air-conditioning, telephone, bath or shower (whirlpool in junior suite), hairdryer, WC, satellite TV, safe and minibar. **Price** Single 990F / 150,92€, double 1290F / 196,66€, junior suite (1-4 pers.) 1590F / 242,39€; –30% (depending on the season) for readers of this guide. **Meals** Breakfast 75F / 11,43€, served 7:00-11:00; snacks available. **Credit cards** All major. **Pets** Dogs allowed. **Facilities** Elevator, bar, laundry service. **Parking** Private, opposite the hotel (150F / 22,87€ /day) and at 169, boulevard Saint-Germain. **How to get there** (Map 1) Bus: 39, 48, 63, 86 and 95 – Metros: Saint-Germain-des-Prés, Rue du Bac. **Open** All year.

Located in the heart of Saint-Germain-des-Prés, the Hôtel Académie has completed a beautiful renovation this year. The ground floor space is very well-used, divided into the reception area, the bar, a warm lounge and a very pleasant breakfast room where food lovers can enjoy a high quality buffet. The bedrooms are classic in various shades of pastel colors; bathrooms are well-equipped, those of the junior suites even have jacuzzi baths. They are quieter on the side of the courtyard, but air-conditioning and soundproofing allow for peaceful sleep on the street side as well, even in summer. Lastly, several rooms have just been redecorated with shimmering fabrics and antique or period furniture. The hotel has thus set a new tone in its style. To these qualities of location and comfort can be added a cheerful welcome.

Hôtel Bersoly's Saint-Germain

28, rue de Lille
75007 Paris
Tel. (0)1 42 60 73 79 - Fax (0)1 49 27 05 55
Mme Carbonnaux

Category ★★★ **Rooms** 16 with soundproofing, air-conditioning, telephone, bath or shower, WC, cable TV, hairdryer, safe. **Price** Single and double 600-750F / 91,47-114,34€; extra bed 150F / 22,87€. **Meals** Breakfast 50F / 7,62€; snacks available. **Credit cards** Visa, Eurocard, MasterCard, Amex. **Pets** Dogs allowed on request. **Facilities** Bar. **Parking** Private; public parking at 9, rue de Montalembert. **How to get there** (Map 1) Bus 24, 27, 39, 48, 68, 69 and 95 – Metro: Rue du Bac, Saint-Germain-des-Prés – RER: Musée d'Orsay. **Closed** 3 weeks in Aug.

There reigns in the small Hôtel Bersoly's an intimate and charming atmosphere due as much to the decor as to the numerous little details for the clientele. To harmonize with the rustic architecture of the house, the reception area and its small corner-lounge mix Louis XIII furniture pieces and sofas with flowered fabrics. For their part, the rooms are each given the name of a painter, and have a colorful decor both bright and very refined; the largest rooms are the twin rooms (most of which can be combined into two-room apartments). They are comfortable and each has an electric kettle as well as cups, a much appreciated initiative on return from a walk or the Musée d'Orsay. The hotel is soundproofed and the street rather quiet. Therefore there is no special advantage to the rooms overlooking the courtyard except that they are slightly cheaper (and slightly darker, apart from those on the upper floor). The welcome is pleasant.

Hôtel Bourgogne et Montana

3, rue de Bourgogne - 75007 Paris
Tel. (0)1 45 51 20 22 - Fax (0)1 45 56 11 98
Mme Martine Monney
E-mail: info@bourgogne-montana.com

Category ★★★ Rooms 26 and 6 suites with air-conditioning, bath, WC, telephone, minibar, cable TV. **Price** Single 930-1300F / 141,78-198,18€, double 1000-1300F / 152,45-198,18€, suite 1800-2000F / 274,41-304,90€; extra bed +370F / 56,41€ – Special rates in Jan, Feb and Aug. **Meals** Breakfast (buffet) included, served 6:30-12:00. **Credit cards** All major. **Pets** Dogs allowed. **Facilities** Elevator. **Parking** Invalides. **How to get there** (Map 1) Bus: 24, 63, 69, 73, 83, 84, 93 and 94 – Metro: Invalides and Assemblée Nationale – RER: Invalides – Les Invalides Air Terminal. **Open** All year.

The Bourgogne et Montana is one of the most beautiful hotels in this neighborhood. A cosmopolitan clientele comes here for the superb location and the smart, refined hotel itself. On the ground floor are the bar, the lounge and the beautiful breakfast room where the use of Third Republic caricatures prefigures the care given to the bedrooms. Freshly refurbished, they are all different but all handsomely laid-out with Empire furniture, beautiful fabrics and irresistible bathrooms. Whether you stay in a bedroom or a suite, all rival each other in charm and comfort (only those with a number ending in a 0 seem a bit small; on the other hand, we quite like the layout of those ending in 4). This very beautiful hotel offers a delicious breakfast buffet, which is included in the room rates.

Hôtel du Champ-de-Mars

7, rue du Champ-de-Mars - 75007 Paris
Tel. (0)1 45 51 52 30 - Fax (0)1 45 51 64 36
M. and Mme Gourdal
Web: www.hotel-du-champs-de-mars.com - E-mail: stg@club-internet.fr

Category ★★ **Rooms** 25 with bath or shower, WC, hairdryer, outlet for modem, telephone and satellite TV. **Price** Single 390F / 59,46€, double 430-460F / 65,55-70,13€. **Meals** Breakfast 35F / 5,34€, served 7:00-10:00. **Credit cards** Visa, Eurocard, MasterCard, Amex. **Pets** Dogs not allowed. **Facilities** Elevator. **Parking** Joffre (École Militaire). **How to get there** (Map 6) Bus: 28, 69, 80, 82, 87 and 92 – Metro: École Militaire – RER: Pont-de-l'Alma, Invalides. **Open** All year.

Acquired by a young and charming couple, this small hotel has been entirely renovated with the rooms given beautiful blue carpeting with small yellow motifs. These two colors are repeated on the wallpaper. The small white bathrooms are new and the whole effect, sustained by the numerous details, is one of brightness and careful maintenance. The lounge, breakfast room and corridors have not been forgotten. They have received the same care and *meridional* style found throughout the house. The courtyard is charming with its recessed walls covered with ivy, small trees and zinc roofs, which all remind us that we are here in the midst of the 7th *arrondissement*, full of life and many little shops. Close by is the rue Cler whose market is known to all Parisians. Add to this the proximity of the Eiffel Tower and the Invalides, and you realize just how well located the Hôtel du Champ-de-Mars really is. However, its excellent value means you must always reserve well in advance.

Hôtel Chomel

15, rue Chomel - 75007 Paris
Tel. (0)1 45 48 55 52 - Fax (0)1 45 48 89 76
M. and Mme Oularbi
E-mail: chomel@cybercable.fr

Category ★★★ **Rooms** 23 with soundproofing, telephone, bath or shower, WC, cable TV, hairdryer, minibar. **Price** Single and double 790-990F / 120,43-150,92€, "de luxe" (1-2 pers.) 1190F / 181,41€; in low season (Jul, Aug, Nov – Feb, excluding trade fair periods) 500-900F / 76,22-137,20€; extra bed 250F / 38,11€. **Meals** Breakfast 60F / 9,15€, served 7:00-10:00. **Credit cards** All major. **Pets** Dogs not allowed. **Facilities** Elevator, laundry service. **Parking** Boucicault (opposite the *Bon Marché* department store). **How to get there** (Map 1) Bus: 39, 63, 68, 70, 83, 84, 87 and 94 – Metro: Sèvres-Babylone. **Open** All year.

The Hôtel Chomel is in a very calm street a few steps away from the Bon Marché department store, very close to Saint-Germain-des-Prés. Its small bedrooms are all decorated on the same principle, without great originality: standard furniture in pale wood, plain fabrics of good quality and thick, beautiful carpets. Well-maintained and renovated, including the bathrooms, they bring you all the necessary comfort. If you want a little more space, you should reserve those with a number ending with a 1 (twin bedrooms) or a 4 (known as "de luxe"). The latter are really large and well-conceived for families; they also have two windows. Lastly, if possible, choose the upper floors, which are more luminous. Despite recent improvements, the reception lounge which stretches into the breakfast room, remains a bit formal. The welcome is attentive, the prices mainly attractive in the low season.

Hôtel Derby Eiffel

5, avenue Duquesne - 75007 Paris
Tel. (0)1 47 05 12 05 - Fax (0)1 47 05 43 43
M. El Bawab
E-mail: reservation@derbyeiffelhotel.com

Category ★★★ **Rooms** 42 and 1 junior suite with air-conditioning, bath or shower, WC, telephone, satellite TV, safe, minibar. **Price** Single 690-750F / 105,19-114,34€, double 750-900F / 114,34-137,20€, triple 900-1200F / 137,20-182,94€, junior suite 1200F / 182,94€, 4 pers. (adjoining rooms) 2000F / 304,90€. **Meals** Breakfast (buffet) 65F / 9,91€, served 7:00-10:30. **Ccredit cards** All major. **Pets** Dogs allowed. **Facilities** Elevator, patio, laundry service. **Parking** École Militaire. **How to get there** (Map 1) Bus: 28, 80, 82, 87 and 92 – Metro: École Militaire. **Open** All year.

This beautiful building faces the Ecole Militaire where, in the morning, you can watch riders training or jumping hurdles in the middle of the sumptuous Court of Honor, designed by the architect Gabriel in 1751. The entrance of the Dereby hotel, renovated last winter in a British spirit, offers a pleasant relaxing space at the corner of the bar. The same care has been put into the bedrooms: beige walls, functional but elegant mahogany furniture, thick beige and pink bedspreads with coordinated curtains and small English engravings with lovely gilt-bronze sconces on either side. An abundant breakfast (with cheese, scrambled eggs, cold cuts) is served in the basement with its exposed-stone walls, where the decor is unfortunately not terribly imaginative, and the lighting not very flattering for morning faces. But if the weather is nice, you can set yourself up in the tiny patio.

Hôtel Duc de Saint-Simon

14, rue de Saint-Simon - 75007 Paris
Tel. (0)1 44 39 20 20 - Fax (0)1 45 48 68 25
M. Lindquist
E-mail: ducdesaint-simon@wanadoo.fr

Category ★★★ **Rooms** 29 and 5 suites (some with air-conditioning, 4 with terrace) with bath (1 with shower), WC, telephone, TV on request, safe. **Price** Single and double 1375-1500F / 209,62-228,67€, suite 1925-1975F / 293,46-301,09€ (2 pers.). **Meals** Breakfast 75F / 11,43€, served from 7:30; snacks available. **Credit cards** All major. **Pets** Dogs not allowed. **Facilities** Elevator, bar, patio. **Parking** Garage de l'Abbaye: at 30, boulevard Raspail. **How to get there** (Map 1) Bus: 63, 68, 69, 83, 84 and 94 – Metro: Rue du Bac. **Open** All year.

The Duc de Saint-Simon is without doubt one of the most charming hotels in Paris. Once you have passed through the portico, you cross the paved courtyard with its wisteria and a few tables, and enter the warm interior recreating the atmosphere of those beautiful residences of earlier days. The bright colors of the polished worked wood and the superb fabrics mix with the paintings and other objects found throughout the house. Lounges, rooms and suites are entirely furnished with antiques of infallible taste. Despite their sometimes small size, the rooms are all extremely comfortable, with an atmosphere of genuine softness. Their superb bathrooms are covered with Salerno tiling. Four of them have beautiful terraces. The vaulted cellar now shelters the breakfast room, bar and numerous little corners fitted-out as small lounges. The whole effect is of total refinement with guaranteed peace and quiet. As for the welcome, it is courteous and most friendly, bringing an additional and indispensable quality to this very beautiful hotel.

Hôtel Duquesne-Eiffel

23, avenue Duquesne - 75007 Paris
Tel. (0)1 47 05 41 86 - Fax (0)1 45 55 54 76
M. Olivier Rioual
E-mail: hotel@duquesneeiffel.com

Category ★★★ **Rooms** 40 with air-conditioning, telephone, bath or shower, WC, hairdryer, minibar, safe, radio, cable and satellite TV. **Price** Single 625-890F / 95,28-135,68€, double 698-950F / 106,56-144,83€, triple 1050F / 160,07€. **Meals** Breakfast (buffet) 50F / 7,62€, served 7:00-11:00 (12:00 in room). **Credit cards** All major. **Pets** Dogs allowed. **Facilities** Elevator, bar, laundry service, room service. **Parking** École Militaire. **How to get there** (Maps 1 and 6) Bus: 28, 80, 82, 87 and 92 – Metro: École Militaire – RER and Les Invalides Air Terminal. **Open** All year.

Royal blue leather sofas set in a square, a large coffee table full of newspapers and magazines, a wall of mirrors, a ceiling with large exposed beams - indeed, the reception lounge of this hotel is extremely comfortable. However it was not included in the recent renovation, and its style is therefore somewhat different from that of the bedrooms. These are truly well-done, with warm and cheerful colors, moderately contemporary furniture and many small details evoking luxury and comfort (the same goes for the bathrooms, where white tiles set off the red marble). In practical terms, there are ten rooms that can communicate and are therefore ideal for families. Those on the *cinquième étage* have balconies and those with a number ending with a 5 have two windows in an angle with a view of the Ecole Militaire and the Eiffel Tower in the background. Lastly, you need not fear the avenue Duquesne. There is not much night traffic, it doses off well before the twelve strokes of midnight.

Eiffel Park Hôtel

17 *bis*, rue Amélie
75007 Paris
Tel. (0)1 45 55 10 01 - Fax (0)1 47 05 28 68
Mme Françoise Testard

Category ★★★ **Rooms** 36 with air-conditioning and soundproofing, telephone, bath or shower, WC, hairdryer, satellite TV, safe and minibar – 2 for disabled persons. **Price** Single 550-700F / 83,85-106,71€, double 550-750F / 83,85-114,34€. **Meals** Breakfast 55F / 8,38€, served 7:00-10:00. **Credit cards** All major. **Pets** Dogs allowed. **Facilities** Elevator, bar, laundry service, terrace. **Parking** Esplanade des Invalides. **How to get there** (Maps 1 and 6) Bus: 28, 69, 80 and 92 – Metro: Latour-Maubourg – RER and Les Invalides Air Terminal. **Open** All year.

The Eiffel Park Hôtel conceals a very pleasant surprise: a solarium-terrace where in warm weather it is quite agreeable to have breakfast. The rest of the hotel would be more banal had the owners not been so fond of Asian furniture (from India or China). As a result, you some very beautiful antique pieces in the lobby and the adjoining lounge bar, and some elegant exotic reminders such as aged and painted furniture pieces in many rooms (naturally those are the ones we advise you to reserve in priority). The other rooms still have, for a short while, modern furniture totally lacking charm, but in all you find an elegant assortment of mural fabrics and curtains. Lastly, when the bad weather keeps you away from the terrace, you can use the pleasant dining room, whose decor is a bit cold, but which extends into a very bright veranda. This is a good address, and the efforts made to break out of commonplace hotel standards are worth acknowledging.

Grand Hôtel Lévêque

29, rue Cler - 75007 Paris
Tel. (0)1 47 05 49 15 - Fax (0)1 45 50 49 36
M. Tourneur
Web: www.hotel-leveque.com - E-mail: info@hotelleveque.com

Category ★ **Rooms** 50 soundproofing with telephone, outlet for modem, satellite TV, safe, hairdryer, fan, 45 with shower and WC, 5 with washstand (private WC outside the room). **Price** Single 300F / 45,73€, double 400-470F / 60,98-71,65€, triple 580F / 88,42€. **Meals** Breakfast 40F / 6,10€, served 7:00-10:30. **Credit cards** Visa, Eurocard, MasterCard, Amex. **Pets** Dogs allowed. **Facilities** Elevator. **Parking** Joffre (École Militaire). **How to get there** (Map 6) Bus: 28, 69, 80, 82, 87 and 92 – Metro: École Militaire – RER: Pont de l'Alma, Invalides. **Open** All year.

The new owners of the Grand Hôtel Lévêque fully renovated it in 1997. Certainly the rooms are not large, as so often in Paris, but all the comforts are here: new bedding, small but impeccable shower rooms, hairdryer, safe, satellite TV, and so on. Still all are designed on the same model. They offer a simple and rather cheerful decor: walls flecked in yellow, light carpeting and printed fabrics. The rooms on the street (pedestrians only) are attractive with their two windows. If you book them in time you can also enjoy all the life of the market in the rue Cler, very picturesque and popular with Parisians. However, if you are afraid of being disturbed by noise, the other rooms at the back are quiet, but do avoid the singles. Breakfast is served in a bistro-style atmosphere. This is a good location for a low price.

Hôtel de La Bourdonnais

111-113, avenue de La Bourdonnais - 75007 Paris
Tel. (0)1 47 05 45 42 - Fax (0)1 45 55 75 54
M. Champetier
Web: www.hotellabourdonnais.com - E-mail: otlbourd@clubinternet.fr

Category ★★★ **Rooms** 57 and 3 junior suites with air-conditioning and soundproofing, bath or shower, WC, telephone, satellite TV, 20 with minibar. **Price** Single 550-580F / 83,85-88,42€, double 720-750F / 109,76-114,34€, junior suite (3-4 pers.) 1100F / 167,69€. **Meals** Breakfast 50F / 7,62€, served 6:00-11:00. **Credit cards** All major. **Pets** Dogs allowed. **Facilities** Elevator, patio, laundry service. **Restaurant** Gastronomic; mealtime specials 240-420F / 36,59-64,12€. **Parking** Joffre (École Militaire). **How to get there** (Map 1) Bus: 28, 69, 80, 82 and 92 – Metro: École Militaire. **Open** All year.

Parallel to the Champ-de-Mars, the avenue de la Bourdonnais is a line of stately buildings, and this hotel is no exception. Some small pointed trees form a guard of honor under the canopy of the entryway and protect the intimacy of the lounge windows. Inside there is one of the best tables of the capital where gourmets meet to thrill their taste buds in total privacy. Marvellously filled plates, top-quality products whose precious flavors are always respected; one leaves feeling at ease, but conquered. The *bourgeois*-style hotel sports a host of squat armchairs in brown leather and antique furniture pieces in the lounge and very classical rooms. These are often large, with a velvety and slightly old-fashioned charm (their size and the low charge for extra guests makes them interesting for families). The veranda-breakfast room, whose wallpaper plays on a *trompe-l'oeil*-theme, opens onto a small garden planted with ivy, ocuba and rhododendrons.

Hôtel de La Motte Picquet

30, avenue de la Motte-Picquet
75007 Paris
Tel. (0)1 47 05 09 57 - Fax (0)1 47 05 74 36
Mme Ireland

Category ★★ **Rooms** 18 and 1 duplex with soundproofing bath or shower, WC (2 outside the room), hairdryer, telephone, satellite TV, safe and minibar. **Price** Single 355-395F / 54,12-60,22€, double 400-490F / 60,98-74,70€, triple 595-670F / 90,71-102,14€, duplex (4 pers.) 780F / 118,91€. **Meals** Breakfast 35F / 5,34€, served 7:00-10:30. **Credit cards** Visa, Eurocard, MasterCard. **Pets** Dogs Allowed (+30F / 4,57€). **Facilities** Elevator. **Parking** Joffre (École Militaire). **How to get there** (Map 6) Bus: 28, 69, 80, 82, 87 and 92 – Metro: École Militaire. **Open** All year.

Mme Ireland has already run four hotels in Paris. She decided to stop, but after three years she began to get bored. Now she is back, at Hôtel de la Motte Piquet, fully renovating eighteen small rooms: beddings, carpets, colorful fabrics, cupboards, white-tiled bathrooms, often with daylight. The result is simple, charming, clean and comfortable (be sure the *premier étage* has been finished before booking there). The windows have been changed as well, and their double-glazing very effectively soundproofs you from the bustle in the avenue. Other rooms overlook a courtyard (avoid numbers 101 and 102 which face a wall) or the rue Cler, which Parisians really like for its lively market. Those with a number ending in 5 have a pleasant corner location, while those ending in 4 seem a bit small. There is also a duplex to accommodate four people. Thoughtful welcome.

Hôtel Latour-Maubourg

150, rue de Grenelle - 75007 Paris
Tel. (0)1 47 05 16 16 - Fax (0)1 47 05 16 14
Victor and Maria Orsenne
Web: www.latour-maubourg.fr - E-mail: info@latour-maubourg.fr

Category ★★★ **Rooms** 9 and 1 suite with soundproofing, bath or shower, WC, hairdryer, telephone, outlet for fax, satellite TV, minibar and fan. **Price** Single 600-700F / 91,47-106,71€, double 850-900F / 129,58 137,20€, suite 1000F / 152,45€; extra bed 200F / 30,49€. **Meals** Breakfast included, served 7:00-19:00; in Aug: 1 pers. 550F / 83,85€, 2 pers. 650F / 99,09€. **Credit cards** Visa, Eurocard, MasterCard. **Pets** Dogs allowed (+50F / 7,62€). **Facilities** Laundry service, baby-sitting, patio, room service (except in Aug). **Parking** Latour-Moubourg. **How to get there** (Maps 1 and 6): Bus: 69 – Metro: Latour-Maubourg – RER: Invalides. **Open** All year.

A square with huge chestnut trees, a tiny little private hotel, a *grille* and three steps - all invite you to push the door and walk in. You would not want to miss it: this is one of our most charming discoveries. The interior reminds you of a private house with a very cozy lounge, old pictures, comfortable chairs and small tables where at any hour you can have a breakfast as good as it is nicely laid-out. Just as enjoyable, the rooms all display their elegant sunny fabrics. They are all of a good size, while the suite is immense and a very good deal. The rooms look out the trees and give a direct view, when the leaves have fallen, of the noble façade of the Invalides under its famous glistening dome. With a sumptuous comfort, they usually have one or two antique furniture pieces in tune with the quality prints and pictures. This is a very fine address run with much flare by M. and Mme. Orsenne, who live on the premises and give the place its inimitable feel of home.

Hôtel Lenox - Saint-Germain

9, rue de l'Université - 75007 Paris
Tel. (0)1 42 96 10 95 - Fax (0)1 42 61 52 83
Christiane Laporte - Claire Colson
Web: www.lenoxsaintgermain.com - E-mail: lenox@gofornet.com

Category ★★★ **Rooms** 34 (4 with mezzanine) with soundproofing and air-conditioning, bath or shower, hairdryer, WC, telephone, safe and TV. **Price** Double 700-1150F / 106,71-175,32€, duplex 1600F /243,92€. **Meals** Breakfast 50 and 75F / 7,62 and 11,43€; snacks available. **Credit cards** All major. **Pets** Samll dogs allowed. **Facilities** Elevator, bar, laundry service, room service. **Parking** At 9, rue Montalembert and opposite 169, boulevard Saint-Germain. **How to get there** (Map 1) Bus: 39, 48, 63, 68, 69 and 95 – Metro: Rue du Bac, Saint-Germain-des-Prés – RER: Musée d'Orsay. **Open** All year.

Well-situated on the corner of the rue du Pré-aux-Clercs, known for its fashion boutiques, and the rue de l'Université, the Lénox has for a long time kept a loyal clientele among the young and the chic. Open till late at night, the hotel bar with its rosewood and 1930s-style plays a big part in the ambiance. The rooms are comfortable and classically decorated (we like less those with a number ending in a 2 or a 6 which are a bit gaudy). The nicely done bathrooms often have a window. On the top floor, the rooms under the roof benefit from the large space. Some are even arranged in duplex but they are also more expensive and not necessarily larger than on the lower floors except for Rooms 54 and 55, which have a small lounge. Lastly, the new management has had air-conditioning installed, an initiative which deserves to be mentioned. The reception is dynamic and professional.

Hôtel Libertel Bellechasse

8, rue de Bellechasse
75007 Paris
Tel. (0)1 45 50 22 31 – Fax (0)1 45 51 52 36
Mme Elfriede Leutwyler

Category ★★★ **Rooms** 41 with telephone, bath or shower, WC, cable TV, minibar – 1 for disabled persons. **Price** Single 964,30F / 147€, double 1029,90-1252,90F / 157-191€ – Special rates in low season on request. **Meals** Breakfast 78,71F / 12€, served 7:00-11:00. **Credit cards** All major. **Pets** Dogs allowed. **Facilities** Elevator, patio, room service. **Parking** Rue du Bac. **How to get there** (Map 1) Bus: 24, 63, 68, 69, 73, 83, 84 and 94 – Metro: Solférino – RER: Musée d'Orsay. **Open** All year.

The Bellechasse is just a few steps from the Musée d'Orsay and the Legion of Honor Museum. The interior decor is influenced by the Empire style. The huge lobby, the exquisite dining room, corridors and bedrooms, all (except for the three rooms on the garden level) have beautiful striped fabrics, sculpted armchairs in the Napoleonic style; pale wood or antique bronze furniture with the famous cross-bars of the Empire epoch. Impeccable bathrooms, pretty lamps and a collection of old engravings further add to the elegance of the Bellechasse. Nevertheless, the rooms are not very large and therefore the prices seem a little high. You can sit in the interior courtyard of the hotel, which has been transformed into a flower garden, or you can take a seat in a deep armchair in the lounge to enjoy a pleasant view of the garden through the bay windows.

Hôtel Libertel Sèvres-Vaneau

86, rue Vaneau
75007 Paris
Tel. (0)1 45 48 73 11 - Fax (0)1 45 49 27 74
Mme Elfriede Leutwyler

Category ★★★ **Rooms** 39 with soundproofing, telephone, bath or shower, WC, cable TV, hairdryer and minibar. **Price** Single 787,20F /120€, double 938F / 143€ – Special rates in low season on request. **Meals** Breakfast (buffet) 78,71F / 12€, served 7:00-10:30; snacks available, served 10:30-22:45. **Credit cards** All major. **Pets** Dogs allowed. **Facilities** Elevator, laundry service. **Parking** Opposite the *Bon Marché* department store. **How to get there** (Map 1) Bus: 39, 70 and 87 – Metro: Vaneau. **Open** All year.

The Sèvres-Vaneau is comfortable, elegant, and well-located. Quite spacious, the bedrooms have white lacquered rattan furniture set off by refined fabrics and wallpaper, which vary depending on the floor. Many still have their original marble fireplaces and some rooms even have beautiful light-colored stained glass. Statuettes and old engravings add a personal touch and lend them the air of a guest room in a private home. The all-white bathrooms, with navy, burgundy or bottle-green friezes, are also very pleasant and well-stocked with toiletries. The corridors are tastefully decorated with English oak-leaf wallpaper, and prettily framed lithographs. The lobby and reception rooms have a new decor, more classic and less British. This new trend will also set the tone for future renovation of the rooms. The welcome is professional and attentive.

Hôtel de Lille

40, rue de Lille - 75007 Paris
Tel. (0)1 42 61 29 09 - Fax (0)1 42 61 53 97
M. Margouilla
E-mail: hotel-de-lille@wanadoo.fr

Category ★★ **Rooms** 20 with soundproofing for the rooms on the street, telephone, bath or shower, hairdryer, WC, cable TV, safe. **Price** Single 540-560F / 82,32-85,37€, double 640-820F / 97,57-125,01€; extra bed 90F / 13,72€. **Meals** Breakfast included, served 7:30-11:00. **Credit cards** All major. **Pets** Dogs not allowed. **Facilities** Elevator, laundry service, bar. **Parking** At 9, rue Montalembert, Orsay. **How to get there** (Map 1) Bus: 24, 27, 39, 48, 68, 69 and 95 – Metro: Rue du Bac – RER: Musée d'Orsay. **Open** All year.

We were enchanted at first sight with this small hotel on the rue de l'Université and its smart yellow walls, 1930s-inspired furniture, lovely green-leather armchairs, mushroom lamps and adorable small bar. Beautiful engravings found in antique shops add a classical note to some bedrooms, while many others are much simpler, with colored bamboo furniture in the smallest, or "burred-wood" furniture in the others. Some have a small folding desk. Most fabrics are bright, and especially lovely are those in the rooms whose numbers end in 1. Rooms with numbers ending in 2, however, are our favorites. Lastly, Room no. 1 (on the ground floor looking out on a fountain) and the rooms on the top floor are the largest and thus the most expensive. The prices nevertheless are very reasonable for this neighborhood, particularly as breakfast is included. The cellar is occupied by a huge barrel-vaulted room with an impressive pillar.

Hôtel Lindbergh

5, rue Chomel – 75007 Paris
Tel. (0)1 45 48 35 53 – Fax (0)1 45 49 31 48
Sophie Guyot and Danièle Mondollot
E-mail: linhotel@club-internet.fr

Category ★★ **Rooms** 26 with soundproofing for the rooms on the street, with telephone, bath or shower, WC and satellite TV. **Price** Single and double 640-760F / 97,57-115,86€, triple 860F / 131,11€, 4 pers. 910F / 138,73€. **Meals** Breakfast (buffet) 45F / 6,86€, served 7:00-10:00. **Credit cards** All major. **Pets** Dogs allowed (+50F / 7,62€). **Facilities** Elevator. **Parking** Boucicaut, opposite the *Bon Marché* department store. **How to get there** (Map 1) Bus: 39, 63, 68, 70, 83, 84, 87 and 94 – Metro: Sèvres-Babylone. **Open** All year.

The Hôtel Lindberg already had the location, the quiet, brand-new bathrooms and a very friendly and relaxed welcome, but it lacked charm. This is no longer the case, and we are delighted to give a place to this small hotel. The owners have hired a decorator who knows how to provide a warm and modern style. This is the spirit in which ten of its twenty-six rooms have been renovated (the only ones we recommend at this point). Chocolate brown carpets, white quilts, fabrics in a large navy blue and brown check, small sleek furniture: simple and chic. Large wardrobes further the comfort even more. The tiny charming lounge is also in harmony with this very successful renovation. The breakfast room is still somewhat dull but refurbishment is underway. This and the rooms which remain to be redone will soon offer the kind of decor we like to find in small Parisian hotels.

Hôtel de Londres Eiffel

1, rue Augereau – 75007 Paris
Tel. (0)1 45 51 63 02 – Fax (0)1 47 05 28 96
Isabelle and Hervé Prigent
Web: www.londres-eiffel.com – E-mail: reservation@londres-eiffel.com

Category ★★★ **Rooms** 30 with telephone, bath or shower, WC, hairdryer, minibar, satellite TV – 1 for disabled persons. **Price** Single 545F / 83,08€, double 645F / 98,33€, triple 725F / 110,53€. **Meals** Breakfast 40F / 6,10€, served 7:00-10:00. **Credit cards** All major. **Pets** Dogs allowed (+50F / 7,62€). **Facilities** Elevator. **Parking** École Militaire. **How to get there** (Map 6) Bus: 28, 42, 69, 80, 82, 87 and 92 – Metro: École Militaire – RER: Pont-de-l'Alma. **Open** All year.

It is always pleasant to see how with some ideas and good taste, a banal neighborhood hotel can be turned into a true hotel of charm. The Londres Eiffel is a great example of this. As if to guarantee a sunny atmosphere in all seasons, the reception lounge is gleaming with orange yellow tones. The decoration and furniture are very much in the style of a private house where ebony framed Napoleon III miniatures and dried floral compositions reflect the attention given to detail. The same cozy characteristics are to be found in the next two rooms, where breakfast is served. A little more sober but just as comfortable and cheery, the bedrooms are quite an achievement. Only their bathrooms have retained the former *café-au-lait* style much in vogue fifteen years ago (they are nevertheless decent and very well maintained). On the street or the courtyard, all rooms are recommendable and their prices excellent for the quality. A welcoming place, worth discovering.

Hôtel Montalembert

3, rue de Montalembert – 75007 Paris
Tel. (0)1 45 49 68 68 – Fax (0)1 45 49 69 49
M. Hubert Bonnier
Web: www.montalembert.com – E-mail: welcome@hotel-montalembert.fr

Category ★★★★ Rooms 50 and 6 suites with air-conditioning, soundproofing, bath, WC, telephone, mobile phone, satellite TV and VCR, hairdryer, safe and minibar. **Price** Single and double 1800-2400F / 274,41-365,88€, suite 2950-4400F / 449,72-671,75€. **Meals** Breakfast 100F / 15,24€, served 7:00-10:30. **Credit cards** All major. **Pets** Dogs allowed on request. **Facilities** Elevator, laundry service, video library, room service, bar, restaurant (250F / 38,11€). **Parking** At 9, rue Montalembert. **How to get there** (Map 1) Bus: 24, 63, 68, 69, 83, 84 and 94 – Metro: Rue du Bac – RER: Gare d'Orsay. **Open** All year.

The Montalembert is one of the best Parisian examples of the new generation of Grand Hotels adapting themselves to the needs of the times. The modern style has been exploited well with discreet luxury that should be approved by all. The sobriety of the entry hall enhances the internal layout. The decoration of the lounge, both chic and welcoming, is organized around a reading room with an open fire. All the rooms offer a very high standard of comfort and aesthetics. Some of them are in retro-style with their furniture in burr wood marquetry, enhanced by delicate gilded bronzes, while others are contemporary, with their smooth dark brown wood panneling perfectly matching the fabrics and carpeting in dark blue, black and fawn tones. However they are often small, notably those with a number ending in 7, but this is fully taken account of in their pricing. Fortunately, the care for details and the high quality of facilities, service and hospitality compensate for any such inconvenience.

Hôtel Muguet

11, rue Chevert - 75007 Paris
Tel. (0)1 47 05 05 93 - Fax (0)1 45 50 25 37
Mme Pelletier
Web: www.hotelmuguet.com - E-mail: muguet@wanadoo.fr

Category ★★ **Rooms** 45 with air-conditioning and soundproofing, bath or shower, WC, telephone, satellite TV, safe, hairdryer – 3 for disabled persons. **Price** Single 520F / 79,27€, double 560-600F / 85,37-91,47€, triple 780F / 118,91€. **Meals** Breakfast 45F / 6,86€, served 7:00-11:00. **Credit cards** Visa, Eurocard, MasterCard, Amex. **Pets** Dogs allowed. **Facilities** Elevator, patio. **Parking** Invalides (300m.). **How to get there** (Map 1) Bus: 28, 69, 80, 82, 87 and 92 – Metro: École Militaire. **Open** All year.

How we would like to be able to offer you more establishments like this one. This little hotel is a real joy. The impeccable bedrooms are renovated and prettily decorated with a fine choice of fabrics and furniture pieces. Each has a charming bathroom tiled right up to the ceiling. Among those giving onto the street, numbers 52, 53, 61 and 62 have a view of the Eiffel Tower, while on the other side you look out onto the Invalides with its shining dome, from numbers 63 and 54. But if the latter are already taken, do not insist: all the rooms are quiet and pleasant (one tip however: those with a middle-size bed are only suitable for singles). Breakfast is served on the verdant patio. When the weather is disappointing the small dining room then takes over, and it is very homey with its rustic cherrywood buffet and Chinese pottery. A precious address with excellent value.

Hôtel d'Orsay

93, rue de Lille - 75007 Paris
Tel. (0)1 47 05 85 54 - Fax (0)1 45 55 51 16
M. Chevalier
E-mail: hotel.orsay@wanadoo.fr

Category ★★ Rooms 52 and 1 suite with bath or shower, WC, hairdryer, telephone, TV, safe and minibar. **Price** Single 485F / 73,94€, double 485-800F / 73,94-121,96€, suite 1500F / 228,67€. **Meals** Breakfast 50F / 7,62€, served from 7:00. **Credit cards** Visa, Eurocard, MasterCard, Amex. **Pets** Dogs not allowed. **Facilites** Elevator, Laundry service, room service. **Parking** At 9, rue de Montalembert. **How to get there** (Map 1) Bus: 24, 63, 68, 69, 73, 83, 84 and 94 – Metro: Solférino and Assemblée-Nationale – RER: Musée-d'Orsay – Les Invalides Air Terminal. **Open** All year.

Two fine buildings from the late 18th century make up this newly renovated hotel close to the Musée d'Orsay. The thick *porte-cochère*, the entry with plate glass doors and walls, the large reception lounge, elegantly furnished and facing a patio-garden "for the pleasure of the eyes only", all make for a beautiful start, and the rest is just as pleasant. Nice bedrooms (the largest are those with a number ending with a 1 or a 2) decorated with beautiful curtains and bedspreads by Canovas or Pierre Frey and Empire or Louis-Philippe style furniture. The effect is completely harmonious. The white bathrooms, enhanced with a frieze, are new and impeccable. Under the beautiful roof structure, there is a superb suite dominating the roofs. It is huge has two small Saint-Tropez-style terraces. If you want to grant yourself an exceptional night, do not hesitate to reserve it; it is rare to find such comfort at this price in Paris. Unquestionably, the Hôtel d'Orsay has become one of the beautiful establishments in this district.

Hôtel du Palais Bourbon

49, rue de Bourgogne - 75007 Paris
Tel. (0)1 44 11 30 70 - Fax (0)1 45 55 20 21
M. Claudon
E-mail: htlbourbon@aol.com

Category ★★ **Rooms** 32 (15 with air-conditioning) with bath or shower, WC, telephone, minibar, satellite TV. **Price** Single 280-500F / 42,69-76,22€, double 330-610F / 50,31-92,99€, triple 710F / 108,24€, 4 pers. 780F / 118,91€ – Special rates in low season. **Meals** Breakfast included, served 7:00-10:00. **Credit cards** Visa, Eurocard, MasterCard. **Facilities** Elevator. **Parking** Invalides. **How to get there** (Map 1) Bus: 69 – Metro: Varenne – RER: Invalides – Les Invalides Air Terminal. **Open** All year.

In this part of the city where the finest private houses have become ministry buildings or embassies, one is surprised and delighted to find a small hotel both simple and economical. The Hôtel du Palais Bourbon is in a state of change in a state of change. Thus, the entry hall has become warmer, but the stairways remain to be improved. The rooms, in contrast, are a welcome surprise. Still fitted-out with comfortable furniture specially made by a Breton cabinet maker, they present large spaces on the "noble" floors- rare in a hotel of that category; those are the one we recommend in priority. Despite the disharmony of some walls speckled with white patches, these are gradually being brightened up by beautiful fabrics, and all the carpeting has already been replaced by a beautiful parquet. The bathrooms are also very well done except in a few single rooms. Air-conditioning has been installed in the rooms on the street side and on the *cinquième étage*. This simple and very friendly hotel is in constant progress.

Hôtel Relais Bosquet - Tour Eiffel

19, rue du Champ-de-Mars - 75007 Paris
Tel. (0)1 47 05 25 45 - Fax (0)1 45 55 08 24
M. and Mme Hervois
Web: www.relaisbosquet.com - E-mail: hotel@relaisbosquet.com

Category ★★★ **Rooms** 40 with soundproofing (13 with air-conditioning), telephone, bath, WC, satellite TV, outlet for modem, radio, safe, minibar – 1 for disabled persons. **Price** Single 600-950F / 91,47-144,83€, double 650-1000F / 99,09-152,45€; extra bed 100F / 15,24€. **Meals** Breakfast 60F / 9,15€, served 7:00-12:00. **Credit cards** All major. **Pets** Dogs allowed. **Facilities** Elevator, patio. **Parking** Some spaces reserved in the lot of École militaire (90F/13,72€ /day). **How to get there** (Map 6) Bus: 28, 69, 80, 82, 87 and 92 – Metro: École militaire. **Open** All year.

Near the avenue Bosquet, this hotel doesn't look like much from the street, but you'll be pleasantly surprised inside. Arranged somewhat like a living room in a private home, the reception area reflects the tasteful, imaginative decor throughout. A soft, green carpet, orange chintz-lined drapes, a skirted pedestal, a table, a *Directoire*-style desk and armchairs all create a lovely setting. The bedrooms are spacious and handsome; they have Directory furniture, pretty prints and charming white-tiled bathrooms with elegant double basins. Thoughtful touches include a selection of magazines, an iron and ironing board in the closet and candies. Breakfasts are served in two ground-floor rooms (one is for non-smokers) which are illuminated by large bay windows and overlook a patio full of plants. The welcome is cheerful.

Hôtel Saint-Dominique

62, rue Saint-Dominique
75007 Paris
Tel. (0)1 47 05 51 44 – Fax (0)1 47 05 81 28

Category ★★ **Rooms** 34 with telephone, bath or shower, WC, cable TV, hairdryer, safe and minibar. **Price** Single 460F / 70,13€, double 540-580F / 82,32-88,42€, "Executive room" 660F / 100,62€. **Meals** Breakfast 40F / 6,10€. **Credit cards** Visa, Eurocard, MasterCard, Amex. **Pets** Dogs allowed. **Facilities** Elevator, patio. **Parking** Esplanade des Invalides. **How to get there** (Maps 1 and 6) Bus: 28, 69, 80 and 92 – Metro: Latour-Maubourg, Invalides – RER: Invalides - Les Invalides Air Terminal. **Open** All year.

Its situation and very carefully thought-out prices make the Saint-Dominique a much sought-after hotel. It is in a building on the lively rue Saint-Dominique, close to Les Invalides. The tone is given right from the entry with its decor in Anglo–American style. The light pinewood furniture matches the soft color shades of the walls and the pink-beige fabrics. The rooms are fitted out in the same style and have a rural charm; their walls are all hung with carefully chosen fabrics: *toile de Jouy*, flowery motifs, or even with a Persian look. The rooms called "executive rooms" have more space. Many look onto the patio and those on the street are soundproofed. The bathrooms have all just been renovated. Although signs of fatigue show in the public areas (corridors and stairways), the renovation should follow there too. No lounge, but in nice weather tables and chairs are set up on the very pleasant patio. Many good qualities, along with a charming and courteous welcome.

Hôtel Saint Germain

88, rue du Bac - 75007 Paris
Tel. (0)1 49 54 70 00 - Fax (0)1 45 48 26 89
M. Michel Malric
Web: www.hotel-saint-germain.fr - E-mail: info@hotel-saint-germain.fr

Category ★★★ **Rooms** 29 with soundproofing, bath, 25 with WC (4 rooms with 2 shared WC outside the rooms), telephone, TV, safe, 24 with hairdryer. **Price** Single 550-800F / 83,85-121,96€, double 550-900F / 83,85 137,20€; extra bed 150F / 22,87€. **Meals** Breakfast 60F / 9,15€, served 7:30-11:30. **Credit cards** Visa, Eurocard, MasterCard, Amex. **Pets** Dogs not allowed. **Facilities** Elevator, patio, room service. **Parking** At 9, rue de Montalembert. **How to get there** (Map 1) Bus: 63, 68, 69, 83, 84 and 94 –Metro: Rue du Bac, Sèvres-Babylone. **Open** All year.

The Hôtel Saint-Germain, which is now completing its renovation, has become one of the best in the neighborhood, and we particularly liked the library and the numerous little corner-lounges of the ground floor. They are decorated with royal-blue armchairs, antique furniture and objects, modern pictures and so on. Such a diverse grouping gives the place the very attractive feel of someone's house. Alongside there is a green courtyard, with its red-ocre tiles and its small fountain, providing access to two rooms on this level, particularly attractive in summer. The others on the upper floors are also very attractive: small alcoves sheltering the beds, Empire or Louis-Philippe chests of drawers, fine double curtains, sunny patinas or more classical wallpaper. They all rival in charm and comfort (we like less those with a number ending with an 0 because they are smaller). A special mention for Rooms 15, 24, 34, 44 and 54 which are large, with a very attractive view on the terrace-garden of the *premier étage*.

Hôtel Saint-Thomas-d'Aquin

3, rue du Pré-aux-Clercs
75007 Paris
Tel. (0)1 42 61 01 22 - Fax (0)1 42 61 41 43
M. Bertrand Plasmans

Category ★★ Rooms 21 with soundproofing, telephone, bath or shower, WC, cable TV, safe. **Price** Single and double 520-610F / 79,27-92,99€. **Meals** Breakfast 45F / 6,86€, served 6:30-10:30. **Credit cards** All major. **Pets** Dogs allowed. **Facilities** Elevator, laundry service. **Parking** At 9, rue Montalembert. **How to get there** (Map 1) Bus: 39, 48, 63, 68, 69 and 95 – Metro: Rue du Bac, Saint-Germain-des-Prés – RER: Musée d'Orsay. **Open** All year.

Numerous fashion boutiques follow one another in the rue du Pré-aux-Clercs. That street is particularly quiet and well-situated between Saint-Germain-des-Prés and the rue de Bac, with the quays of the Seine close by. The Saint-Thomas-d'Aquin is a very simple hotel, regularly renovated, well-maintained and offering very fair prices for the district. Excepting their sizes, which do vary, the rooms are all laid out on the same mode: light wallpaper, standard furniture and a touch of brightness with the fabrics, with a dominating touch of yellow, green and pink in the floral motives. The quilted bedspreads have been matched with the curtains, always with the same colors and motifs. They enjoy large windows, moulded ceilings and impeccable bathrooms. The twin rooms have a particularly attractive layout but are a little more expensive. On the ground floor, an L-shaped room is shared between a corner for breakfasts and a lounge. A two star hotel with a good feeling to it, and which, due to the change of owner, will further improve from renovation work planned for the winter 2000/2001.

Hôtel de Suède

31, rue Vaneau - 75007 Paris
Tel. (0)1 47 05 00 08 - Fax (0)1 47 05 69 27
M. Pialoux
E-mail: hotsuede@aol.com

Category ★★★ Rooms 38 and 1 suite with air-conditioning, with bath or shower, WC, telephone, satellite TV, hairdryer, safe. **Price** Single 606F / 92,51€, double 752F / 114,80€, triple 970F / 147,88€, suite (1-2 pers.) 1200F / 182,94€. **Meals** Breakfast 50F / 7,62€, served 6:30-11:00; snacks available. **Credit cards** Amex, Visa, Eurocard, MasterCard. **Pets** Dogs allowed (+ 40F / 6,10€). **Facilities** Elevator, patio. **Parking** At 30, boulevard Raspail, square Boucicaut, opposite the *Bon Marché* department store. **How to get there** (Map 1) Bus: 69, 82, 87 and 92 – Metro: Saint-François-Xavier, Sèvres-Babylone. **Open** All year.

The Hôtel de Suède enjoys the peace and quiet found in this district of embassies, the Invalides and the Rodin Museum. Classical in its style, the reception area is very large and entirely wainscotted, as are the numerous corner-lounges with sofas, armchairs and other wing chairs allowing one to relax in full comfort. Breakfasts are served here, but in fine weather you may prefer to eat on the flowery patio with a few tables. The very elegant rooms are for their part much more "Gustavian": grey-white and sky-blue monochromes, Directory-style furniture pieces painted in ivory, the whole brightened up by beautiful fabrics (by Pierre Frey) for the bedspreads and curtains. Rooms with a double bed usually have a shower, while the twin-bed rooms are the largest and there are more of them. If you reserve in good time, ask first for those giving onto the courtyard or those on the upper floors with a view over the Matignon gardens. The welcome is very courteous.

Thoumieux

79, rue Saint-Dominique
75007 Paris
Tel. (0)1 47 05 49 75 – Fax (0)1 47 05 36 96
M. Bassalert

Category ★★★ **Rooms** 10 with bath, WC, telephone, TV. **Price** Single 550-650F / 83,85-99,09€, double 600-800F / 91,47-121,96€; extra bed 70F / 10,67€. **Meals** Breakfast 45F / 6,86€, served 7:00-11:00. **Credit cards** Visa, Eurocard, MasterCard, Amex. **Pets** Dogs allowed. **Facilities** Laundry service, bar service in bedroom. **Restaurant** Mealtime specials 92 and 170F / 14,04 and 25,92€, also a la carte. **Parking** Invalides. **How to get there** (Maps 1 and 6): Bus: 28, 69, 80, 92 – Metro: Latour-Maubourg, Invalides – RER: Invalides – Les Invalides Air Terminal. **Open** All year.

Thoumieux is a veritable institution, patronized by people from the nearby embassies and ministries who enjoy the bistro atmosphere and the excellent Corrèze specialties that have been popular for three generations. Eclipsed perhaps by this gastronomic reputation and due to the fact that it doesn't advertise, the hotel is less well known. Yet its bedrooms, many of which are very large, are comfortable, and bathrooms are gorgeous. Cosseted and comfortable, soberly decorated with textured wallpaper, all of the rooms are recommendable, even though the 70s decor in some is becoming a bit old-fashioned. Number 2 is very elegant, with autumnal Persian fabrics and two large windows overlooking the street; and the large Rooms 5 and 10 with a corner sitting areas and windows overlooking the courtyard. You will be properly received, but don't expect an overabundance of attention since most of the staff is very busy in the bustling restaurant.

Hôtel Le Tourville

16, avenue de Tourville - 75007 Paris
Tel. (0)1 47 05 62 62 - Fax (0)1 47 05 43 90
M. Bouvier - M. Jacquet
Web: www.hoteltourville.com - E-mail: hotel@tourville.com

Category ★★★★ Rooms 30 with air-conditioning (4 with terrace), bath, WC, telephone, satellite TV, hairdryer. **Price** Single and double 690-1 090F / 105,19-166,17€, room with terrace 1190F-1390F / 181,41-211,90€, junior suite 1490-1990F / 227,15-303,37€ (low season: Mid Nov to end Feb and in Aug); extra bed 100F / 15,24€. **Meals** Breakfast 60F / 9,15€. **Credit cards** All major. **Pets** Dogs allowed. **Facilities** Elevator. **Parking** Place de l'École Militaire. **How to get there** (Map 1) Bus: 28, 80, 82, 87 and 92 – Metro: École Militaire. **Open** All year.

A beautiful building situated between the Invalides Dome and the Rodin Museum shelters the Hôtel Le Tourville. The atmosphere is plush in the refined lounge whose decoration was carried out by the David Hicks studio. The subdued lighting and slightly sharp colors give a lot of charm to the elegant, comfortable rooms. Small or large, they are all personalized by kilim-style carpets and antique furniture pieces and pictures. The bathrooms are also impeccable with beautiful white faience and grey-veined marble. Four of the rooms open onto attractive flower-covered and well-laidout terraces. Even if their prices are difficult to justify in the winter period, with good weather they become particularly attractive, serving as genuine living areas due to their large space and quiet. This is a fine hotel with reasonable prices allowing you to appreciate the charms of the Left Bank; both welcome and service are very attentive.

Hôtel de la Tulipe

33, rue Malar
75007 Paris
Tel. (0)1 45 51 67 21 - Fax (0)1 47 53 96 37
M. Fortuit

Category ★★ **Rooms** 22 with soundproofing for the rooms on the street, bath or shower, WC, telephone, satellite TV, minibar – 1 for disabled persons. **Price** Single and double 550-700F / 83,85-106,71€. **Meals** Breakfast 48F / 7,32€. **Credit cards** Amex, Visa, Eurocard, MasterCard. **Pets** Dogs allowed. **Facilities** Small garden, laundry service, tea room. **Parking** Private (80F / 12,2€ /day). **How to get there** (Map 6) Bus: 28, 63, 69, 80, 83 and 92 – Metro: Latour-Maubourg, Invalides – RER: Pont de l'Alma – Les Invalides Air Terminal. **Open** All year.

This small hotel is installed in an ancient convent, but only a little paved courtyard now remains from the original structure, covered in greenery. This courtyard is the central feature of the hotel and several staircases lead off from it to the rooms. Naturally some tables have been placed here so that breakfasts and other meals can be served outside on fine days. Inside, the rural character of the building has been preserved, with its wooden beams and stone walls also found in some of the rooms. These are small but calm (those looking onto the street, with few passers-by, are soundproofed) and well-maintained. Their cane furniture is generally brightened up with Provençal fabrics, while their pretty, brand-new bathrooms are worth mentioning. Note that if you reserve in good time, you can ask for the largest rooms, since they all cost the same price. Lastly, a lively and hospitable management has created a relaxed and friendly atmosphere.

Hôtel de l'Université

22, rue de l'Université - 75007 Paris
Tel. (0)1 42 61 09 39 - Fax (0)1 42 60 40 84
Mme Bergmann
Web: www.hoteluniversité.com

Category ★★★ **Rooms** 27 (2 with terrace) with air-conditioning, bath or shower, WC, telephone, TV, safe. **Price** Single 500-750F / 76,22-114,34€, double 900-950F / 137,20-144,83€, rooms with terrace 1200 and 1300F / 182,94 and 198,18€ (2 pers.), triple 1100-1500F / 167,69-228,67€. **Meals** Breakfast 50F / 7,62€; snacks available. **Credit cards** Visa, Eurocard, MasterCard, Amex. **Pets** Dogs not allowed. **Facilities** Elevator, bar. **Parking** At 9, rue de Montalembert. **How to get there** (Map 1) Bus: 39, 48, 63, 68, 69 and 95 – Metro: Rue du Bac, Saint-Germain-des-Prés – RER: Musée d'Orsay. **Open** All year.

The Hôtel de l'Université enjoys a privileged location with antique shops and art galleries in the neighboring streets and with the Louvre and Musée d'Orsay a few paces away. Saint-Germain-des-Prés is also close by. In addition, this is a hotel full of character which the management has insisted on personalizing to give it all the charm of a private house. The ancient vaulting with supporting pillars in oak, the staircase and fireplaces have all been conserved. Damask and velvet in ocre cover the sofas and armchairs of the small lounges, and the same tones are found in the rooms which are comfortable and decorated with antique furniture and small objects. Often large, they usually have bathrooms in marble. All are air-conditioned and well-soundproofed from any street noise, while some of them look over the back courtyard. The two suites with their Mansard roofs on the top floor also have small private terraces. The welcome is extremely attentive.

Hôtel de Varenne

44, rue de Bourgogne
75007 Paris
Tel. (0)1 45.51.45.55 – Fax (0)1 45.51.86.63
M. Janin

Category ★★★ **Rooms** 24 with air-conditioning and soundproofing for the rooms on the street, bath or shower, WC, telephone, hairdryer, satellite TV. **Price** Single 630F / 96,04€, double 660-760F / 100,62-115,86€; extra bed 120F / 18,29€. **Meals** Breakfast 52F / 7,93€, served at any time. **Credit cards** Visa, Eurocard, MasterCard, Amex. **Pets** Dogs allowed. **Facilities** Elevator, patio, laundry service. **Parking** Invalides. **How to get there** (Map 1) Bus: 69 – Metro: Varenne, Invalides – RER: Invalides – Les Invalides Air Terminal. **Open** All year.

The garden courtyard of the charming Hôtel de Varenne stretches out lengthwise in the axis of the entrance portico. Its abundant bushes leave enough space for guests to sit and enjoy their breakfast or a drink, according to the time of day. On the side is the entrance to the hotel with a simple, refined lobby, and to its right a dining room with a somewhat British feel. This is mainly due to the engravings and mahogany furniture strongly contrasting with the rose wall fabrics. Upstairs, most of the rooms overlook the garden. Some are large, others are smaller, but they are all arranged with much care, in soft colors. Their atmosphere is both classic and peaceful. Equivalent care has been given to the bathrooms, which are covered up to the ceiling with beige tiles, very functional and perfectly maintained. These qualities, added to the quiet and to Mme Cherruy-Cohen's sense of welcome, make the Hôtel de Varenne a much valued address.

Hôtel Verneuil

8, rue de Verneuil - 75007 Paris
Tel. (0)1 42 60 82 14 - Fax (0)1 42 61 40 38
Sylvie de Lattre
E-mail: verneuil@cybercable.fr

Category ★★★ **Rooms** 26 with soundproofing (15 with air-conditioning), telephone, bath or shower, WC, cable TV, hairdryer, safe, minibar. **Price** Single and double 690-1030F / 105,19-157,02€. **Meals** Breakfast 60F / 9,15€, served 7:00-10:30. **Credit cards** All major. **Pets** Dogs not allowed. **Facilities** Elevator, laundry service, bar. **Parking** Rue Montalembert (special rates). **How to get there** (Map 1) Bus: 24, 27, 39, 48, 63, 68, 69 and 95 – Metro: Saint-Germain-des-Prés, Rue du Bac. **Open** All year.

The rue de Verneuil is marvellously situated in the quiet area between Saint-Germain-des-Prés and the Seine, right in the heart of the Left Bank *carré*. The Hôtel de Verneuil is in an old building that has conserved all its charm: French-style ceilings and stone walls, but as so often is the case with older buildings, the rooms are not always very large. This is why you find several room sizes; those with a number ending in 3 are charming but really small and would prove difficult for any lengthy stay. Fitted with small but modern bathrooms in marble, they are however all very pleasant, comfortable and warmly decorated. Always different, they are hung with superb fabrics and fitted out with refinement, and one particularly notes the ravishing series of prints. The largest rooms often have a canopied bed. As for the lounges, they are in the image of the house: classical, well-arranged with taste and skill, and one feels as if in a private home. An excellent welcome confirms this good impression on all counts; this is really a fine place to stay.

Hôtel de l'Arcade

9, rue de l'Arcade
75008 Paris
Tel. (0)1 53 30 60 00 - Fax (0)1 40 07 03 07
Mme Dirce Chiesa

Category ★★★★ **Rooms** 37 and 4 duplexes with air-conditioning, soundproofing, telephone, bath, WC, hairdryer, satellite TV, minibar, safe. **Price** Single 820-920F / 125,01-140,25€, double 1040F / 158,55€, triple and duplex 1230F / 187,51€ – Special rates in Aug and at Christmas. **Meals** Breakfast (buffet) 55F / 8,38€, served 7:00-10:30. **Credit cards** All major. **Pets** Small dogs allowed. **Facilities** Elevator, laundry service. **Parking** Place de la Madeleine. **How to get there** (Map 7) Bus: 24, 42, 43, 52, 84, 94 – Metro: Madeleine – RER: Auber – Train station: Gare Saint-Lazare. **Open** All year.

An atmosphere of great tranquility emanates from the Hôtel de l'Arcade. The long lobby-lounge is a very open and airy place where benches, small sofas and armchairs create attractive little corners for relaxation and conversation. The soft colors predominate with a pinky beige for the seating, light green carpet and grey-blue for the cerused wall panelling, all adding to this impression of peace and quiet. The small breakfast room next door has the same character, and the bedrooms are just as elegant. They only differ in size, with the singles naturally the smallest, although the bed is still a double. The double and triple rooms are larger and very pleasant (the duplexes turn out to be less rational with their mezzanine beds). There is a lot of comfort in the very well-equipped marble bathrooms (they even have a telephone). The general maintenance is excellent, the lady in charge uncompromising about details. Courteous welcome.

Hôtel Balzac

6, rue Balzac – 75008 Paris
Tel. (0)1 44 35 18 00 – Fax (0)1 44 35 18 05
M. Christian Falcucci
E-mail: hotelbalzac@wanadoo.fr

Category ★★★★ **Rooms** 56 and 14 suites with air-conditioning, soundproofing, 2 telephones, bath, WC, hairdryer, cable TV, minibar. **Price** Single 2000F / 304,90€, double 2200-2500F / 335,39-381,12€, suite (2 pers.) 3800-6000F / 580,15-916,03€ – Special rates for weekends or 5 night stays at certain periods **Meals** Continental breakfast 120F / 18,29€, american 180F / 27,44€, served from 6:00. **Credit cards** All major. **Pets** Dogs allowed. **Facilities** Elevator, laundry service, room service (24h). **Restaurant** *Pierre Gagnaire*. **Parking** Private garage and Champs-Elysées or Friedland. **How to get there** (Map 6) Bus: 22, 30, 31, 52, 73, 92 – Metro: George V and Charles de Gaulle-Étoile – RER: Charles de Gaulle-Étoile. **Open** All year.

The Hôtel Balzac is in a beautiful building near the Champs-Elysées, just off the Étoile. A few steps lead up to the revolving doors. Areas for the concierge and reception are followed by a beautiful lounge with a glass roof. The decor is inspired by Italy, with sienna walls and palm trees in large glazed earthenware pots. The walls of the bar feature a beautiful collection of architects' drawings of gardens; this is also where breakfast is served. The bedrooms are truly palatial: large, very refined, with immense beds, thick carpets, marble bathrooms and room service at any time of day. Lastly, all gourmets will delight in lunching or dining in Pierre Gagnaire's restaurant inside the hotel.

Hôtel Beau Manoir

6, rue de l'Arcade
75008 Paris
Tel. (0)1 42 66 03 07 – Fax (0)1 42 68 03 00
Mme Teil – Mme Duhommet

Category ★ ★ ★ ★ Rooms 32 with air-conditioning, soundproofing, bath, WC, telephone, satellite TV, hairdryer, safe and minibar. **Price** Single 995-1155F / 151,69-176,08€, double 1155-1365F / 176,08-208,09€, suite 1465-1700F / 223,34-259,16€. **Meals** Breakfast (buffet) included, served 7:00-11:00. **Credit cards** All major. **Pets** Dogs allowed. **Facilities** Elevator, bar, laundry service. **Parking** Place de la Madeleine, rue Chauveau-Lagarde. **How to get there** (Map 7) Bus: 24, 42, 52, 84 and 94 – Metro: Madeleine – RER: Auber – Train station: Gare Saint-Lazare. **Open** All year.

Using their know-how, the owners have succeeded in creating a genuine small prestige hotel with the Beau Manoir. Once across the threshold you can admire the quality of the craftsmen who worked here. In the lounge old worked wood pieces enhance the greeneries of an 18th-century Aubusson tapestry, while damask-covered sofas and wing chairs also add to an atmosphere both luxurious and intimate. Polished walnut furniture in the Louis XIII-style has been chosen for the rooms, whose decor blends happily with a mix of coordinated prints. All are perfectly soundproofed (notice the heavy doors and double glazing), spacious and comfortable; they often have a small corner lounge and a marble bathroom. Our favorites are those with a number ending with a 1. This is a fine hotel just a few steps away from the Madeleine.

Hôtel Bedford

17, rue de l'Arcade – 75008 Paris
Tel. (0)1 44 94 77 77 – Fax (0)1 44 94 77 97
M. Gérard Berrut
E-mail: bedresa@clubinternet.fr

Category ★★★★ **Rooms** 135 and 11 apartments with air-conditioning, telephone, bath or shower, WC, hairdryer, satellite TV, minibar. **Price** Single 880F / 134,16€, double 980-1300F / 149,40-198,18€, triple 1300F / 198,18€, apartment (3-4 pers.) 1800F / 274,41€. **Meals** Breakfast 75F / 11,43€, served 7:00-10:30. **Credit cards** Amex, Visa, Eurocard, MasterCard. **Pets** Small dogs allowed. **Facilities** Elevator, laundry service, restaurant, bar-grill. **Parking** Place de la Madeleine. **How to get there** (Map 7) Bus: 24, 42, 52, 84 and 94 – Metro: Madeleine – RER: Auber – Train station: Gare Saint-Lazare. **Open** All year.

The Bedford has all the airs of a Grand Hotel with its liveried personnel in the lobby and the vast hall with corner-lounges. These are both soberly furnished, and combine the grey and beige tones which are also found in all the rooms. Classically modern and with a discreet elegance, the rooms have a velvet-like comfort. However, the hotel is in the course of renovation, and for the present we recommend those on the *cinquième étage* (our favorites) and below, but avoid the *sixième étage* which has not yet been worked on. You should note that the hotel offers interesting arrangements for families as certain rooms can be linked together. There are also apartments. The breakfast room is really astonishing in that it has conserved its rich "pastry decoration" in grey stucco, while the bar is more modern and an attractive place for relaxing or meetings. The service is stylish and friendly.

Hôtel Bradford-Élysées

10, rue Saint-Philippe-du-Roule
75008 Paris
Tel. (0)1 45 63 20 20 – Fax (0)1 45 63 20 07
M. Mathieu Clayeux

Category ★★★★ **Rooms** 50 with air-conditioning, telephone, bath or shower, WC, hairdryer, satellite TV, safe, minibar. **Price** Single 890-1390F / 135,68-211,90€, double 1090-1690F / 166,17-257,64€, triple 1290-1890F / 196,66-288,13€. **Meals** Breakfast 100F / 15,24€; snacks available. **Credit cards** All major. **Pets** Dogs not allowed. **Facilities** Elevator, laundry service. **Parking** 60, rue de Ponthieu. **How to get there** (Map 6) Bus: 32, 52, 83 and 93 – Metro: Saint-Philippe-du-Roule. **Open** All year.

The elegant Hôtel Bradford-Elysées is in a very fine building between the Champs-Elysées and rue du Faubourg-Saint-Honoré. The recent renovation has not interfered with the internal architecture. The now larger reception area leads to two lounges decorated with fine fabrics and high quality reproductions of ancient paintings. The breakfast room has been installed in a pretty lounge of a neoclassical style with a glass roof. The beautiful flight of stairs leading up to the rooms has also gained in scale. The bedrooms have kept their size and period furniture pieces. Excepting those with numbers ending with a 2, which are the singles, the rooms are really very comfortable and *soigné*, with impeccable bathrooms. Our preference is for those on rue Saint-Philippe-du-Roule, very sunny in the morning. Some rooms can be used by families without feeling too cramped. A high quality hotel where you will be assured of a pleasant stay.

Demeure Marignan-Élysées

12, rue de Marignan - 75008 Paris
Tel. (0)1 40 76 34 56 - Fax (0)1 40 76 34 34
M. Patrick Langlois
E-mail: marignan@cie.fr

Category ★★★★ **Rooms** 56 and 17 suites with air-conditioning, bath, WC, hairdryer, cable TV, safe, minibar, 3 telephone and outlet for fax. **Price** Double 2328,65-2820,62F / 320-387€, suite 3673,36F / 560€. **Meals** Breakfast (buffet) 150F / 22,87€, served 6:30-11:00. **Credit cards** All major. **Pets** Dogs allowed. **Facilities** Elevator, laundry service, room service 24h, bar. **Restaurant** *Spoon Food and Wine*, around 300F / 45,73€. **Parking** Rue François-Iᵉʳ. **How to get there** (Map 6) Bus: 32, 42, 73 and 80 – Metro: Franklin-Roosevelt – RER: Charles de Gaulle-Étoile. **Open** All year.

The Marignan-Elysées is a luxury hotel with a beautiful, classic and opulent decor. The lounges are richly furnished: 17th-century chests of drawers with gilted bronzes fixtures, 15th-century wall clocks, Beauvais tapestries. The whole space is luminous; even the breakfast room (which turns into a pleasant tearoom in the afternoon) is bathed in light, thanks to a large glass ceiling. The bedrooms have been entirely redecorated with Louis XVI furniture. The decor mainly makes use of fabrics reproducing ancient documents, notably Persian with Chinese motifs, on the walls and the headboards, in monochromes of beige and soft green. The largest and most luxurious (which better justify their price) are the duplex rooms on the two lower floors. The bathrooms are all very comfortable but nevertheless small; The famous Spoon, Food and Wine restaurant is located in this hotel: it serves cuisine from the whole world over, with a selection of 120 wines from the four corners of the planet.

Hôtel de L'Élysée

12, rue des Saussaies – 75008 Paris
Tel. (0)1 42 65 29 25 – Fax (0)1 42 65 64 28
Mme Lafond
E-mail: hotel.de.l.elysee@wanadoo.fr

Category ★★★ **Rooms** 30 and 2 junior suites with air-conditioning, telephone, bath or shower, WC, hairdryer and satellite TV. **Price** Single 660-820F / 100,62-125,01€, double 660-1280F / 100,62-195,13€; junior suite 1500F / 228,67€ – Special rates the weekends and in low season, prices on request. **Meals** Breakfast 45-75F / 6,86-11,43€, served 7:00-11:00. **Credit cards** All major. **Pets** Dogs allowed (+40F/6,10€). **Facilities** Elevator, laundry service, bar. **Parking** Hôtel Bristol. **How to get there** (Map 7) Bus: 32, 52, 83 and 93 – Metro: Madeleine, Miromesnils. **Open** All year.

Ideally situated between the Faubourg Saint-Honoré, the Madeleine church and the Champs-Elysées, the Hôtel de l'Elysée of course owes its name to the Presidential Palace close by. Its decor is very definitely Directory-style, with *trompe-l'oeil* paintings on the stairs, and the lounge with its rounded tables and late-18th-century "*gendarme hat*"-style chairs set around an open fireplace, topped by the traditional mirror framed with candle-sticks. The rooms are all different, regularly renovated in the same refined country style: cherry wood furniture, padded or canopied four-postered beds coordinated with floral or *toile de Jouy* fabrics. Generally, they are not very large but they all seem quite charming. For a little more space, choose those ending in 1, located in a corner on the street side (they have a window in the bathroom). There are also two junior suites with a mansard ceiling on the last floor. The owners are very attentive and eager to improve both comfort and service. A dependable address.

Hôtel Élysées Matignon

3, rue de Ponthieu - 75008 Paris
Tel (0)1 42 25 73 01 - Fax (0)1 42 56 01 39
Jean-François Cornillot
Web: www.elyseesmatignon.com - E-mail: hcv@centrevillehotels.com

Category ★★★ Rooms 21 and 4 junior suites with air-conditioning (20 with soundproofing) telephone, bath or shower, WC, hairdryer, cable TV, minibar and safe. **Price** Single 890F / 135,68€, double 990F / 150,92€, junior suite (1-3 pers.) 1300F / 198,18€. **Meals** Breakfast 55F / 8,38€, served 7:00-11:00. **Credit cards** All major. **Pets** Dogs allowed. **Facilities** Elevator, bar, laundry service, room service. **Parking** Rue Rabelais. **How to get there** (Map 6) Bus: 32, 42, 52, 73, 80, 83 and 93 – Metro: Franklin-Roosevelt. **Open** All year.

In the twenties, lovers used the Élysées-Matignon as a discreet meeting place. The hotel has now settled down but has not forgotten its former references. Paintings dedicated to feminine elegance, geometric mosaics, mirrors, warm and intimate colors, a long with floral compositions. All it lacks is a Charleston tune to bring back the carefree life between the two world wars. Nevertheless, it should be specified that the bedrooms have just been renovated with carefully chosen fabrics, beautiful carpets and light wood veneer designer furniture. It is chic and well-thought-out. A small entrance gathers the minibar, the dressing-room and WC. The pale-blue tiled bathrooms with retro chrome faucets are irresistible. The romantic fresco above the headboard in some of the rooms dates back to that period, and certainly could tell many stories. Also from the *Belle Epoque* is the incredible bar with crimson velvet, kilim wall seats and a collection of drawings by Bernard Buffet in the library corner. You may come across a celebrity who has come for a last drink before the place turns off its lights, only to reopen for breakfast.

Hôtel Élysées-Mermoz

30, rue Jean-Mermoz - 75008 Paris
Tel. (0)1 42 25 75 30 - Fax (0)1 45 62 87 10
M. Breuil
E-mail: elymermoz@worldnet.fr

Category ★★★ Rooms 27 with air-conditioning, soundproofing, telephone, bath, WC, hairdryer, TV, safe – 2 for disabled persons. **Price** Single 750-810F / 114,34-123,48€, double 810-920F / 123,48-140,25€, suite (1-4 pers.) 1230F / 187,51€. **Meals** Breakfast 60F / 9,15€, served 7:00-10:30. **Credit cards** All major. **Pets** Small dogs allowed. **Facilities** Elevator, laundry service. **Parking** Rond Point des Champs-Élysées and rue Rabelais. **How to get there** (Map 6) Bus: 28, 32, 42, 52, 73, 80, 83 and 93 – Metro: Franklin-Roosevelt and Saint-Philippe-du-Roule. **Open** All year.

The Hôtel Elysées Mermoz is located between the Rond Point des Champs-Elysées and the rue du Faubourg Saint-Honoré. From the charming entrance and veranda, you catch a glimpse of a small library-lounge, with *trompe-l'œil*-painted books, where breakfasts are served. Much care has been given to the comfort of the bedrooms, which are decorated in bright, sunny colors, featuring a predominance of yellow and blue, or yellow and red. There are handsome modern amenities, and the bathrooms have beautiful white tiles with blue borders, and even heated towel racks. The bedrooms are fairly large, and the suites can accommodate four people. Noise is no problem, regardless of the season; all the bedrooms are sound-proofed and air-conditioned.

Hôtel Étoile-Friedland

177, rue du Faubourg-Saint-Honoré – 75008 Paris
Tel. (0)1 45 63 64 65 – Fax (0)1 45 63 88 96
M. Jean-Bernard Denis
E-mail: friedlan@paris-honotel.com

Category ★★★★ **Rooms** 40 with air-conditioning and soundproofing, telephone, bath or shower, WC, hairdryer, cable and satellite TV, minibar, safe – 2 for disabled persons. **Price** Single and double 950-1300F / 144,83-198,18€. **Meals** Breakfast 80F / 12,20€, served 6:45-12:00. **Credit cards** All major. **Pets** Dogs allowed. **Facilities** Elevator, laundry service, bar, room service from 11:00AM to 10:45PM. **Parking** 163, boulevard Haussmann. **How to get there** (Map 3) Bus: 22, 43, 52, 83 and 93 – Metro: Saint-Philippe-du-Roule – RER: Charles de Gaulle-Étoile. **Open** All year.

Very close to the Étoile, the hotel is in a building on the corner of avenue de Friedland and rue du Faubourg-Saint-Honoré. Recently renovated, the hotel has rediscovered a new and lively spirit perceptible from the entrance. At the reception Bernard greets you with all due attention, and both room and bar service are just as efficient and cheerful. This brightness is also seen in the light and colorful decor. The largest rooms are on the top floor. Their Mansard ceilings give them extra charm. All are air-conditioned and soundproofed, so you should not be disturbed by the heavy traffic of avenue de Friedland. However, to be on the safe side, reserve the upper floors. This is a convivial hotel with a good, humorous atmosphere.

Hôtel Folkestone Opéra

9, rue Castellane – 75008 Paris
Tel. (0)1 42 65 73 09 – Fax (0)1 42 65 64 09
M. Michel Léger – Mlle Anne-Marie Gerbault
E-mail: folkestone@paris-hotels-opera.com

Category ★★★ **Rooms** 50 with soundproofing and air-conditioning, telephone, bath, WC, satellite TV, hairdryer, safe, minibar. **Price** (depending on the season) Single 735-900F / 112,05-137,20€, double 750-950F / 114,34-144,83€, triple 950-1200F / 144,83-182,94€, "de Luxe" (1-4 pers.) 1200-1500F / 182,94-228,67€. **Meals** Breakfast (buffet) 50F / 7,62€, served 7:00-11:00. **Credit cards** All major. **Pets** Dogs allowed. **Meals** Elevator, bar, laundry service. **Parking** Place de la Madeleine and rue des Mathurins. **How to get there** (Map 7) Bus: 24, 42, 52, 84 and 94 – Metro: Madeleine, Havre-Caumartin – RER: Auber – Train station: Gare Saint-Lazare. **Open** All year.

No need to sing the praises of this quarter of the Madeleine, where rue de Castellane runs into rue Tronchet, an obligatory track for shopping fanatics. The Folkestone Opéra is a pretty little hotel where the space has been very well utilized; by the time you reach the reception you have already passed through two very cozy small lounges. Bordeaux red and blue or green and yellow are the colors used in the printed fabrics decorating the rooms to create a comfortable and elegant atmosphere. This compensates for their small space and storage capacity. A copious breakfast buffet with house gateaux is laid out in a room in the basement, but guests staying on the *sixième étage* can also have it on their balcony when the weather is nice.

Hôtel Franklin-Roosevelt

18, rue Clément-Marot – 75008 Paris
Tel. (0)1 53 57 49 50 – Fax (0)1 47 20 44 30
M. and Mme Le Boudec
Web: www.franklin-roosevelt.com – E-mail: franklin@iway.fr

Category ★★★ **Rooms** 45, 2 junior suites and 1 apartment with soundproofing (some with air-conditioning), telephone, bath or shower, WC, TV, hairdryer – 1 for disabled persons. **Price** "Standard" 945-1200F / 144,06-182,94€, "supérieure" 1500-2200F / 228,67-335,39€, junior suite 2500-2800F / 381,12-426,86€, apart. 3000-3500F / 457,35-534,35€ – Low season from Nov to Feb (excluding trade fair periods) and in Jul-Aug. **Meals** Breakfast 75F / 11,43€, buffet 120F / 18,29€. **Credit cards** Amex, Visa, Eurocard, MasterCard. **Pets** Dogs not allowed. **Facilities** Bar, room service until 20:00. **Parking** Rue François-Iᵉʳ. **How to get there** (Map 6) Bus: 32, 42, 63, 80 and 92 – Metro: Franklin-Roosevelt and Alma-Marceau – RER: Pont de l'Alma. **Open** All year.

The Franklin-Roosvelt has given itself a new look. The reception area, leading into the reading lounge, the bar and the breakfast room, opens onto a winter garden. A very plush, comfortable and warm English style has been chosen along with dark wood and deep red fabrics, diffused lights, thick carpeting. The "de luxe" rooms on the *cinquième étage* are extremely refined. Their colors are more neutral but they exude an atmosphere of great comfort and well-being which guest certainly enjoy. On the top floor there is a luxurious suite with a lounge, a jacuzzi, a sophisticated shower and a king size bed. Of course, the rates rise along with the services and amenities. Standard rooms are just as charming, with a romantic atmosphere and panoramic wallpaper – and everybody can enjoy the public rooms. A very lovely address.

Hôtel La Galerie

16, rue de la Pépinière – 75008 Paris
Tel. (0)1 53 04 96 96 – Fax (0)1 40 08 07 77
M. Michel Agid
E-mail: hotel.lagalerie@wanadoo.fr

Category ★★★ **Rooms** 49 with air-conditioning and soundproofing, telephone, bath or shower, WC, hairdryer, satellite TV, safe, minibar. **Price** Single 750F / 114,34€, double 900F / 137,20€; extra bed 180F / 27,44€ –Special rates in low season. **Meals** Breakfast 55F / 8,38€, buffet 70F / 10,67€, served 7:00-10:00. **Credit cards** All major. **Pets** Dogs allowed. **Facilities** Elevator, bar, laundry service, patio, room service. **Restaurant** Mealtime specials 90-110F / 13,72-16,77€. **Parking** Place Bergson. **How to get there** (Map 4) Bus: All to Saint-Lazare – Metro: Saint-Augustin, Saint-Lazare – Train station: Gare Saint-Lazare. **Open** All year.

The ambiance is chic and contemporary behind the walls of this fine 19th-century building in cut stone. The Hôtel La Galerie has just been refurbished and the charm comes more from the harmony of the materials and colors. First of all, there is the ravishing patio with tables and parasols, ideal for breakfast, lunch or dinner. Then there is the small lounge bar and dining room on either side of the entry area, with their comfortable vivid red armchairs. There are smooth and somber panels in exotic woods that show off the paintings. Decorated very carefully in the same style, the rooms all have very sober and integrated furniture, while the bathrooms are covered in pretty faience-mosaics with small grey and white banding. Whatever their size (no. 708 is the largest) the comfort level is always excellent. This is a great address to discover and you can also dine very well here.

Hôtel Galiléo

54, rue Galilée
75008 Paris
Tel. (0)1 47 20 66 06 - Fax (0)1 47 20 67 17
M. Buffat

Category ★★★ **Rooms** 27 with air-conditioning and soundproofing, telephone, bath, hairdryer, WC, outlet for fax, safe, cable TV and minibar – 2 for disabled persons. **Price** Single 800F / 121,96€, double 950F / 144,83€. **Meals** Breakfast (buffet) 50F / 7,62€ served 7:15-11:00. **Credit cards** Amex, Visa, Eurocard, MasterCard. **Pets** Dogs not allowed. **Facilities** Elevator, winter garden, bar, room service. **Parking** George V-Champs-Elysées. **How to get there** (Map 6) Bus: 22, 30, 31, 52, 73 and 92 – Metro: George V and Charles de Gaulle-Étoile – RER: Charles de Gaulle-Étoile. **Open** All year.

Well-situated between the Champs-Elysées and avenue Georges V, the Galiléo is a truly charming hotel. Refinement and modernity have guided the furnishing and decoration. In the lounge an 18th-century fireplace and a verdant Aubusson tapestry can be found. In the basement there is a breakfast room with soft lighting and colors, and a pretty view onto the cleverly laidout garden. To these qualities should be added that of well-thought-out comfort in the bedrooms where you will appreciate the airconditioning, reading lamps, fax lines and even radios in the bathrooms. Certain rooms are more spacious: the two on the ground floor and the luminous 501 and 502 on the *cinquième étage* with adorable verandas are our favorites.

Hôtel Lancaster

7, rue de Berri - 75008 Paris
Tel. (0)1 40 76 40 76 - Fax (0)1 40 76 40 00
M. John Petch
Web: www.hotel-lancaster.fr – E-mail: pippaona@hotel-lancaster.fr

Category ★★★★ **Rooms** 50 and 10 suites with air-conditioning, soundproofing, telephone, bath or shower, WC, hairdryer, cable TV, minibar and safe. **Price** Single 1672,69-1967,87F / 255-300€, double 2492,64-2886,21F / 380-440€, suite 3214,19-10495,31F / 490-1600€. **Meals** Breakfast 131,19F / 20€, served from 7:00. **Credit cards** All major. **Pets** Small dogs allowed on request. **Facilities** Elevator, bar, laundry service, garden, room service (24h). **Restaurant** For residents only. Dishes from 150F / 22,87€, also à la carte. **Parking** 5, rue de Berri. **How to get there** (Map 6) Bus: 32 and 73 – Metro: George V – RER: Charles de Gaulle-Étoile. **Open** All year.

The Lancaster continues to be one of the leading examples of Parisian Grand Hôtels, thanks to a remarkable restoration that has conserved more than one thousand antique articles and pieces accumulated by its founder, E. Wolf. The rooms are vast, the suites immense, and all are decorated with very beautiful fabrics, period furniture and pictures often of an exceptional quality. The bathrooms are in the modern style but have kept a noble sobriety. The main salon and dining room have been rejuvenated with subtlety, notably by a choice of rather matte colors tending to give a more modern touch to the furniture, carpets and old pictures. The garden adds to the refinement with its atmosphere of great calm; portions of the walls are covered by large brown reeds and giant plants collected from all five continents. There is also the sound of splashing water.

Hôtel Le Lavoisier

21, rue Lavoisier - 75008 Paris
Tel. (0)1 53 30 06 06 - Fax (0)1 53 30 23 00
M. Bouvier
Web: www.hotellavoisier.com - E-mail: info@hotellavoisier.com

Category ★★★★ (certification pending). **Rooms** 27 (2 with terrace), 2 junior suites and 1 suite with air-conditioning and soudproffing, with telephone, satellite TV, bath or shower, WC and hairdryer – 2 for disabled persons. **Price** Single and double 1190F / 181,41€, junior suite (2-3 pers.) 1490 and 1890F / 227,15 and 288,13€, suite (1-4 pers.) 2500F / 381,12€; extra bed 100F / 15,24€. **Meals** Breakfast 70F / 10,67€, served 7:00-11:00. **Credit cards** All major. **Pets** Dogs allowed. **Facilities** Elevator, bar, laundry service, room service. **Parking** Malesherbes. **How to get there** (Maps 4 and 7) Bus: 22, 32, 43, 80, 84 and 94 – Metro: Saint-Augustin – Train station: Gare Saint-Lazare. **Open** All year.

The Hôtel Le Lavoisier is one of the most beautiful creations of the year. Jean-Philippe Nuel has asserted here, with even more refinement, his taste for classicism; he has employed a symmetrical use of space and architectural motifs in an antique style. The Georgian-style lobby leads to two small lounges decorated in monochromes of beige and red, with flannel bordered sisal carpets and a collection of 19th century paintings of children. Behind the reception area, there is a very confidential library-bar with a black *parquet*, a brown leather sofa and diffused lighting. The elegant bedrooms are less sophisticated: light, fairly large, with blackened pear wood furniture and an occasional piece from the 19th-century. They all have comfortable, white marbled bathrooms. Rooms in the rear have a nice view over buildings covered with Virginia creeper. Some rooms also have a nice terrace with teak furniture. The same chic is to be found in the breakfast room where one comes across a rich and trendy clientele.

Hôtel Lido

4, passage de la Madeleine
75008 Paris
Tel. (0)1 42 66 27 37 - Fax (0)1 42 66 61 23
Mme Teil

Category ★★★ **Rooms** 32 with air-conditioning, soundproofing, bath, WC, telephone, outlet for modem, satellite TV, hairdryer, safe, minibar. **Price** Single 830-980F / 126,53-149,40€, double 930-1100F / 141,78-167,69€. **Meals** Breakfast (buffet) included, served 7:00-11:00. **Credit cards** All major. **Pets** Dogs allowed. **Facilities** Elevator, Laundry service, bar. **Parking** Place de la Madeleine and rue Chauveau-Lagarde. **How to get there** (Map 7) Bus: 24, 42, 52, 84 and 94 – Metro: Madeleine – RER: Auber – Train station: Gare Saint-Lazare. **Open** All year.

The first hotel in a small group including the Beau Manoir next door, the Lido is a good example of personalized hotel keeping, and a lot of the atmosphere is due to Mme. Teil who personally looks after the well-being of her clients. Carpets, an 18th-century Aubusson tapestry and *Haute Époque*-style chairs furnish the warm reception area and lounge. The rooms have kept their ceiling beams and have recently been refurbished. The walls are usually draped with damask silks or *toile de Jouy*, along with the double curtains. Their style mixes rusticity and refinement, and is always well-thought-out, with functional cupboarding and comfortable bathrooms in marble offering numerous welcoming product lines. You should note that rooms with numbers ending with a 3 are the largest. A good breakfast is served in a vaulted room, with house pastries and home-made jams.

Hôtel-Résidence Lord Byron

5, rue Chateaubriand
75008 Paris
Tel. (0)1 43 59 89 98 – Fax (0)1 42 89 46 04
E-mail: lord.byron@escapade-paris.com

Category ★★★ **Rooms** 31 with telephone, bath or shower, WC, hairdryer, satellite TV, minibar and safe. **Price** Single 690-860F / 105,19-131,11€, double 890-990F / 135,68-150,92€, junior suite 1390F / 211,90€ (2 pers.). **Meals** Breakfast 65F / 9,91€, served 7:15-12:00. **Credit cards** All major. **Pets** Dogs not allowed. **Facilities** Elevator, laundry service, garden. **Parking** 5, rue de Berri. **How to get there** (Map 6) Bus: 22, 30, 31, 52, 73 and 92 – Metro and RER: Charles de Gaulle-Étoile. **Open** All year.

On a quiet street near the Étoile and between the avenue de Friedland and the Champs-Elysées, the Résidence Lord Byron is an attractive hotel. A fine entryway in classical style with carved wood pieces, moldings, antique furniture and English carpeting leads through to the reception. The hotel splits its rooms between the main building with most of them, and a second building on the other side of the garden. This is where our favorite rooms are. Recently renovated, they enjoy the proximity and quiet of the garden, abundant with flowers in the summer. The perspective of its partitions attracts the eye as you walk into the hotel. Breakfast and drinks are served there in the fine weather. The rooms are pleasantly decorated, flowery, bright and very light on the garden side. You get either bathtub or shower depending on room category and size; the smallest rooms are on the top floor but have the charm of Mansard ceilings. You will be well-received here, and if it's full, you should know that the same management runs the hotel next door, the Mayflower, which is fully comparable with the Lord Byron, except for the garden.

New Orient Hôtel

16, rue de Constantinople - 75008 Paris
Tel. (0)1 45 22 21 64 - Fax (0)1 42 93 83 23
Mme Wehrle
E-mail: new.orient.hotel@wanadoo.fr

Category ★★ **Rooms** 30 with soundproofing, telephone, bath or shower, WC, satellite TV. **Price** Single 395-485F / 60,22-73,94€, double 490-620F / 74,70-94,52€, triple 650F / 99,09€. **Meals** Breakfast (buffet) 39F / 5,95€, served 7:00-12:00. **Credit cards** All major. **Pets** Dogs allowed. **Facilities** Elevator, bar. **Parking** Europe, avenue de Villiers. **How to get there** (Map 4) Bus: 30 and 53 – Metro: Europe, Villiers, Saint-Lazare – Train station: Gare Saint-Lazare. **Open** All year.

On a street where hotels are numerous, the New Orient immediately stands out with its abundantly flowered façade. This charming little hotel owes much of its personality to its owners, as Catherine and Sepp Wehrle have chosen to fit it out with the same care as for a private house, and to this end spend part of their free time in acquiring and restoring retro furniture pieces. All the results are here and each landing displays a fine antique cupboard, while in a good number of the rooms you find late-19th-century headboards along with Napoleon III chairs and small furniture pieces. This creates a very personal overall effect, warm and bright, and even if the bathrooms could do with a bit more attention to details, they are nevertheless well-maintained. All these qualities, the reasonable prices, and the friendly welcome make the New Orient Hôtel a precious little address in this district.

Hôtel Newton Opéra

11 *bis*, rue de l'Arcade - 75008 Paris
Tel. (0)1 42 65 32 13 - Fax (0)1 42 65 30 90
M. Simian
E-mail: newtonopera@easynet.fr

Category ★★★ **Rooms** 31 with air-conditioning (2 with terrace), telephone, outlet for modem, bath, WC, hairdryer, satellite TV, radio, minibar, safe. **Price** Single and double 760-860F / 115,86-131,11€, junior suite with terrace 1500F / 228,67€ – Special rates in Aug. **Meals** Breakfast (buffet) 60F / 9,15€, served 6:45-10:00. Snacks available. **Credit cards** All major. **Pets** Small dogs allowed. **Facilities** Elevator, laundry service, room service. **Parking** Place de la Madeleine, rue Chauveau-Lagarde. **How to get there** (Map 7) Bus: 24, 42, 52, 84 and 94 – Metro: Madeleine – RER: Auber – Train station: Gare Saint-Lazare. **Open** All year.

Among the many hotels on the rue de l'Arcade, the Newton Opéra is possibly the least luxurious, but offers excellent comfort at the best prices. You'll find a somewhat country atmosphere with rustic painted furniture and fabrics in bright, floral motifs. What's surprising about this small hotel are the services offered: air-conditioning, private safe, trouser-press and room service with Hédiard tray-meals. Much attention has been given over to detail; in the bathrooms various accessories have been added along with a delicate scent of vanilla. On arrival a small carafe of mandarin liqueur awaits you. In the summer, if you reserve in good time, you may be able to get one of the two rooms with a terrace. Their table and deck chairs, are ideal for any longer stay. You will find a generous breakfast buffet—all you can eat—served in the vaulted room in the cellar. What's not surprising is that this family-run hotel has attracted many faithful customers over the years.

Hôtel Queen Mary

9, rue Greffulhe – 75008 Paris
Tel. (0)1 42 66 40 50 – Fax (0)1 42 66 94 92
M. Byrne - M. Tarron
Web: www.hotelqueenmary.com – E-mail: hotelqueenmary@wanadoo.fr

Category ★★★ **Rooms** 35 and 1 suite with air-conditioning, soundproofing, telephone, bath, WC, hairdryer, cable TV, minibar and safe (extra charge). **Price** Single 780F / 118,91€, double 915-995F / 139,49-151,69€, suite (1-3 pers.) 1400F / 213,43€; extra bed 250F / 38,11€. **Meals** English breakfast 85F / 12,96€, served 7:30-10:00. **Credit cards** All major. **Pets** Dogs not allowed. **Facilities** Elevator, patio, room service. **Parking** Place de la Madeleine. **How to get there** (Map 7) Bus: 22, 24, 32, 84 and 94 – Metro: Madeleine and Havre-Caumartin – RER: Auber – Train station: Gare Saint-Lazare. **Open** All year.

Close to the lively quarter of the Grands Magasins but sheltered from the traffic, the Queen Mary has just completed a very successful renovation. You will appreciate the elegance and very cozy comfort of the small lounge and bar where plush sofas, molded ceilings, ravishing yellow and blue wall hangings make for a warm and cheerful atmosphere. You will equally like the atmosphere of the bedrooms decorated in an English style, in tones perfectly harmonizing with the mahogany furniture and the fabrics of the chairs, drapes and bedspreads. The same attention has been given to the white bathrooms. The comfort is perfect for the price, and you will also approve of such details as the trouser-press and carafe of sherry wine awaiting your arrival. You should also note the very tiny patio where you can have a drink during the day, along with the basement breakfast room prettily decorated in green and yellow tones. This is a very agreeable small hotel with an attentive and available staff.

Résidence Monceau Hôtel

85, rue du Rocher
75008 Paris
Tel. (0)1 45 22 75 11 – Fax (0)1 45 22 30 88
Mme Touber – Mme Loreau

Category ★★★ **Rooms** 50 and 1 suite with soundproofing, telephone, bath or shower, WC, hairdryer, satellite TV, minibar – 2 for disabled persons. **Price** Single and double 760F / 115,86€, junior suite 900F / 137,20€ (3 pers.). **Meals** Breakfast (buffet) 50F / 7,62€, served 7:00-11:00. **Credit cards** All major. **Pets** Dogs not allowed. **Facilities** Elevator, laundry service, bar, individual safes at reception, garden. **Parking** Boulevard des Batignolles, avenue de Villiers. **How to get there** (Map 4) Bus: 30 – Metro: Villiers – Train station: Gare Saint-Lazare. **Open** All year.

The Résidence Monceau is located midway between the Arc de Triomphe and Sacré-Cœur. A large, convivial area groups together the lounge, reception area and bar. Rattan window boxes and furniture brighten the lounge corner, while the bar is more modern. It has black and mahogany furniture along with a series of photos of chairs on the walls. There is a spacious breakfast room extending into a veranda, for enjoyment of the garden all year round. On the other side, the few bedrooms recently renovated are excellently done; decor in tones of blue, comfortable bathrooms with well-chosen furniture and tiles (the double rooms on the street side can connect with singles overlooking the garden). The rooms upstairs are more ordinary, with conventional furniture in burr walnut or oak veneer, but all are comfortable. It is nevertheless preferable to sleep on the courtyard side, especially in summer. Note that Room 117 is not spacious, but it does have a large terrace. The welcome is very hospitable.

Hôtel du Rond-Point des Champs-Élysées

10, rue de Ponthieu
75008 Paris
Tel. (0)1 53 89 14 14 - Fax (0)1 45 63 99 75
M. Villette

Category ★★★ **Rooms** 43 (2 with terrace) and 1 junior suite with soundproofing, telephone, bath or shower, WC, satellite TV, 40 with minibar, 30 with hairdryer and safe. **Price** single 650F / 99,09€, double 775F / 118,15€, twin and room with terrace 885F / 134,92€, junior suite (2 pers.) 995F / 151,69€, triple 1005-1115F / 153,21-169,98€. **Meals** Breakfast 50F / 7,62€, served 7:30-11:00. **Credit cards** All major. **Pets** Dogs not allowed. **Facilities** Elevator, laundry room. **Parking** (At 100m). **How to get there** (Map 6) Bus: 32, 42, 52, 73, 80, 83 and 93 – Metro Franklin-Roosevelt. **Open** All year.

The Hôtel du Rond-Point des Champs-Élysées has retained a very engaging simplicity. This beautiful 1930 building has saved all the decorative elements of the period while the renovation work has started to make this place more comfortable. The three first floors have been entirely redecorated; new wall paintings and carpeting harmonize with pretty floral fabrics or pompoms. It has also kept its spaciousness. Thus, the bedrooms are sizeable and airy, with large bathrooms also overlooking the street. The upper floors remain to be refurbished but they are nevertheless very recommendable, notably the rooms on the *septième étage* with furnished balconies. However the hotel is not air-conditioned; therefore in July or August you had better sleep on the courtyard side where it is cooler. On the other hand, the rest of the year you can enjoy the sun, or at least its luminosity.

Hôtel Royal Opéra

5, rue de Castellane - 75008 Paris
Tel. (0)1 42 66 14 44 - Fax (0)1 42 66 48 47
M. Michel Léger - Mlle Anne-Marie Gerbault
E-mail: royal@paris-hotels-opera.com

Category ★★ Rooms 30 with soundproofing, telephone, bath or shower, WC, satellite TV, safe and minibar. **Price** (depending on the season) Single 490-590F / 74,70-89,94€, double 520-650F / 79,27-99,09€, triple 620-730F / 94,52-111,29€. **Meals** Breakfast 30F / 4,57€, served 7:00-10:30. **Credit cards** All major. **Pets** Dogs allowed. **Facilities** Elevator, laundry service. **Parking** Place de la Madeleine and rue des Mathurins. **How to get there** (Map 7) Bus: 24, 42, 52, 84 and 94 – Metro: Madeleine, Havre-Caumartin – RER: Auber – Train station: Gare Saint-Lazare. **Open** All year.

Close to the Place de la Madeleine, the Opera and the department stores on boulevard Haussmann, this little hotel (which has been entirely renovated since 1998) has the advantage of giving you your money's worth. There is not an excess of charm, but the establishment has sought to add a little elegance to its "two-star" category standard. Thus the breakfast room has on its walls a fine series of architectural drawings of various Parisian monuments, while the rooms are simple, comfortable and perfectly maintained. Rare at this price level, each even has a small safe and a minibar. The small white bathrooms are brand-new and also impeccable. As the street is very quiet, we recommend that you choose a room on that side because on the courtyard they seem a little dark. A continental breakfast is served with house *pains au chocolat* and croissants.

Hôtel San Régis

12, rue Jean-Goujon - 75008 Paris
Tel. (0)1 44 95 16 16 - Fax (0)1 45 61 05 48
M. Maurice Georges
Web: www.hotel-sanregis.fr - E-mail: message@hotel-sanregis.fr

Category ★★★★ Rooms 41 and 3 suites (with terrace) with telephone, bath or shower, WC, cable and satellite TV, minibar, hairdryer (34 with air-conditioning). **Price** Single 1800F / 274,41€, double 2400-3200F / 365,88-487,84€, suite (2-3 pers.) 3500-6100F / 534,35-931,29€. **Meals** Breakfast 120F / 18,29€, served 7:00-10:30. **Credit cards** All major. **Pets** Dogs not allowed. **Facilities** Elevator, bar, laundry service, room service 24h. **Restaurant** À la carte (250-350F / 38,11-53,36€, except drinks). **Parking** Rue François-Iᵉʳ. **How to get there** (Map 6) Bus: 42, 72, 80, 83 and 93 – Metro: Franklin-Roosevelt and Champs-Elysées-Clémenceau. **Open** All year.

Apart from the luxurious and celebrated rue Montaigne and rue François I, which house the really big names of *Haute Couture*, the district also has its own charming small hotel in the San Régis. The welcome is spontaneous and very attentive as you are led through the large lounge or small dining room of the hotel restaurant. The velvety ambiance, antique furniture and pictures, and abundance of fine fabrics with pretty motifs go to make for a very "British" atmosphere. This same feeling of comfort is in both the corridors and rooms, where the deep-pile carpeting dampens any noise. The suites and rooms are all spacious, and each has its own special decor, created by by a very fine choice of well-coordinated fabrics. The singles, in another wing of the house, are more sober and smaller. They are all equally comfortable and could even suit a couple looking for a more reasonable price. The personnel is particularly attentive and on-hand to offer you all the establishment's services.

Hôtel Sydney Opéra

50, rue des Mathurins – 75008 Paris
Tel. (0)1 42 65 35 48 – Fax (0)1 42 65 03 07
M. Michel Léger – Mlle Anne-Marie Gerbault
E-mail: sydney@paris-hotels-opera.com

Category ★★★ **Rooms** 38 with soundproofing and air-conditioning, telephone, bath or shower, WC, satellite TV, safe and minibar. **Price** Single 735-900F / 112,05-137,20€, double 800-1000F / 121,96-152,45€, triple 1000-1500F / 152,45-228,67€, "de Luxe" (1-4 pers.) 1200-1500F / 182,94-228,67€. **Meals** Breakfast (buffet) 50F / 7,62€, served 7:00-11:00. **Credit cards** All major. **Pets** Dogs allowed. **Facilities** Elevator, bar, laundry service. **Parking** Opposite the hotel. **How to get there** (Map 7) Bus: All to Saint-Lazare – Metro: Madeleine – RER: Auber – Train station: Saint-Lazare. **Open** All year.

Golden yellow walls with green ribbon edging, 1930s-style armchairs and seats covered with very elegant fabrics, the rounded acajou style of the bar-reception hall of the Hôtel Sydney Opéra well illustrates the quality of the recently completed renovation. Certainly some sacrifices have been made to today's tastes, but the result is bright, warm and comfortable, and it is a real triumph. You will not be disappointed by the fittings in the bedrooms, which have been totally renewed: thick burgundy carpeting with small motifs, yellow ocre walls to highlight the gilt wall-lamps and the dark browns of the smooth and modern furniture, pretty flowery or tartan fabrics. The same care has been given over to the all-white bathrooms with just a tiny yellow streaking. Lastly, because one cannot overestimate the importance of breakfast, we should give credit to the elegance and size of the dining room stemming out from the lounge, lit by a glass roof. There a self-service buffet awaits the clientele.

Hôtel Tronchet

22, rue Tronchet – 75008 Paris
Tel. (0)1 47 42 26 14 – Fax (0)1 49 24 03 82
Mme Sophie Charlet
Web: www.hotel-tronchet.com – E-mail: trontel@club-internet.fr

Category ★★★ Rooms 34 with air-conditioning and soundproofing, telephone, bath or shower, WC, hairdryer, cable TV, minibar and safe. **Price** Single 940-1040F / 143,30-158,55€, double 960-1060F / 146,35-161,60€; extra bed (until 12 year) 150F / 22,87€. **Meals** Breakfast (buffet) 70F / 10,67€, served 7:00-9:30. **Credit cards** All major. **Pets** Dogs allowed. **Facilities** Elevator, laundry room. **Parking** Place de la Madeleine. **How to get there** (Map 7) Bus: 24, 27, 29, 42, 84 and 94 – Metro: Madeleine – RER: Auber – Train station: Gare Saint-Lazare. **Open** All year.

The rue Tronchet goes from the Madeleine to the boulevard Haussmann where the large department stores are. For those who enjoy shopping, it is a necessary stop, especially when *Erès* releases its new bathing suit collection. Behind an impersonal façade, but with pretty geraniums (in the summer) lies a veritable small hotel of charm. The reception area abounding in blooming hydrangea is small, the cerused oak wood library-lounge where you can consult the papers and Paris guides is small. Small too are the bedrooms, brightened up by well-chosen fabrics. The white marble bathrooms are comfortable. Those called "superior" are a bit larger, have more sophisticated furniture and a Jacuzzi bath to relax in. As is often the case, breakfasts are served in a vaulted room in the cellar. A well-tended hotel.

Hôtel Vernet

25, rue Vernet - 75008 Paris
Tel. (0)1 44 31 98 00 - Fax (0)1 44 31 85 69
M. Gabriel Lousada
Web: www.hotelvernet.com - E-mail: hotelvernet@jetmultimédia.fr

Category ★★★★ **Rooms** 42 and 9 suites with air-conditioning, soundproofing, telephone, bath with whirlpool, WC, hairdryer, cable TV, minibar and safe. **Price** Single 1950-2300F / 297,28-350,63€, double 2300-2900F / 350,63-442,10€, suite 3500-4800F / 534,35-732,82€. **Meals** Continental breakfast 130F / 19,82€, served 7:00-10:30. **Credit cards** All major. **Pets** Small dogs allowed. **Facilities** Elevator, laundry service, bar, room service (24h). **Restaurant** Gastronomic, mealtime specials 480F / 73,18€ (lunch), 530-840F / 80,80-128,06€ (diner), also à la carte. **Parking** Private. **How to get there** (Map 6) Bus: 22, 30, 31, 52, 73 and 92 – Metro and RER: Charles de Gaulle-Étoile. **Open** All year.

The Étoile-Champs-Elysées area remains the most prestigious quarter of international Paris and most of the luxury hotels are found here. What makes the difference with Hotel Vernet is a welcome that does not end with simple conventional courtesies or the close attention given to clients. The hotel is located in a building from the 1920s where there is a superb glass roof over the Les Elysées restaurant. The Mediterranean-style cuisine of Alain Soliveres has been awarded a two-star rating. An Italian-type gallery with an antique decor leads to the lounges and bar. With the open fire and piano or harp music, you are only too glad to linger here some evenings. The bar is now near the entry in a lounge opening onto the street. The rooms are regularly renovated and offer the latest comforts in a refined setting. In all of them, you are greeted with seasonal fruits and cakes prepared in the kitchen. The service is - obviously - perfect.

Hôtel Vignon

23, rue Vignon
75008 Paris
Tel. (0)1 47 42 27 65 – Fax (0)1 47 42 04 60
M. Fouillade

Category ★★★ **Rooms** 30 with air-conditioning and soundproofing, telephone, bath or shower, WC, hairdryer, satellite TV, minibar and safe – 2 rooms for disabled persons. **Price** Single 700-800F / 106,71-121,96€, double 830-950F / 126,53-144,83€, triple 1050-1200F / 160,07-182,94€. **Meals** Continental breakfast 55F / 8,38€, buffet 70F / 10,67€, served 7:00-10:30. **Credit cards** Amex, Visa, Eurocard, MasterCard. **Pets** Dogs not allowed. **Facilities** Elevator, bar, laundry service. **Parking** Place de la Madeleine. **How to get there** (Map 7) Bus: All to Saint-Lazare – Metro: Madeleine – RER: Auber – Train station: Gare Saint-Lazare. **Open** All year.

Located in a quiet street of the Madeleine quarter, right behind a shopping street, the rue Tronchet, the Hôtel Vignon has just reopened, all bright spanking new. The small lounge opening onto the street is already very charming and inviting, with caramel colored, leather-upholstered armchairs and thickly woven floor mats. The decorator has pushed the refinement even further in the finely honed bedrooms. For a luminous and airy ambiance, he has combined browns and yellows or browns and greens, depending on the floors. You will find a low chair covered with white damask in each room. Comfort comes next, with air-conditioning and voluptuous white marbled baths. Here again, breakfast is served in a basement room with bright red seats for an invigorating morning start.

Austin's Hôtel

26, rue d'Amsterdam - 75009 Paris
Tel. (0)1 48 74 48 71 - Fax (0)1 48 74 39 79
M. Hamidi
E-mail: austins.hotel@wanadoo.fr

Category ★★ **Rooms** 36 with soundproofing, telephone, bath or shower, WC, hairdryer, satellite TV. **Price** Single 410F / 62,50€, double 480F / 73,18€ – Special rates Friday, Saturday and Sunday. **Meals** Breakfast (buffet) 35F / 5,34€, served 7:00-10:00. **Credit cards** All major. **Pets** Dogs not allowed. **Facilities** Elevator, bar. **Restaurant** Mealtime specials 74-104F / 11,28-15,85€. Specialties: traditional cooking, couscous. **Parking** Gare Saint-Lazare. **How to get there** (Map 4) Bus: All to Saint-Lazare – Metro and train station: Gare Saint-Lazare – RER: Auber. **Open** All year.

Here is a good example to prove that with a small budget you can still live well in Paris. In the very animated quarter of the Gare Saint-Lazare, Austin's Hôtel is in a small street running along one of the sides of this imposing building, and the hotel is equally close to the department stores of Boulevard Haussmann. The interior is however very quiet and the comfort offered is exemplary considering its price. Even though it is recommended to sleep in a room on the courtyard (especially in summer if you want to open your windows), the rooms overlooking the street have very effective double-glazing. The rooms are generally small but prettily decorated with stripes or printed paper in dominant greens or blues. The bathrooms are impeccable and the service very professional, with tray-meals on request. A very good breakfast is served for you in an attractive bistro-style room, and this is a good new recruit for the inexpensive section of our guide.

Hôtel de Châteaudun

30, rue de Châteaudun – 75009 Paris
Tel. (0)1 49 70 09 99 – Fax (0)1 49 70 06 99
Mme Lassalle
E-mail: hotel.chateaudun@wanadoo.fr

Category ★★★ **Rooms** 26 with air-conditioning and soundproofing, telephone, bath or shower, WC, hairdryer, cable TV, safe and minibar. **Price** Single 680F / 103,67€, double 810F / 123,48€, triple 1020F / 155,50€, 4 pers. 1420F / 216,48€. **Meals** Breakfast (buffet) 50F / 7,62€, served 7:00-10:00. **Credit cards** All major. **Pets** Dogs allowed. **Faciles** Elevator, laundry service, room service (tray-meal 100F / 15,24€). **Parking** Rue Chauchat. **How to get there** (Map 4) Bus: 26, 32 and 43 – Metro: Notre-Dame-de-Lorette and Le Peletier. **Open** All year.

The rue de Châteaudun is midway between the quarter of the Grands Magasins and that of Pigalle and Montmartre. The hotel, named after the street, still reflects its choice to be original even though this now goes back a few years. The lobby, where one finds both the reception area and the lounge, sets the tone: bright blue, Charles Eames' sofa and armchairs in black leather, with carpets by McConnico. The bedrooms are fitted out with interesting furniture especially made for the hotel, reasonably sophisticated, taking its rightful place in the white and blue decor. As far as comfort is concerned, the classical amenities are fully provided. The corner rooms are more pleasant because they have bathrooms with daylight. Families should note that the rooms ending with a 5 or 6 can be connected. The whole is well-maintained (the carpeting, painting and wallpaper have just been changed on most floors), and the concept still holds together.

Hôtel Chopin

10, boulevard Montmartre (46, passage Jouffroy)
75009 Paris
Tel. (0)1 47 70 58 10 – Fax (0)1 42 47 00 70
M. Philippe Bidal

Category ★★ **Rooms** 35 with telephone, bath or shower, TV and 34 with WC. **Price** Single 405-455F / 61,74-69,36€, double 450-520F / 68,60-79,27€, triple 595F / 90,71€. **Meals** Breakfast (buffet) 40F / 6,10€, served 7:15-9:45. **Credit cards** Visa, Eurocard, MasterCard. **Pets** Dogs allowed. **Facilities** Elevator. **Parking** Rue Chauchat. **How to get there** (Map 7) Bus: 20, 39, 48, 67, 74 and 85 – Metro: Richelieu-Drouot. **Open** All year.

On the boulevard Montmartre between the Musée Grévin and the Hard Rock Café, the glass roofing of Passage Jouffroy shelters numerous bookshops (including one to delight all movie fans), along with the Hôtel Chopin. The place has a great deal of charm. The hotel lobby has a piano and two portraits of the celebrated couple of Chopin and George Sand. It's up a few steps to the dining room, where breakfasts are served, and to the elevator for the floors above. The rooms, more or less on the small side, have almost all been renovated: simply but comfortably furnished, often brightened up with fabrics and wallpaper of tonic colors, with new carpeting for most of them. (however those on the *premier étage* and with a number ending in 2 get less light). They are all well-maintained and very quiet (not one of them opens onto the street). A friendly address with a good quality-price ratio.

Hôtel des Croisés

63, rue Saint-Lazare
75009 Paris
Tel. (0)1 48 74 78 24 - Fax (0)1 49 95 04 43
Mme Bojena

Category ★★ Rooms 24 and 3 junior suites with soundproofing on street side, telephone, bath, WC, hairdryer, satellite TV and minibar. **Price** Single 420F / 64,12€, double 470-500F / 71,65-76,22€, junior suite 580F / 88,42€ (2 pers.), 675F / 102,90€ (3 pers.); extra bed 95F / 14,48€. **Meals** Breakfast (buffet) 39F / 5,95€, served 6:45-11:00. **Credit cards** All major. **Pets** Dogs allowed. **Facilities** Elevator. **Parking** Trinité. **How to get there** (Map 4) Bus: All to Saint-Lazare – Metro: Trinité – RER: Auber – Train station: Gare Saint-Lazare. **Open** All year.

This is a surprising hotel which we can recommend now that the bathrooms (which needed a renovation) have all been redone, retaining their spaciousness as well as the porcelain. To have kept its initial style is what makes the charm of the Hôtel des Croisés. A beautiful freestone entry with wood panelling, a period elevator, wrought iron lamps and 19th-century paintings bring back the atmosphere of the early 20th-century that fills the whole building. The bedrooms are for the most part very large and very retro. Some have furniture from the school of Nancy with stoneware fireplaces which might be by Bigot (Room 23). Others have kept the *Barbès* furniture with sycamore or mahogany veneer. Some have an unusual layout, with the entrance to the bathroom hidden in the wood panelling (no. 25) or a lounge corner set up on a platform. In summer your can enjoy the coolness of the rooms at the back (no. 2, 4 and 12). This hotel should delight all antique lovers.

Hôtel du Léman

20, rue de Trévise - 75009 Paris
Tel. (0)1 42 46 50 66 - Fax (0)1 48 24 27 59
M. Legrand
E-mail: lemanhot@aol.com

Category ★★★ Rooms 24 with soundproofing, telephone, bath or shower, WC, hairdryer, satellite TV and minibar. **Price** (depending on the season and excluding trade fair periods) Single 410-490F / 62,50-74,70€, double 490-540F / 74,70-82,32€, double with king-size bed 540-720F / 82,32-109,76€; extra bed 130F / 19,82€. **Meals** Breakfast (buffet) 45F / 6,86€, served 7:00-10:45; snack availables. **Credit cards** All major. **Pets** Dogs allowed. **Facilities** Elevator, laundry service. **Parking** Rue Richer. **How to get there** (Map 4) Bus: 26, 32, 42, 43, 48 and 74 – Metro: Cadet, Grands-Boulevards. **Open** All year.

Between the Grands Boulevards, the popular boulevard Montmartre and the world-famous Folies Bergères, the rue de Trévise on which Le Léman stands is actually a very quiet street. The hotel reception area conserves some of the souvenirs of its globe-trotting owners, such as the fine Italian marble marquetry panels surrounding the office. All the bedrooms have just been pleasantly freshened up with new carpeting that harmonizes with a panel of printed wallpaper behind the bed. The rooms on the top floor have mansard ceilings, notably no. 66, and are very popular. The restful atmosphere that M. Legrand wanted for his guests has been preserved. The buffet breakfast is copious, the welcome very attentive, and snacks are always available should you get hungry.

Hôtel Libertel Franklin

19, rue Buffault
75009 Paris
Tel. (0)1 42 80 27 27 – Fax (0)1 48 78 13 04
Mme Esnault

Category ★★★ **Rooms** 68 and 9 suites with soundproofing, telephone, bath or shower, WC, hairdryer, minibar, cable TV – 2 for disabled persons. **Price** Single 918,34F / 140€, double 989,34F / 150€, suite 1052F / 160€ (3 pers.) – Special rates from Nov to end Mar (excluding trade fair periods). **Meals** Breakfast (buffet) 78,71F / 12€, served 7:00-10:30. **Credit cards** All major. **Pets** Dogs allowed. **Facilities** Elevator, laundry service, garden, room service. **Parking** Rue Buffault, square Montholon. **How to get there** (Map 4) Bus: 26, 32, 42, 43 and 85 – Metro: Cadet. **Open** All year.

Very welcoming, the large reception area of the Libertel Franklin has an unexpected and rather naive panorama on its walls, but the hotel itself is mainly inspired by the Napoleonic era. No richly decorated furniture pieces in mahogany to recall the Empire, but rather, wrought iron chairs and tables more typical of a military campaign. The rooms are papered in wide gray or dark red stripes, and soberly but elegantly fitted with cerused furniture. The themes chosen for the rooms have been reflected in the prints. They are very comfortable with perfect bathrooms that have recently renovated. Very well organized, the hotel had adapted itself to clientele needs. There are non-smoking floors and room service that provides tray-meals for the exhausted business clientele, or those not wishing to miss the TV soccer match at any price. Guests will find a kettle with tea and coffee as well as the programs of Parisian events placed in the desk-blotters.

Hôtel Libertel Lafayette

49-51, rue Lafayette
75009 Paris
Tel. (0)1 42 85 05 44 - Fax (0)1 49 95 06 60
Mme Dessors

Category ★★★ Rooms 96 and 7 suites, (1 floor for non-smokers, 28 rooms with air-conditioning) with telephone, bath or shower, WC, hairdryer, satellite TV, minibar, safe, trouser-press – 2 for disabled persons. **Price** Single 1016,73F / 155€, double 1082,33F / 165€, "supérieure" 2000,65F / 305€, suite 2505,75F / 382€; in Jul, Aug and from Nov to Mar (excluding trade fair periods) 695,31F / 106€ (1-2 pers.). **Meals** Breakfast (buffet) 78,71F / 12€, served 6:30-10:30; snacks available. **Credit cards** All major. **Pets** Small dogs allowed. **Facilities** Elevator, laundry service. **Parking** Rue Buffault. **How to get there** (Map 4) Bus: 26, 32, 42, 43, 67, 74 and 85 – Metro: Le Peletier and Cadet. **Open** All year.

The Libertel Lafayette is close to the Grands Boulevards and the *Grands Magasins*. The decoration was inspired by the elegance and comfort of *bourgeois* residences across the Channel. Thus two windows, with cobalt-blue lacquered molding, frame the entrance with its two large copper lanterns. The lobby leads through to the bar and a smoking lounge lit by a skylight covered in clever *trompe-l'oeil*. The space is light and airy, in a beige monochrome. The floor is stone, with cerused furniture, the walls covered with linen fabrics printed with medallions, and there are mahogany furniture pieces. The rooms are just as well-done and quiet. Six of the ten rooms on each floor overlook the courtyard. The blue, green or beige *toile de Jouy* gives them a cozy country atmosphere. Nothing is lacking for comfort, including an electric kettle with tea or coffee for moments of relaxation. The suites, very well conceived, are almost all fitted out with a kitchenette. Both welcome and service are attentive.

Hôtel Libertel Moulin

39, rue Fontaine
75009 Paris
Tel. (0)1 42 81 93 25 - Fax (0)1 40 16 09 90
Mme Frédérique Péchenart

Category ★★★ **Rooms** 48 and 2 junior suites with soundproofing, telephone, bath or shower, WC, minibar, cable TV and 20 with hairdryer. **Price** Single 885F /135€, double 951F/ 145€, junior suite 1298F / 190€ (2 pers.), in Jul, Aug and Nov to end Mar (excluding trade fair periods and national holidays): 1 pers. 600F / 91,47€, 2 pers. 800F / 121,96€. **Meals** Breakfast (buffet) 78,71F / 12€, served 7:00-10:30. **Credit cards** All major. **Pets** Dogs allowed (+50F / 7,62€). **Facilities** Elevator, laundry service, room service: 11AM–2PM, 6:30PM–10:30PM. **Parking** Rue Mansart. **How to get there** (Map 4) Bus: 30, 54, 68 and 74 – Metro: Blanche. **Open** All year.

The Moulin Rouge district is certainly just what you would expect: popular, touristy and noisy, but the Hôtel Libertel Moulin is set back from all the agitation. It must also be added that you are close to all that gives this district its full charm (provided you have good legs): the rue Lepic market, the bistros in the rue des Abbesses, the Butte Montmartre and Sacré-Coeur church. The hotel interior is carefully maintained with a combined reception area and comfortable lounge, filled mainly with black leather "club" armchairs. Most of the rooms have just been redone, and they are not large but are cozy with their warm brick tones; all have comfortable bathrooms in bicolored *travertin*. Rooms on the street are very light but those on the courtyard are quieter - each side of the hotel has its advantages. Both welcome and service are attentive, the breakfast-buffet is copious, and the rates are attractive.

Hôtel Pulitzer-Opéra

23, rue du Faubourg-Montmartre
75009 Paris
Tel. (0)1 53 34 98 10 - Fax (0)1 53 34 98 11
Mlle Yolanda Herrero

Category ★★★ (categorization pending) **Rooms** 43 and 1 suite with air-conditioning and soundproofing, telephone, bath or shower, WC, hairdryer, satellite TV and 15 with minibar – 2 for disabled persons. **Price** Single 550-950F / 83,85-144,83€, double 750-1150F / 114,34-175,32€, triple 1300F / 198,18€, suite (4 pers.) 1600F / 243,92€. **Meals** Breakfast (buffet) 65F / 9,91€, served 7:00-11:00. **Credit cards** All major. **Pets** Dogs allowed. **Facilities** Elevator, bar, laundry service, room service. **Parking** Rue Chauchat. **How to get there** (Map 7) Bus: 20, 39, 48, 67, 74 and 85 – Metro: Grands Boulevards. **Open** All year.

This working-class district lacked a good hotel. Although fast food and cheap stores fill the whole street, one should not overlook its proximity to the Drouot auction sales room as well as, on the other side of boulevard Montmartre, the rue Vivienne directly leading to La Bourse and the Palais-Royal Gardens. The Pulitzer-Opéra has just opened. The choice of decoration is simple, sober and contemporary, without much personality but always very comfortable. In the bedrooms, you will appreciate the parquet floor, the soundproofing, the well-devised layout as well as the new and pretty bathrooms. They are all luminous, impeccable, and most have the advantage of overlooking the courtyard. Our favorites are no. 511, which is among the largest, with a truly successful use of space, and those in with a number ending in 6, which have two windows on the courtyard. The lounge, bar and breakfast room make up a beautiful reception space, opening wide onto the vegetation of the patio.

Résidence du Pré

15, rue Pierre-Sémard
75009 Paris
Tel. (0)1 48 78 26 72 - Fax (0)1 42 80 64 83
Mme Dupré

Category ★★★ **Rooms** 40 with soundproofing, telephone, bath or shower, WC, satellite TV and 4 with safe. **Price** Single 445F / 67,84€, double 495-530F / 75,46-80,80€, triple 645F / 98,33€. **Meals** Breakfast (buffet) 50F / 7,62€ (free of charge between mid Nov and mid Mar), served 7:30-10:00. **Credit cards** All major. **Pets** Dogs not allowed. **Facilities** Elevator, bar, patio. **Parking** Rue Mayran (60F / 9,15€ /day). **How to get there** (Map 4) Bus: 26, 32, 42, 43, 48 and 85 – Metro: Cadet. **Open** All year.

Around the Square Montholon, four hotels are called "du Pré" after the family who owns them. To the William's du Pré, which we have already selected for its view over the square, we have added the Résidence du Pré, which has been, for the most part, refurbished. The spacious entry was totally redesigned to create a convivial bar lounge: salmon colors for the comfortable sofas, green carpeting, and lights adjustable to the intimate atmosphere desired. The rooms are distributed between what is called the "main" building and the annex, although the latter is an integral part of the hotel. Most of them have new decoration (in the annex, Rooms 17, 27, 18 and 28, in the main building rooms ending in 1 and 6). The often large bathrooms have also been redone. The whole effect is friendly, and all these efforts have not brought about a price increase, a decisive factor in the choice of this hotel. Good welcome and availability on the part of the reception staff.

Hôtel Riboutté-Lafayette

5, rue Riboutté
75009 Paris
Tél. (0)1 47 70 62 36 – Fax (0)1 48 00 91 50
Mme Claudine Gourd

Category ★★ **Rooms** 24 (with soundproofing on the street) with telephone, bath or shower, WC, hairdryer, satellite TV. **Price** Single 370-425F / 56,41-64,79€, double 390-470F / 59,46-71,65€; extra bed 150F / 22,87€. **Meals** Breakfast 35F / 5,34€, served 7:00-10:00. **Credit cards** Visa, Eurocard, MasterCard and Amex. **Pets** Dogs allowed. **Facilities** Elevator. **Parking** Rue Mayran (square de Montholon). **How to get there** (Map 4) Bus: 26, 32, 42, 43, 48 and 85 – Metro: Cadet. **Open** All year.

The small Hôtel Riboutté-Lafayette also enjoys the proximity of the Montholon square and its precious parking lot. It is a simple hotel which has kept up its decoration in an 80s style, judging by the durable Japanese wallpaper that still remains in some places. Yet there is a concern to update the decor of the hotel: colorful bedspreads brighten up the bedrooms, each of which is personalized with a small piece of furniture or a mirror found at a second-hand sale (even though some of these elements could do with refurbishing or re-varnishing). The small mansard rooms on the top floor are very popular for their "under the roofs of Paris" charm, but in summer you had better sleep on the courtyard side, where the rooms are quieter, cooler and still very luminous. A pleasant hotel for small budgets.

Hôtel de La Tour d'Auvergne

10, rue de La Tour d'Auvergne
75009 Paris
Tel. (0)1 48 78 61 60 – Fax (0)1 49 95 99 00
M. Duval

Category ★★★ **Rooms** 24 with telephone, bath, WC, hairdryer, TV. **Price** Single 600-750F / 91,47-114,34€, double 700-850F / 106,71-129,58€. **Meals** Breakfast (buffet) 55F / 8,38€, served 7:00-10:00. **Credit cards** All major. **Pets** Dogs allowed (+50F / 7,62€). **Facilities** Elevator, laundry service. **Parking** Square de Montholon. **How to get there** (Map 4) Bus: 26, 30, 42, 54, 67 and 85 – Metro: Cadet and Anvers. **Open** All year.

Not very far from the Butte Montmartre, with its theaters, and, of course, Sacré Coeur, or from the Opera, the Hôtel de la Tour d'Auvergne has just been extensively renovated. The decor is eclectic and no room is like the other. According to your taste, you can choose bright colors (no. 41 in turquoise and yellow is quite audacious) or soft tones, *toile de Jouy* (no. 55 under the roof) or Persian fabrics, floral motifs or stripes, a country or baroque atmosphere. All the rooms have comfortable bathrooms. As is always the case in Paris, you'll be sure to have a quiet room on the courtyard, but the view there is somewhat gray. We prefer the rooms on the street side, particularly as there is not much traffic. The bar is pleasant and the staff charming.

Hôtel William's du Pré

3, rue Mayran/Square de Montholon
75009 Paris
Tel. (0)1 48 78 68 35 - Fax (0)1 45 26 08 70
M. Dupré

Category ★★★ **Rooms** 30 with soundproofing, telephone, bath or shower, WC, hairdryer and TV. **Price** Single 425F / 64,79€, double 480-510F / 73,18-77,75€, triple 630F / 96,04€. **Meals** Breakfast (buffet) 50F / 7,62€ (free of charge between mid Nov and mid Mar), served 8:00-10:00. **Credit cards** All major. **Pets** Dogs allowed. **Facilities** Elevator. **Parking** Rue Mayran (60F / 9,15€ /day). **How to get there** (Map 4) Bus: 26, 32, 42, 43, 48 and 85 – Metro: Cadet. **Open** All year.

The Square Montholon is a pleasant oasis of greenery and gardens in this neighborhood located half-way between the Opéra and Sacré-Coeur. All the bedrooms of the Hôtel William's du Pré enjoy a lovely view of the gardens. Decorated in shades of pink or blue, depending on the floor, the rooms have tinted furniture with beds and drapes in coordinated, floral cotton-satin; the decor may not be remarkable, but the rooms are comfortable. Those on the *deuxième* and *cinquième étages* open onto a balcony, and the higher up you are, the better your view of the Square. The breakfast room in the basement is where you'll be served a delicious buffet. Note that there is a public parking lot just in front of the hotel, an added bonus.

Hôtel Libertel Champagne Mulhouse

87, boulevard de Strasbourg
75010 Paris
Tel. (0)1 42 09 12 28 - Fax (0)1 42 09 48 12
Mme Simone Foerst

Category ★★ **Rooms** 31 (1 floor for non-smokers) with soundproofing, telephone, bath or shower, WC, hairdryer, cable TV. **Price** Single 570,68F / 87€, double 636,28F / 97€ – Speciale rates on request **Meals** Breakfast (buffet) 49,20F / 7,50€, served 7:00-10:30. **Credit cards** All major. **Pets** Dogs allowed. **Facilities** Elevator, room service. **Parking** Gare de l'Est. **How to get there** (Map 4) All bus to Gare de l'Est – Metro and train station: Gare de l'Est. **Open** All year.

The Champagne-Mulhouse is almost right on the Gare de l'Est square, in one of the last buildings on the Boulevard de Strasbourg. It has a discrete entrance behind the terraces of the brasseries surrounding it. A few steps up is a bell to open the door, and a beautiful sculptured-oak railing leads to the reception area. In the small reception lounge, the carpet, sofa, and armchairs by McConnico are in bright shades of cherry red, carmine, vermilion, and orange, while the breakfast room is decorated in bold shades of green, lavender blue, and turquoise. The bedrooms are equally cheerful, with yellow or almond-green striped fabrics and bedspreads in floral chintz or tartan cotton. They are very comfortable and have practical, pivoting reading lamps, cable television and, a pleasant detail, toiletries in the bathroom. A copious breakfast buffet confirms the quality of this small hotel, which offers more than just good value.

Hôtel Libertel Terminus Nord

12, boulevard de Denain
75010 Paris
Tel. (0)1 42 80 20 00 - Fax (0)1 42 80 63 89
M. Didier Picaud

Category ★★★ **Rooms** 236 (1 floor for non-smokers) with soundproofing, telephone, bath, WC, satellite TV and safe – 5 for disabled persons. **Price** Single 1095,45F / 167€, double 1161,04F / 177€, "prestige room" 1731,73F / 264€; extra bed 150F / 22,87€. **Meals** Breakfast (buffet): 82F / 12,5€, served 6:30-10:30. **Credit cards** All major. **Pets** Small dogs allowed. **Facilities** Elevator, Laundry service, office facilities, room service (24 h). **Parking** Gare du Nord. **How to get there** (Map 4) Bus: all to Gare du Nord – Metro, RER and train station: Gare du Nord. **Open** All year.

One of the most beautiful monuments in Paris, the Gare du Nord train station has become the crossroads of Europe with the opening of the Channel Tunnel and the Eurostar Paris-London train. This explains the large numbers of English people who frequent the Terminus Nord, which is in front of the station and next to the famous *Brasserie Terminus Nord* (oyster lovers shouldn't miss it). This is a hotel in the grand style, with porters and bellboys to greet you and courteous receptionists behind the large desk. The huge lobby is very Art Nouveau with its skylight and the original stained glass that was discovered when the hotel was renovated. It opens onto several lounges. The bar, the private lounges, and the breakfast room are on the *premier étage*. A variety of fabrics and colors are nicely coordinated; the decor throughout is both sumptuous and comfortable. The bedrooms and suites are exquisite: quilted, floral chintz in shades of red, dark-wood furniture in some and painted furniture with white and blue fabrics in others. Our favorite rooms are those on the *quatrième étage* and up, with a view over the Gare du Nord.

Hôtel Beaumarchais

3, rue Oberkampf
75011 Paris
Tel. (0)1 53 36 86 86 – Fax (0)1 43 38 32 86
M. Alain Quintard

Category ★★ **Rooms** 29 and 2 junior suites with soundproofing (28 with air-conditioning), telephone, bath or shower, WC, hairdryer, satellite TV and safe. **Price** Single 350-450F / 53,36-68,60€, double 490-550F / 74,70-83,85€, junior suite 700F / 106,71€. **Meals** Breakfast 35F / 5,34€, served 7:00-11:00. **Credit cards** Amex, Visa, Eurocard, MasterCard. **Pets** Dogs allowed. **Facilities** Elevator, patio, room service. **Parking** Private (at 30m). **How to get there** (Map 8) Bus: 20, 56, 65 and 96 – Metro: Oberkampf, Filles du Calvaire. **Open** All year.

Not far from the Cirque d'Hiver (Winter Circus), the small white façade of the Hôtel Beaumarchais conceals a very pleasant discovery. An architect recently converted into a hotel owner, Alain Quintard wanted to maintain the extremely reasonable prices of the establishment but also to offer a good level of comfort and an attractive decor; and that's just what he did! The reception lounge and breakfast room open straight onto a flowery patio, and they show a pronounced taste for the South (coatings in red-ochre stucco, bright colors, and so on) and contemporary art. The rooms retain a bit of this bright and youthful style, and are simple and well-maintained. The hotel offers services rare in the "two-star" category, such as air-conditioning, private safes, hairdryers, etc. The bathrooms have been entirely refurbished in the same spirit of creativity and tastefulness. A ceramic decor in a patchwork of tile pieces surrounds the brand-new bathtubs and sinks. The reception is charming and attentive. A hotel well in the style of the rue Oberkampf.

Home Plazza Saint-Antoine

289, rue du Faubourg Saint-Antoine – 75011 Paris
Tel. (0)1 40 09 40 00 – Fax (0)1 40 09 11 55
Mme Valérie Thromat
E-mail: resanation@home-plazza.com

Category ★★★ **Rooms** 89 with soundproofing and air-conditioning, telephone, bath, WC, hairdryer (on request), cable TV, minibar, safe, kitchenette – 2 for disabled persons. **Price** Single 457-826F / 69,77-126,1€, double 494-939F / 75,41-143,35€, triple and 4-5 pers. 794-1591F / 121,22-242,9€. **Meals** Breakfast (buffet) 65F / 9,91€, served 7:00-10:00. **Credit cards** All major. **Pets** Dogs allowed (80F / 12,20€). **Facilities** Elevator, laundry service, patio. **Parking** On the premises (95F / 14,48€ /day). **How to get there** Bus: 56, 57 and 86 – Metro and RER: Nation. **Open** All year.

This is the perfect spot for tourists or business people wishing to spend a long time in the capital, or for families who find it constraining to dine out every night. Indeed, the Plazza Saint-Antoine provides suites which are interesting in that they can not only be booked for a night but they can also be turned private apartments for four to five people. Whatever their size, all are equipped with a kitchenette, refrigerator, hot plates, a microwave, dishes, and a breakfast nook. The largest also have a small living room with a convertable sofa and bunk beds. Divided up among the three buildings which surround the garden-courtyard, the bedrooms have a pleasant decor in tones of red or blue, and are all very comfortable. The buffet breakfast is quite copious. The staff is always at your service, and will greet you in the large, light, reception area furnished with chairs and decorated with engravings and a large painting by Bernard Buffet. The family-oriented Home Plazza is a practical place to stay.

Hôtel Libertel Croix de Malte

5, rue de Malte
75011 Paris
Tel. (0)1 48 05 09 36 - Fax (0)1 43 57 02 54
Mlle Stéphanie Biagini

Category ★★ **Rooms** 29 with soundproofing, telephone, bath or shower, hairdryer, WC, cable TV – 1 for disabled persons. **Price** Single 570,70F / 87€, double 636,30F / 97€ – Specail rates in Jul to Aug and Nov to end Feb (excluding trade fair periods). **Meals** Breakfast (buffet) 49,20F / 7,5€, served 7:00-10-30. **Credit cards** Amex, Visa, Eurocard, MasterCard. **Pets** Dogs not allowed. **Facilities** Elevator, bar. **Parking** Place de la République. **How to get there** (Map 8) Bus: 20, 46, 65 and 96 – Metro: Oberkampf and Filles du Calvaire. **Open** All year.

The hotel is sited on one of the three sections making up the rue de Malte, between rue Oberkampf and boulevard Voltaire. The rooms are split between two small buildings, each facing a veranda framed by two small courtyards painted with an attractive decor of tropical forests in *trompe l'oeil*. Drinks from the bar are served here along with breakfast, but do not leave it too for late as the buffet is not always fully restocked. The whole hotel rather smacks of the exotic as shown by the colored reproductions by Wallace Ting. In the blue and white area with its elevator, the rooms are rather standard and not very large, but they are well-thought-out and always come with a small desk and well-equipped bathrooms. In the other building, with two floors but no elevator, there is the same decor but in green and orange. In the rooms on the upper floor, the bathrooms are reached by a rather steep spiral staircase. They have mansard ceilings and charm, but one needs to be quite agile all the same. Rooms on the ground floor open onto the small courtyards. This is an attractive hotel.

203

Hôtel Belle Époque

66, rue de Charenton
75012 Paris
Tel. (0)1 43 44 06 66 - Fax (0)1 43 44 10 25
Mme Isabelle Frouin

Category ★★★ **Rooms** 28 and 2 junior suites with air-conditioning and soundproofing, telephone, bath, WC, hairdryer, satellite TV, safe and minibar. **Price** Single 810F / 123,48€, double 830F / 126,53€, triple 1000F / 152,45€, junior suite 1200F / 182,94€; in low season: 1 pers. 600F / 91,47€, 2 pers. 660F / 100,62€. **Meals** Breakfast (buffet) 55F / 8,38€, buffet 75F / 11,43€, served 7:00-11:00. **Credit cards** All major. **Pets** Dogs allowed. **Facilities** Elevator, bar, patio. **Parking** Rue du Faubourg Saint-Antoine. **How to get there** (Map 2) Bus: 20, 29, 61, 65, 76, 86, 87 and 91 – Metro: Ledru-Rollin and Bastille – RER and train station (TGV): Gare de Lyon. **Open** All year.

Just five minutes from the Place de la Bastille and its Opera, the Hôtel Belle Epoque is completely dedicated to the Art Deco style. The space on the ground floor has just been renovated; it comprises the reception area, the bar and the lounge where breakfast is served, and gives onto a small green courtyard with some tables in summertime for the breakfast brunch. The rooms are in a 1900s-style while the furniture is 1930s copies, with the best found in the *chambre d'époque* suite with a bed, wardrobe and chairs in the Printz style. The others are more sober and recall the furniture of Ruhlman. All are large enough and have marble bathrooms, while some also have small balconies. Generally speaking, it is better to sleep on the courtyard side but thanks to the double-glazing and air-conditioning you need not fear the noise from the street. The welcome is extremely convivial.

Hôtel Libertel Nation

33, avenue du Docteur-Arnold-Netter
75012 Paris
Tel. (0)1 40 04 90 90 - Fax (0)1 40 04 99 20
Rodolphe Leroux

Category ★★★ **Rooms** 49 with air-consitioning and soundproofing with telephone, bath
or shower, WC, hairdryer, satellite TV. **Price** (–30% for readers of this guide). Single
885,54F / 135€, double 951,14F / 145€, triple 1082,33F / 165€. **Meals** Breakfast
78,71F / 12€, served 7:00-10:30. **Credit cards** All major. **Pets** Dogs allowed. **Facilities**
Elevator, bar, laundry service, room service. **Parking** Underneath the hotel 70F/10,67€
/day. **How to get there** (Map 11) Bus: 29, 56 and 62 – Metro: Picpus. **Open** All year.

Although it is in the neighborhood of the Opera Bastille and the
Palais Omnisport de Bercy, as well as that of the Bois de
Vincennes and the *Coulée Verte* (a verdured pedestrian path leading to
the Bastille), most tourists would not consider such a hotel, so far
away from the city center. Yet the Libertel Nation presents many
advantages to those who wish to stay in the east of Paris. This
modern, comfortable establishment offers luminous rooms, both
impeccable and very functional. They all have the same yellow and
blue decor and the same comfort - only their size and aspect vary. We
prefer those at the rear, which are generally larger and calmer (ask for
one on the upper floors). We also quite like those ending in 1 on the
street side for their corner location. While the bedrooms are pleasant
but with no special character, the warm and modern atmosphere that
emanates from the lounge and breakfast room deserves a special
mention. The staff is concerned with your well-being.

Nouvel Hôtel

24, avenue du Bel-Air
75012 Paris
Tel. (0)1 43 43 01 81 – Fax (0)1 43 44 64 13
M. and Mme Marillier

Categorie ★★ Rooms 28 with soundproofing, telephone, 4 with bath, 24 with shower, WC and TV. **Price** Single 375-405F / 57,17-61,74€, double 450-580F / 68,60-88,42€. **Meals** Breakfast 43F / 6,56€, served 7:00-10:30. **Credit cards** All major. **Pets** Dogs allowed. **Facilities** Garden and patio. **Parking** Garage Renault: 24, avenue de Saint-Mandé (at 100m). **How to get there** (Map 8) Bus: 29, 56, 57, 86 and 351 for terminal Roissy-Charles-de-Gaulle – Metro and RER: Nation. **Open** All year.

The avenue du Bel-Air is one of the wide streets that lead to the large Place de la Nation. The verdant façade of the Nouvel Hôtel intices you to walk into the reception area where you will be very amicably greeted. You will then discover a small, countrified breakfast room with double table cloths and floral wallpaper brightened by a beautiful frieze with fruit motifs. M. and Mme Marilliet have chosen coordinated fabrics from Laura Ashley for the bedrooms. These are fresh, cheerful and cozy, all differently decorated and very well maintained. Their very correct size and the well-conceived storage space make them fully sufficient for longer occupation. Most overlook the garden or the patio. No. 109 is quite sought-after because guests have direct access to the garden and almost total privacy once the breakfast service there is finished, but it is also the least bright. We should add that much care is put into the breakfast and the welcome is particularly attentive. One of the best places in Paris for a low price.

Hôtel Paris Bastille

67, rue de Lyon
75012 Paris
Tel. (0)1 40 01 07 17 - Fax (0)1 40 01 07 27
Mme Isabelle Frouin

Category ★★★ **Rooms** 37 with air-conditioning and soundproofing, telephone, bath, WC, hairdryer, satellite TV, minibar and safe – 2 for disabled persons. **Price** Single 810F / 123,48€, double 830F / 126,53€; triple 1000F / 152,45€, junior suite (2 pers.) 1200F / 182,94€; in low season: 1 pers. 600F / 91,47€, 2 pers. 660F / 100,62€. **Meals** Breakfast 55F / 8,38€, buffet 75F / 11,43€, served 7:00-11:00. **Credit cards** All major. **Pets** Dogs allowed. **Facilities** Elevator, laundry service, bar, room service until 22:00. **Parking** Opéra Bastille (in front of the hotel). **How to get there** (Map 2) Bus: 20, 29, 65, 87 and 91 – Metro: Bastille – RER and train station (TGV): Gare de Lyon (300 m). **Open** All year.

Just like its neighbor next door, described on the next page, the Paris Bastille is just in front of the Bastille Opera with its controversial architecture. It is one of the last of the Parisian *Grands Travaux* projects providing Paris with new monuments and has now become the capital's temple of all the lyric arts. The large reception area is very light and opens onto the street; it leads through to the lounge-bar where breakfast is also served. The decor is simple with Japanese panels, light wood furniture and colors various in shades of grey. You find the same contemporary spirit and colors in the rooms. They are spacious and comfortable with their only fantasy shown in the flowery quilted bedspreads. Such elegant sobriety creates an atmosphere of well-being, while the welcome from the personnel is courteous and very professional.

Hôtel Le Pavillon Bastille

65, rue de Lyon - 75012 Paris
Tel. (0)1 43 43 65 65 - Fax (0)1 43 43 96 52
M. and Mme Arnaud - Mme Fournier
E-mail: hotel-pavillon@akamail.com

Category ★★★ **Rooms** 25 with air-conditioning and soundproofing, telephone, bath, WC, hairdryer, satellite TV, minibar and safe – 1 for disabled persons. **Price** Single and double 840F / 128,06€, "privilège" 955F / 145,59€, suite (2-4 pers.) 1375F / 209,62€; from Jan to Mar, mid Jul to end Aug and Nov to Dec 22: −10 % (excluding trade fair periods). **Meals** Breakfast (buffet) 75F / 11,43€. **Credit cards** All major. **Pets** Dogs allowed. **Facilities** Elevator, laundry service, courtyard-garden, room service. **Parking** Opposite the hotel. **How to get there** (Map 2) Bus: 20, 29, 65, 87 and 91 – Metro: Bastille – RER and train station (TGV): Gare de Lyon (at 500m). **Open** All year.

Modernity and efficiency are the two words best qualifying Le Pavillon Bastille, even if a beautiful 17th-century fountain has been conserved in the pretty entry courtyard of the hotel. "Baroque Modernity" describes the extremely bright decor in the reception hall, all in contrasting colors, materials and lighting. The rooms are softer, and offer all the extras that you might wish for: international TV, minibar and so on. You find the same style in the bathrooms with very comfortable bath robes provided from the famous House of Porthault. The reception team is efficient and offers 24-hour room service. You can also ask the management to reserve your tickets for the Bastille Opera, and take advantage of the special evening rates and weekend rates offered by the hotel. The Bastille district is one of the trendy areas of Paris with its "avant-garde" galleries (Jousse-Seguin, Durand, and others), restaurants (Café de l'Industrie, Chez Paul) and late-closing cafés.

Hôtel La Manufacture

8, rue Philippe-de-Champagne - 75013 Paris
Tel. (0)1 45 35 45 25 - Fax (0)1 45 35 45 40
Mme Géraldine Le Bobinnec
E-mail: lamanufact@aol.com

Category ★★ Rooms 57 with air-conditioning and soundproofing, telephone, bath or shower, WC, hairdryer and satellite TV – 3 for disabled persons. **Price** Single 450F / 68,60€, double 550F / 83,85€, big room 800F / 121,96€, triple 750F / 114,34€, Adjoining rooms (4 pers.) 1000F / 152,45€ – Special rates for readers of this guide. **Meals** Breakfast (buffet) 42F / 6,41€, served 7:00. **Credit cards** All major. **Pets** Dogs not allowed. **Facilities** Elevator, bar, laundry service. **Parking** Place d'Italie. **How to get there** (Map 10) Bus: 27, 47, 57, 67 and 83 – Metro: Place d'Italie. **Open** All year.

This charming hotel is on a choice spot: on one side, Les Gobelins with the famous tapestry manufacture and the lively quarter of the rue Mouffetard, on the other. Beyond the Place d'Italie, you will find the Parisian Chinatown and its numerous restaurants. The hotel has just opened and is quite an achievement. One is charmed by the warm and reasonably modern decor of the reception area opening onto the bar lounge. As in many hotels, classicism and Art deco styles are softly blended. Bright colors have boldly been foldly combined with delicate tones. The rooms are often small (except those on the septième étage which are all large), but charming and comfortable. They offer good amenities and services for this two-star category (the hotel is fully air-conditioned). In order to make the maximum use of the space, the pretty furniture in natural materials was specially designed for each room. The bathrooms are also very charming and well-planned. The welcome is friendly and professional, well in tune with this simply refined hotel for a moderate price.

Résidence Le Vert Galant

41, rue Croulebarbe
75013 Paris
Tel. (0)1 44 08 83 50 - Fax (0)1 44 08 83 69
Mme Laborde

Category ★★★ Rooms 15 with soundproofing, telephone, bath or shower, WC, hairdryer, minibar, cable TV, some with kitchenette – 1 for disabled persons. **Price** Single 400F / 60,98€, double 450-500F / 68,60-76,22€. **Meals** Breakfast 40F / 6,10€, served 6:30-11:00. **Credit cards** All major. **Pets** Dogs not allowed. **Facilities** Laundry service, bar, garden. **Restaurant** Specialties: Southwest cuisine – Mealtime specials 100F / 15,24€ for readers of this guide; also à la carte. **Parking** Private. **Hout to get there** (Map 10) Bus: 27, 47 and 83 – Metro: Gobelins, Corvisart. **Open** All year.

Facing the René Le Gall Park and a few paces from the Manufacture des Gobelins, the hotel is next to the excellent Basque inn, the *Etchegorry*, under the same ownership. From the entrance one notes the pretty garden onto which all the rooms face from both the ground floor and the *premier étage*. Of a pleasant size, all are comfortable and fitted-out very elegantly. Decorated in the same style, they offer varying tones, but always very soft with the dominant color found even in the little knots attaching the pillow case ties. The most expensive have discreetly concealed small kitchenettes. All the colors have been chosen with care, with small carpets or rugs and reproductions of Impressionist works hanging almost everywhere in the house. Breakfasts are eaten in the reception area which is set up as a winter garden with small bistro tables. A quiet atmosphere reigns here, while the charm and excellent price-quality relationship make this address one of our favorites.

Résidence Les Gobelins

9, rue des Gobelins - 75013 Paris
Tel. (0)1 47 07 26 90 - Fax (0)1 43 31 44 05
M. and Mme Poirier
E-mail: goblins@cybercable.fr

Category ★★ **Rooms** 32 with bath or shower, WC, telephone, satellite TV. **Price** Single 325-395F / 49,55-60,22€, double 425-455F / 64,79-69,36€, triple 555F / 84,61€; −10% in Feb and Aug. **Meals** Breakfast 39F / 5,95€. **Credit cards** All major. **Pets** Dogs not allowed. **Facilities** Patio. **Parking** Place d'Italie and rue Censier. **How to get there** (Map 10) Bus: 27, 47, 83 and 91 – Metro: Gobelins – RER: Port-Royal. **Open** All year.

Close to the Manufacture Royale des Gobelins, the hotel is in a quiet area despite the lively and colorful district. The rue Mouffetard and its market are close by as well as all the *souks*, *Turkish* baths, cafés and restaurants surrounding the Paris Mosque. The decoration of the hotel is beginning to date a little, while the rooms are well-maintained and furnished with colored bamboo furniture, yellow wallpaper, blue frames and white *piqué* bedspreads. The bathrooms are not brand-new but not lacking in comfort. On the upper floors, the rooms facing the courtyard (those on the last floor have a mansard ceiling) have a view of the garden. Thanks to its large windows, the breakfast room looks directly onto the flowery patio covered by a luxurious honeysuckle. Well-arranged with its teak furniture and parasols, this would be the ideal spot to relax and have a drink. This very simple place is therefore particularly attractive in the summer. It should be noted that the rates are truly sensible and the welcome is very amiable.

Hôtel Aiglon

232, boulevard Raspail – 75014 Paris
Tel. (0)1 43 20 82 42 – Fax (0)1 43 20 98 72
M. Jacques Rols
Web: www.aiglon.com

Category ★★★ Rooms 47 and 9 suites (with soundproofing and air-conditioning,) with bath or shower, WC, telephone, satellite TV, hairdryer and minibar. **Price** Single or double 490-850F / 74,70-129,58€, suite (2 pers) 1060F / 161,60€; extra bed +120F / 18,29€, apart. (1-4 pers.) 1480F / 225,62€. **Meals** Breakfast 40F / 6,10€, served 7:00- 11:00. **Credit cards** All major. **Pets** Dogs allowed. **Facilities** Elevator, bar, laundry service. **Parking** In the hotel (8 spaces, 80F / 12,20€ /day) or boulevard Edgar-Quinet. **How to get there** (Map 10) Bus: 68 and 91 – Metro: Raspail. **Open** All year.

In front of the Montparnasse Cemetery, on the corner of the Raspail and Edgar Quinet Boulevards, the Aiglon is a comfortable hotel near the great brasseries which were the hallmarks of this neighborhood's Golden Age. Empire style was chosen for the reception areas, with mahogany woodwork, green leather and gilt interlacing motifs, along with period furniture. The lobby, lounge, library-bar and beautiful dining room reflect the same style. Classic inspiration can also be seen in the bedroom decor, with custom–made cherry wood or burr furniture, headboards in the shape of an ancient pediment; our favorites have a charming assortment of green and yellow fabrics. Always luminous and tasteful, they have protective double-glazing, and those on the cemetery side have a better view of trees and greenery. The suites are most pleasant to stay in and the corner bedrooms have an amusing use of space. Excellent value (and the least expensive rooms are not the least attractive) and a very cordial welcome.

Hôtel de Bretagne Montparnasse

33, rue Raymond-Losserand - 75014 Paris
Tel. (0)1 45 38 52 59 - Fax (0)1 45 38 50 39
M. Jean-Luc Houdré
E-mail: bwbm@bwbretagnemontparnasse.com

Category ★★★ **Rooms** 44 with soundproofing, telephone, bath or shower, WC, hairdryer, cable TV and minibar. **Price** Depending on the season. Single 520-720F / 79,27-109,76€, double 580-800F / 88,42-121,96€, triple 730-950F / 111,29-144,83€, junior suite 1050F / 160,07€. **Meals** Breakfast (buffet) 50F / 7,62€, served 5:30-11:30. **Credit cards** All major. **Pets** Dogs allowed. **Facilities** Elevator, bar, laundry service, room service (24h). **Parking** Gaîté. **How to get there** (Map 10) Bus: 28, 58, 88 and Air France Montparnasse – Metro: Pernety, Gaîté – Train station (TGV): Gare Montparnasse. **Open** All year.

The Hôtel de Bretagne has chosen to present you with a modern decor. The lobby leads into a small sienna lounge with Le Corbusier black leather sofas and armchairs. The bedrooms are more standardized: all have pale wood furniture, yellow-, orange- and blue-striped fabrics, and very soft straw-yellow wall upholstery. They are often small; the largest are more pleasant and have a sofa bed. Lovely colors have been used for the modern bathrooms. You should avoid the ground floor rooms, which are small and less luminous. Breakfasts are served in a barrel-vaulted cellar room, nicely decorated in an Italian style. The hotel is near the Montparnasse TGV train station, and the new business districts, but the rates they charge are a little pricey in high season.

Hôtel Broussais-Bon Secours

3, rue Ledion
75014 Paris
Tel. (0)1 40 44 48 90 - Fax (0)1 40 44 96 76
Karine Blanchetête

Category ★★ (categorization pending) **Rooms** 25 and 1 suite, with soundproofing, shower, WC, telephone and TV. **Price** Single 250F / 38,11€, (205F / 31,25€, the weekend), double 295F / 44,97€, suite (3-4 pers.) 480F / 73,18€. **Meals** Breakfast 30F / 4,57€, served 7:00-11:00. **Credit cards** All major. **Pets** Small dogs allowed. **Facilities** Patio. **Parking** Porte d'Orléans, 36, rue Friant. **How to get there** (Map 10) Bus: 58, 62, PC – Metro: Alésia and Plaisance. **Open** All year.

It is mostly the excellent quality-price arrangement, the charm of its interior courtyard and Karine's welcome which made us select this small hotel, a bit out of the way, but with easy access to Montparnasse, Saint-Germain-des-Prés or Porte de Versailles. Recently refurbished, the hotel provides small rooms with beige walls and plain, white furniture; the little plus comes from the lighting and pretty duvets. It is fresh and younthful, without pretence and well-maintained. The white-tiled bathrooms remain in the same spirit, but some may show signs of age. On the ground floor, the breakfast room is arranged in a bistro style, but in nice weather, you can have the pleasure of sitting outside on the small patio-terrace. One of the lowest rates in the capital.

Hôtel Delambre

35, rue Delambre - 75014 Paris
Tel. (0)1 43 20 66 31 - Fax (0)1 45 38 91 76
M. Patrick Kalmy
Web: www.hoteldelambre.com

Category ★★★ **Rooms** 30 and 1 suite with soundproofing, telephone, bath or shower, WC, hairdryer, satellite TV, outlet for PC and safe – 1 for disabled persons. **Price** Single 395-550F / 60,22-83,85€, double 460-550F / 70,13-83,85€, junior suite (1-4 pers.) 750F / 114,34€. **Meals** Breakfast (buffet) 42F / 6,41€, served 7:30-10:30. **Credit cards** Visa, Eurocard, Mastercard, Amex. **Pets** Dogs allowed. **Facilities** Elevator, laundry service, bar. **Parking** Tour Montparnasse, boulevard Edgar-Quinet. **How to get there** (Map 10) Bus: 28, 58, 68, 82 and 91 – Metro: Vavin, Edgar Quinet, Montparnasse – Train station (TGV): Gare Montparnasse. **Open** All year.

It is difficult not to be attracted by this small hotel entirely renovated in 1996 by the architect-decorator, Jean-Philippe Nuel. For each room he chose cerused beech furniture with curving lines wrought iron work enhancing the straw yellow of the walls, while the flecked carpeting and fabrics are mainly in blues or brick red. The bathrooms are clear and sleek- just as impeccable. All the rooms are pleasant but if you reserve in good time, you should ask for number 7 for its size and private terrace. Numbers 1 and 2 are recommended in the summer for their small, private, furnished courtyards. The hall–lounge and breakfast room are in the image of the rest of the house, which means comfortable, soft and warm. The fine overall effect thus once again proves to us that charming hotels really do exist in Paris at reasonable prices, well–situated and well–planned.

Hôtel Istria

29, rue Campagne-Première
75014 Paris
Tel. (0)1 43 20 91 82 - Fax (0)1 43 22 48 45
Daniel and Odile Crétey

Category ★★ **Rooms** 26 with soundproofing, bath or shower, WC, telephone, satellite TV, outlet for PC, hairdryer, safe. **Price** Single 505F / 76,99€, double 584-617F / 89,16-94,19€ – Special rates in low season and on weekend by request. **Meals** Breakfast 46F / 7,02€, served 7:00-10:00. **Credit cards** All major. **Pets** Dogs not allowed. **Facilities** Elevator, laundry service, drink service. **Parking** Boulevard du Montparnasse (at 150 m). **How to get there** (Map 10) Bus: 68 and 91 – Metro: Raspail – RER: Port-Royal **Open** All year.

On a quiet street just off crowded Montparnasse with its movies, theaters, and famous brasseries, this small, family-style hotel adjoins a beautiful building occupied by artists' studios. The hotel's lovely reception and lounge area is furnished with deep, black-leather sofas. Well-fitted-out and soundproofed, the bedrooms are more sober. They have Korean straw on the walls, elm wood headboards, small desks and wardrobes in a more rustic style. There are quilted bedspreads with colorful motifs. Even though the bedrooms are rather small (those on the street are larger), you will be comfortable here, especially as the rooms are bright, very well kept, and have beautiful new bathrooms. Some rooms, located in a small house, open onto the patio at ground level; they are quiet but with less light and seem less pleasant. Breakfasts are served in a barrel-vaulted room in the cellar. A small, unpretentious hotel, where Daniel and Odile Crétey will greet you in a most attentive and hospitable way.

Hôtel de l'Orchidée

65, rue de l'Ouest
75014 Paris
Tel. (0)1 43 22 70 50 - Fax (0)1 42 79 97 46
M. and Mme Mollière

Category ★★★ **Rooms** 40 with soundproofing, telephone, bath or shower, WC, hairdryer on request, cable TV – 2 for disabled persons. **Price** Single 456-556F / 69,61-84,88€, double 502-602F / 76,64-91,90€, triple 608-708F / 92,82-108,09€. **Meals** Breakfast 35F / 5,34€, served 7:00-12:00. **Credit cards** All major. **Pets** Dogs not allowed. **Facilities** Elevator, laundry service, garden, bar, room service, sauna, whirlpool. **Parking** Private. **How to get there** (Map 10) Bus: 28, 58, 88 and 91 – Metro: Pernety. **Open** All year.

The "Orchid" hotel stands on a small, tree-lined square near the Montparnasse high-speed train (TGV) station. When you walk in, you will find a large, bright room bar with many green plants, a luminous skylight and bay windows overlooking the garden. This is both the lounge and bar. The breakfast room is hiding behind a curtain of vegetation, but in good weather, it's delightful to have breakfast in the garden. The luminous bedrooms are decorated in the same style as the lounge. They have salmon, green, or blue cerused bamboo furniture, fresh fabrics that vary from floor to floor and warm tones on the walls of the rooms recently refurbished. They are very well-maintained and have small, modern baths. Those with numbers ending in 5, 6, or 7 overlook the garden at the rear and some have a small balcony. The hotel has the added bonuses of a relaxation bathtub and a sauna in the basement, not to mention the welcome, which is truly friendly.

Hôtel du Parc-Montsouris

4, rue du Parc-Montsouris - 75014 Paris
Tel. (0)1 45 89 09 72 - Fax (0)1 45 80 92 72
Mme Piguet - M. Grand
Web: hotel-parc-montsouris.com - E-mail: hotel-parc-montsouris@wanadoo.fr

Category ★★ **Rooms** 35 with bath or shower, WC, telephone, cable TV. **Price** Single and double 350-410F / 53,36-62,50€, twin (2-3 pers.) 460F / 70,13€, apart. (3-4 pers.) 550F / 83,85€. **Meals** Breakfast 38F / 5,80€. **Credit cards** Amex, Visa, Eurocard, MasterCard. **Pets** Dogs allowed. **Facilities** Elevator. **Parking** On private street. **How to get there** (Map 10) Bus: 88, PC and Orlybus – Metro: Porte d'Orléans – RER: Cité Universitaire. **Open** All year.

While staying in this part of the 14th *arrondissement* you will discover another aspect of the capital: its quiet cul-de-sacs and 1930s villas, some fine architecture from Sauvage, Le Corbusier and Lurçat, as well as two immense parks, the International University City and Parc Montsouris. The hotel has been opened in one of these villas, and its columns and Art Deco pictures recall the earlier character of the house. Comfortable but soberly fitted-out with standard furniture, the rooms are luminous and well-maintained. Their light walls have numerous reproduction pictures adding to their pleasant atmosphere; we prefer those in the main building where most of them have a view onto Parc Montsouris. No. 633 has a fine panorama over Paris and its monuments. The rooms in the small house behind are bright enough in the summer but otherwise seemed rather somber to us. You should also note the seven apartments with their two communicating rooms, much appreciated by families. This is a hotel where you can be assured of nice quiet nights.

Hôtel Raspail Montparnasse

203, boulevard Raspail - 75014 Paris
Tel. (0)1 43 20 62 86 - Fax (0)1 43 20 50 79
Christiane Martinent
E-mail: raspailm@aol.com

Category ★★★ **Rooms** 36 and 2 junior suites with air-conditioning, soundproofing, bath or shower, WC, telephone, hairdryer, cable TV, minibar, safe. **Price** Single 560F / 85,37€, double 760-860F / 115,86-131,11€, "luxe" 950F / 144,83€, junior suite 1200F / 182,94€. **Meals** Breakfast 50F / 7,62€. **Credit cards** All major. **Pets** Dogs not allowed. **Parking** At 116, boulevard du Montparnasse. **How to get there** (Map 10) Bus: 58, 68, 82 and 91 – Metro: Vavin, Raspail – RER: Port-Royal. **Open** All year.

A little before his death, the famous decorator Serge Pons was attracted by this Art Deco hotel and in 1992 he renovated the vast and airy vestibule, with its large rounded bay windows and ceilings lined with fine geometrical mouldings. He opened up the monumental staircase, renovated the corner lounge-bar, and had the superb coat of arms on the façade reworked. The rooms and the pretty bathrooms have a studied decor, their furniture inspired by the 1930s. All have the name of and a fine reproduction by some painter who lived in Montparnasse, and each floor has its own color scheme. You move from blue, very well-done, through sienna, very warm, while passing through creams and grays. The *troisième étage*, recently renovated, displays an elegant harmony of green and beige. You should note the corner rooms, which are particularly large with their three windows. Other qualities to be stressed are excellent sound-proofing along with a professional and relaxed welcome in this very "Montparnasse" hotel.

Hôtel de l'Avre

21, rue de l'Avre – 75015 Paris
Tel. (0)1 45 75 31 03 – Fax (0)1 45 75 63 26
M. Bernard Vialettes
Web: www.hoteldelavre.com

Category ★★ **Rooms** 26 with soundproofing, telephone, bath or shower, WC, TV, hairdryer. **Price** Single 345-395F / 52,59-60,22€, double 395-450F / 60,22-68,60€, triple 560F / 85,37€; extra bed 100F / 15,24€. **Meals** Breakfast 37F / 5,64€ (free of charge weekends for readers of this guide), served 7:30-10:30. **Credit cards** All major. **Pets** Small dogs allowed. **Facilities** Elevator, garden. **Parking** 104, rue du Théâtre. **How to get there** (Map 6) Bus: 80 – Metro: La Motte-Picquet-Grenelle. **Open** All year.

Bernard Vialettes has taken over the Hôtel de l'Avre and it is with an obvious pleasure that he receives his guests. He has redone the breakfast room, bought pretty crockery, laid out colored tablecloths and flowered his garden. In the rooms the renovations have also been completed and the wallpapering, which, depending on the floor is blue (very cheerful), yellow (very light) or ivory, goes well with the pretty curtains. The furniture is sober, the bedding new, the bathrooms impeccable. The whole effect is cheerful, neat and pleasant. All is irreproachably maintained. The soundproofed rooms ensure little noise, not only in those overlooking the verdant garden, but even in those on the street side, as there is little traffic in this usually quiet district. You should note that the garden is bathed in sunlight in the mornings, and breakfast is served there in fine weather. The constant efforts towards the comfort of each guest, as well as carefully chosen prices, make this small hotel a highly recommendable address close to the center of Paris and to the Porte de Versailles exhibition center.

Hôtel Bailli de Suffren-Tour Eiffel

149, avenue de Suffren - 75015 Paris
Tel. (0)1 56 58 64 64 - Fax (0)1 45 67 75 82
Mme Tardif
E-mail: bailli.suffren.hotel@wanadoo.fr

Category ★★★ **Rooms** 25 with soundproofing, bath or shower, WC, hairdryer, telephone, satellite TV, minibar and safe. **Price** Single 610-690F / 92,99-105,19€, double 735-815F / 112,05-124,25€; extra bed 100F / 15,24€, apart. (4 pers.) 1400-1600F / 213,43-243,92€; −15% for weekend (2 nights). **Meals** Breakfast 65F / 9,91€, served 7:00-11:00; snacks availables (95F / 14,48€). **Credit cards** All major. **Pets** Small dogs allowed (+50F / 7,62€). **Facilities** Elevator, laundry service, bar. **Parking** Rue François Bonvin. **How to get there** (Map 1) Bus: 39, 70 and 89 — Metro: Ségur and Sèvres-Lecourbe. **Open** All year.

In this district of UNESCO, on the boundary of the 15th and 7th *arrondissements*, the hotel has been tastefully renovated on the theme of the bailiff *(Bailli)* of Suffren. M. and Mme. Tardif have renewed most of the bathrooms which are now very functional and well-furnished, some having particularly large bathtubs. The rooms are all personalized, warm and comfortable. The new rooms, such as "Versailles", the "Bailli" suite and some others, have been successfully done, while the older rooms also have their charm, and are being renovated as occasion arises. The quietest and brightest are on the courtyard side and certain rooms are convertible into two-room apartments ideal for families. The lounge matches the rest of the house, refined with beautiful furniture. You find here all the newspapers and magazines, and all the discreet attention of the owners. They are ready to make your stay as happy as possible, so it is no surprise that both service and welcome are faultless.

Hôtel Charles Quinze

37, rue Saint-Charles / 36–38, rue Rouelle
75015 Paris
Tel. (0)1 45 79 64 15 - Fax (0)1 45 77 21 11
M. and Mme Fournerie

Category ★★ **Rooms** 30 with soundproofing, telephone, bath or shower, WC, hairdryer, cable TV, minibar. **Price** (Depending on the season) Single 435-450F / 66,32-68,60€, double 535-560F / 81,56-85,37€, triple 685-710F / 104,43-108,24€. **Meals** Breakfast 45F / 6,86€, served 7:00-10:30. **Credit cards** All major. **Pets** Dogs allowed. **Facilities** Elevator, laundry service, patio. **Parking** Beaugrenelle (rue Linois). **How to get there** (Map 6) Bus: 42 – Metro: Dupleix and Charles-Michels – RER: ligne C. **Open** All year.

Astone's throw from the Front de Seine business complex, the Charles Quinze is a lovely small hotel. In all the bedrooms, you will find honey-colored English-pine furniture. These are small and all laid-out in the same way, only the colors of the fabrics and sponge-painted wallpaper vary. Some floors are thus yellow, blue or pink, with a delicate touch of identical color on the tiled friezes in the white bathrooms. Breakfasts are served in a basement room decorated in the same spirit, with Haitian primitive paintings on the walls. In good weather, you can choose to have your breakfast on the small patio with pretty plants. Just nearby, adjoining the reception area, there is the lounge corner with beautiful blue sofas and armchairs. A simple, welcoming and comfortable hotel in a quiet spot between the Eiffer Tower and Porte de Versailles.

Hôtel Fondary

30, rue Fondary
75015 Paris
Tel. (0)1 45 75 14 75 – Fax (0)1 45 75 84 42
M. Bosson

Category ★★ Rooms 21 with telephone, bath or shower, WC, TV and minibar. **Price** Single 390-410F / 59,46-62,50€, double 390-425F / 59,46-64,79€; −10% for the weekends and in Jul and Aug. **Meals** Breakfast 38F / 5,80€, served 7:00-10:00. **Credit cards** Amex, Visa, Eurocard, MasterCard. **Pets** Small dogs allowed. **Facilities** Elevator, laundry service, bar, patio. **Parking** Garage de la Poste (104, rue du Théâtre). **How to get there** (Map 6) Bus: 80 – Metro: Émile Zola and La Motte-Picquet-Grenelle. **Open** All year.

Behind La Motte-Picquet and not far from the Parc des Expositions at Porte de Versailles - also not far from the center of Paris - the Fondary proposes small, beautifully kept bedrooms. These are simple but all different, many with rattan furniture; the bathrooms are pleasant. The bedrooms on the street (fairly quiet) are slightly larger but those at the back overlook a flower-filled patio, prettily arranged, where guests can enjoy being outside. The large room downstairs is divided into a reception area, a small corner lounge, the breakfast room and bar, and a small veranda opening onto the patio. well-served by public transport, this economical, unpretentious hotel is very popular with a clientele of regulars. Your will receive the best welcome.

Hôtel Montcalm

50, avenue Félix-Faure
75015 Paris
Tel. (0)1 45 54 97 27 - Fax (0)1 45 54 15 05
Mme Taillère

Category ★★★ **Rooms** 40 and 1 suite with bath or shower, WC, telephone, satellite TV, minibar and safe – 1 for disabled persons. **Price** Single 470-680F / 71,65-103,67€, double 745F / 113,57€, family suite (4 pers.) 1250F / 190,56€; In low season (Jan to end Mar, in Jul to Aug and Nov to Christmas Day): 1 pers. 420-490F / 64,12-74,70€, 2 pers. 520F / 79,27€, family suite (4 pers.) 870F / 132,63€. **Meals** Breakfast (buffet) 55F / 8,38€. **Credit cards** All major. **Pets** Small dogs allowed. **Facilities** Elevator, garden, laundry service. **Parking** At 50 m. **How to get there** (Map 9) Bus: 42 and 62 – Metro: Boucicaut. **Open** All year.

Not far from the Parc des Expositions at the Porte de Versailles, the Montcalm has a somewhat banal brick and stone façade, which conceals a pleasant surprise. Beyond the small entrance hall, and to its right the lounge with brown sofas set in a square, you come upon a small garden: hydrangeas, large basins overflowing with flowers, soft carpets of green plants with leaves like duckweed, and a magnolia tree. The perfect spot to relax and enjoy a drink. The small house set in the garden is ideal for families. The bedrooms are identically decorated with old-pink fabric on the walls, ash furniture and woodwork. Standard, but recently refurbished and pleasant (equal care has been given to the small bathrooms). We prefer the rooms overlooking the garden and the particularly charming Room 4 on the ground floor. There is a pleasant dining room, all wood-paneled on a below the ground level.

Hôtel Pasteur

33, rue du Docteur-Roux
75015 Paris
Tel. (0)1 47 83 53 17 – Fax (0)1 45 66 62 39
Mme Pinhas

Category ★★ **Rooms** 19 with telephone, bath or shower, WC, hairdryer, cable TV, minibar and safe. **Price** Single and double 370-590F / 56,41-89,94€, 4 pers. 790F / 120,43€. **Meals** Breakfast 40F / 6,10€, served 7:00-12:00. **Credit cards** Visa, Eurocard, MasterCard. **Pets** Dogs allowed. **Facilities** Elevator. **Parking** At 81, rue Falguière. **How to get there** (Maps 9 and 10) Bus: 39, 48, 70, 88, 89 and 95 – Metro: Pasteur and Volontaires. **Open** All year.

Adjoining the Pasteur Institute, this small hotel is named after the renowned scientist (there is a museum in his former apartment inside the institute). The bedrooms are small and very simple but well kept, some of them prettily redecorated, and there are modern amenities. The decor is nothing to write home about; the tones are often autumnal yet the rooms have all the necessary comforts, and number 22 is very large. The same, pleasant provincial atmosphere can be found in the reception lounge which could just as well be that of a private apartment, both quaint and friendly. The main attraction of the hotel lies outside in the garden, where tables, chairs, armchairs, umbrellas and even some deck chairs are set up in good weather - a delightful spot to read or enjoy a drink. The welcome you will find here is one of the many charms of this hotel, which is very convenient if you want quiet and the proximity to the Porte de Versailles. The hotel is also well-served by public transport to the center of Paris.

Hôtel Tour Eiffel - Dupleix

11, rue Juge – 75015 Paris
Tel. (0)1 45 78 29 29 – Fax (0)1 45 78 60 00
M. Lebailly
E-mail: dupleix@club-internet.fr

Category ★★ **Rooms** 40 with soundproofing, telephone, bath or shower, WC, hairdryer, cable TV. **Price** Single and double 490-690F / 74,70-105,19€; in low season: 390-590F / 59,46-89,94€. **Meals** Breakfast (buffet) 45F / 6,86€, served 6:30-10:30 (weekend 7:00-11:00) **Credit cards** All major. **Pets** Dogs allowed (+50F / 7,62€). **Facilities** Elevator, laundry service, patio. **Parking** At 50 m. **How to get there** (Map 6) Bus: 42 – Metro: Dupleix. **Open** All year.

This hotel is close to the new *Front de Seine* buildings and UNESCO. Following the reception area there is a small and warm lounge with lattice-work wicker armchairs and little tables. The breakfast room, where a beautiful buffet is set out every morning, is pleasantly decorated in a bistro style. It has yellow walls, light wood parquet floor and generously wide windows that open onto a patio, where tables and chairs are of course set out in good weather. As for the rooms, they have all been decorated in an identical way with ivory walls, fabrics in blue tones and polished wood furniture. Often small, with those on the *sixième étage* generally larger, they are bright, well-maintained and comfortable. Those with a number ending in 2 have a tiny shower room, but nevertherless, all the necessary amenities (they are also the least expensive). The welcome and services are professional and close to those of a three-star hotel.

Villa Toscane

36–38, rue des Volontaires
75015 Paris
Tel. (0)1 43 06 82 92 - Fax (0)1 40 56 33 23
Mlle Christelle Le Mentec

Rooms 7 with telephone, shower, WC, TV, hairdryer and safe. **Price** Single 380F / 58,01€, double 480F / 73,18€. **Meals** Breakfast 49F / 7,48€, served 7:30-10:30. **Credit cards** Visa, Eurocard and MasterCard. **Pets** Dogs allowed. **Restaurant** Italian – Mealtime specials 130F / 19,82€, also à la carte (around 200F / 30,49€). **Parking** Rue François Bonvin. **How to get there** (Map 9) Bus: 39, 48, 70, 88, 89 and 95 – Metro: Volontaires. **Open** All year.

The rue des Volontaires is quiet and airy, with its alignment of one- or two-story buildings. La Villa Toscane is no exception to this rule and one enters the reception area via some small steps serving both hotel and restaurant. Making a virtue of the narrowness of the house, Christelle Le Mentec has made this a most intimate place; in the small dining rooms, tables and chairs are found in the littlest corners. Upstairs the seven rooms are in the same style, rather small but cozy and amply decorated with heavy-design fabrics. They all have a 1930s chest of drawers or dressing table, a copper bedstead covered by yellow or red quilts. Only certain small shower rooms have started to show signs of fatigue. But nothing has been forgotten to make travelers comfortable. Sampling excellent Italian cuisine here is undeniably one more extra. What more to say, but that the welcome is extremely friendly and the very favorable prices make La Villa Toscane an address to discover.

Hôtel Alexander

102, avenue Victor Hugo
75116 Paris
Tel. (0)1 45 53 64 65 - Fax (0)1 45 53 12 51
M. Christian Cartier

Category ★★★★ **Rooms** 60 and 2 suites with bath or shower, WC, telephone, cable TV, minibar. **Price** Single and double 1390-1790F / 211,90-272,88€, junior suite 2500F / 381,12€; −15% for the readers of this guide (excluding trade fair periods). **Meals** Breakfast (buffet) 100F / 15,24€, snack availables. **Credit cards** All major. **Pets** Dogs not allowed. **Facilities** Elevator, small garden, laundry service, room service. **Parking** Avenue Victor Hugo (at 50 m). **How to get there** (Map 6) Bus: 52, 82 — Metro: Victor Hugo — RER: Charles de Gaulle-Étoile. **Open** All year.

Supremely classic, the Alexandre is a small, four-star hotel that is elegant without being ostentatious. The beautiful lobby, entirely paneled in natural oak with a handsome reproduction of 18th-century woodwork, leads to the sitting areas, which face a small garden. Small arm chairs in a Louis XV style, crystal wall sconces, wood paneling and soft carpeting with floral motifs make up most of its decor. All the bedrooms are spacious, and many overlook several neighboring gardens. (mostly Numbers 105, 123, 142, 152, 161, and 182). They are decorated with Louis XV or Louis XVI furniture (with one or two contemporary exceptions), and they are all very comfortable, even though some details of aging have started to show (notably in the bathrooms). A renovation program is scheduled for the year 2000. Lastly, guests are pampered with a new variation on the "delicious breakfast".

Hôtel Ambassade

79, rue Lauriston
75116 Paris
Tel. (0)1 45 53 41 15 - Fax (0)1 45 53 30 80
Mme Enault

Category ★★ **Rooms** 38 with telephone, bath or shower, WC, hairdryer, satellite TV. **Price** Single 505-525F / 76,99-80,04€, double 580-645F / 88,42-98,33€; Weekends: −10% and −15% in Jan and Feb. **Meals** Breakfast 45F / 6,86€, served 7:00-10:30. **Credit cards** All major. **Pets** Small dogs allowed. **Facilities** Elevator, laundry service. **Parking** Avenue Kléber. **How to get there** (Map 6) Bus: 22, 30, 52 and 82 − Metro: Boissière, Victor Hugo. **Closed** Aug.

Midway between the Place de l'Etoile and the Trocadero, you will find the Hôtel Ambassade, an attractive accommodation well-run by a lively manageress who would like to prove that one can still find charm in a "two-star" hotel. Certainly space is in rather short supply and the few tables in the reception area double for breakfast use. The rooms are not large and only have showers, but the decor is pleasant: the colors are soft, the prints discreet and the bedspreads well-chosen. One tip, however: avoid the ground floor rooms as they are too close to the street; as a general rule reserve those on the courtyard. You will be welcomed with a hospitable smile.

Au Palais de Chaillot Hôtel

35, avenue Raymond-Poincaré - 75116 Paris
Tel. (0)1 53 70 09 09 - Fax (0)1 53 70 09 08
Thierry and Cyrille Pien
Web: auchaillotel.com - E-mail: hapc@club-internet.fr

Category ★★ **Rooms** 28 with soundproofing, telephone, bath or shower, WC, hairdryer, satellite TV. **Price** Single 480F / 73,18€, double 570-640F / 86,90-97,57€; extra bed 140F / 21,34€. **Meals** Breakfast 42F / 6,41€, served 7:00-11:00. **Credit cards** All major. **Pets** Dogs not allowed. **Facilities** Elevator, laundry service, room service. **Parking** At 50m. **How to get there** (Map 6) Bus: 22, 30, 63 and 82 – Metro: Trocadéro, Victor Hugo. **Open** All year.

The Palais de Chaillot Hôtel, entirely renovated down to the smallest detail, reopened its doors in 1996. Right in the middle of a business district and a few paces from the Trocadero and numerous museums, this is a place that will appeal to those who appreciate comfort as much as simplicity, and who insist that a reasonable price should not preclude tasteful decor. The small rooms are pleasantly arranged with navy blue carpeting against a background of yellow walls, white and blue bathrooms and furniture especially designed for the hotel. A large number of the rooms face the avenue, but those doubtful about the real efficacy of double-glazing can always ask for one at the back (the double rooms overlooking the courtyard are also larger). The ground floor is where breakfast is served and it has received the same care and innovative decoration. As for the welcome, it is youthful and really aimiable, while this is also one of the best price-quality offerings in the capital.

Hôtel Boileau

81, rue Boileau - 75016 Paris
Tel. (0)1 42 88 83 74 - Fax (0)1 45 27 62 98
M. Mahé Guirec
E-mail: boileau@cybercable.fr

Category ★★ **Rooms** 30 (some with soundproofing) with telephone, bath or shower, WC, hairdryer and cable TV. **Price** Single 400F / 60,98€, double 470F / 71,65€, triple 650F / 99,09€; –20 % Jul 15 to end Aug. **Meals** Breakfast 40F / 6,10€, served 7:00-10:00. **Credit cards** All major. **Pets** Dogs allowed. **Facilities** Bar, laundry service, room service. **Parking** Avenue de Versailles. **How to get there** (Map 9) Bus: 22, 62, 72 and PC – Metro: Exelmans. **Open** All year.

We appreciate the Hôtel Boileau for the convivial atmosphere found here thanks to its young owner, Mahé Guirec, who is always eager to make improvements. We also like the warmth of the ground floor area where family furniture, pictures and other objects give a "lived-in" feel. You enter first into the reception area and its corner lounge, then into the bar, and finally into the very attractive and airy breakfast room lit from the patio. You cannot enter the latter, but it forms an integral part of the decor. There are thirty rooms, but for the moment we would only recommend those which have been fully or partially renovated with all-new bathrooms and colorful wallpapers and fabrics. Some have cerused oak furniture; in others you might find a headboard from the auction sale of a palace. For the moment, the rest of them retain their standard furniture. On our last visit only Rooms 111, 112, 121, 122, 231, and 302 had not been refurbished, but they may have been since then. The area is quiet, the rates are reasonable and Oscar, the house parrot, will not fail to liven up breakfast conversation.

Hôtel du Bois

11, rue du Dôme - 75116 Paris
Tel. (0)1 45 00 31 96 - Fax (0)1 45 00 90 05
M. Byrne - M. Tarron
Web: hoteldubois.com - E-mail: hoteldubois@wanadoo.fr

Category ★★★ **Rooms** 41 with soundproofing, bath or shower, WC, hairdryer, telephone, cable TV, minibar, safe (+10F / 1,52€). **Price** Single 550-585F / 83,85-89,18€, double 595-770F / 90,71-117,39€; extra bed 220F / 33,54€. **Meals** Breakfast 58F / 8,85€, served 7:30-10:00. **Credit cards** All major. **Pets** Dogs allowed. **Facilities** Laundry service, room service. **Parking** 8, avenue Foch. **How to get there** (Map 6) Bus: 22, 30, 52, 73, 92 and bus for Roissy-Charles de Gaulle – Metro: Kléber, Charles de Gaulle-Étoile – RER: Charles de Gaulle-Étoile. **Open** All year.

A few meters from the Etoile you reach the little rue du Dôme from the Avenue Victor Hugo via a flight of steps, which gives a slight air of Montmartre to the area, even though it is in the most classical quarter of them all. The hotel is somewhat British in its style, not really surprising as the manager, Mr Byrne, comes from England. Spring-like fabrics and thick carpeting from across the Channel have been chosen for the room decor to give them a very soft character, and even though they are not large you always feel at home in them. Some rooms can sleep up to four people, and all are comfortable and soundproofed to better isolate the hotel from the noise of the major avenues around the Etoile. There is a ravishing lounge which doubles as the breakfast room, facing the reception area, and the welcome is both courteous and friendly. This offers very good value for a hotel of charm in such a favored district.

Hôtel Chambellan-Morgane

6, rue Keppler
75116 Paris
Tel. (0)1 47 20 35 72 - Fax (0)1 47 20 95 69
Mme Christine de Lapasse

Category ★★★ **Rooms** 20 with soundproofing and air-conditioning, bath or shower, WC, telephone, cable TV, minibar, 11 with hairdryer. **Price** Single and double 800-1000F / 121,96-152,45€ – Special rates in low season and weekends on request. **Meals** Breakfast (buffet) 60F / 9,15€, served 7:00-10:00. **Credit cards** All major. **Pets** Small dogs allowed. **Facilities** Elevator, laundry service, room service, bar. **Parking** George-V and at avenue Marceau. **How to get there** (Map 6) Bus: 92 for Roissy – Metro: George-V and Kléber – RER: Charles de Gaulle-Étoile. **Open** All year.

Just behind avenue Marceau and close to the Etoile, rue Keppler is very quiet. You pass through a little hall before entering the Hôtel Chambellan-Morgane itself, where you discover a very pretty lounge entirely redecorated in yellow and blue tones, covered with painted worked wood and furnished in the Louis XVI-style. Breakfast from a copious buffet is also served here. The bedrooms have also been refurbished with patinated walls and cerused oak furniture. There has been no hesitation in using color, and the whole effect is cheerful, elegant and harmonious. Very comfortable and light, they are pleasantly sized and have impeccable bathrooms. In addition, whether on the back or even on the street, all are quiet and well-sound-proofed. The welcome is very friendly and everything will be done to ease your stay.

Hôtel Étoile Maillot

10, rue du Bois-de-Boulogne
75116 Paris
Tel. (0)1 45 00 42 60 - Fax (0)1 45 00 55 89
M. Delfau

Category ★★★ **Rooms** 22, 5 junior suites (with air-conditioning) and 1 suite, with soundproofing, telephone, bath or shower, WC, hairdryer and cable TV. **Price** Single 570-700F / 86,90-106,71€, double 600-730F / 91,47-111,29€, suite and junior suite 820F / 125,01€ (1 pers.), 850F / 129,58€ (2 pers.); extra bed 120F / 18,29€. **Meals** Breakfast 65F / 9,91€ (included some weekends in Jul and Aug and some weekends throughout the year), served 6:30-11:30. **Credit cards** All major. **Pets** Dogs allowed. **Facilities** Elevator, laundry service, bar. **Parking** Avenue Foch. **How to get there** (Map 3) Bus: 73, 82 and bus for Roissy – Metro: Argentine – RER: Charles de Gaulle-Étoile, Porte-Maillot. **Open** All year.

In a quiet spot between the Arc de Triomphe and the Palais des Congrès, the Étoile Maillot is having a full face-lift. A country flavor has swept into the hotel: two huge climbing geraniums frame the entrance door, and the reception area followed by the breakfast room are henceforth in a pleasant rustic style with pretty armchairs around the fireplace. Rooms 5, 10, 15, 20 and 24 have been fully refurbished in a dominating late 18th-century *bijou* style. The space is cunningly laid out, with a small entry and telephone corner that can sleep a child, and to the right, a comfortable bathroom with separate toilet. We like these rooms very much, and they are the only ones we recommend at the moment. Those with a number ending in 3 have also been renovated, but in a more classic and less cozy style. There is much left to be done, but the aesthetic standpoint is certainly promising. The reception is very cordial.

Hôtel Frémiet-Eiffel

6, avenue Frémiet - 75016 Paris
Tel. (0)1 45 24 52 06 - Fax (0)1 42 88 77 46
Mme Fourmond
E-mail: hotel.fremiet@wanadoo.fr

Category ★★★ Rooms 34 (20 with air-conditioning) and 2 suites with bath or shower, WC, telephone, TV, hairdryer and minibar – 1 for disabled persons. **Price** Single 550-990F / 83,85-150,92€, double 690-1200F / 105,19-182,94€, suite 990F / 150,92€ (1 pers), 1650F / 251,54€ (2pers); low season: Nov to end Feb (excluding trade fair periods and national hoildays and from mid Jul to end Aug); extra bed +170F / 25,92€ (free for children under 12). **Meals** Breakfast 65F / 9,91€, served 6:30-12:00; snacks avalaible. **Credit cards** All major. **Pets** Dogs allowed. **Facilities** Elevator, laundry service. **Parking** At 200m. **How to get there** (Map 6) Bus: 32, 72 – Metro: Passy. **Open** All year.

The Hôtel Frémiet is located in one of the small, very quiet streets built at the turn of the century to connect the quays of the Seine with the Passy hill. Classic and cozy are the key words at the Frémiet, which has 18th-century-style furniture, wood panelling, high molded ceilings and a beautiful stairway. The bedrooms are quite cheerful, often large and always impeccably maintained. They are very comfortable and elegantly decorated with charming, famous-name fabrics, gleaming bathrooms (the last ones will be redone this winter), and well-chosen furniture, some of which has been designed by the owners' daughter. On each floor, there are two adjoining rooms, an ideal space for families. Guests in the two Etamine suites—one decorated in blue, the other in *écru*—will enjoy outstanding quality for the price. Note that there are many museums nearby. A beautiful hotel with an attentive welcome.

Hôtel Garden Élysées

12, rue Saint-Didier - 75116 Paris
Tel. (0)1 47 55 01 11 - Fax (0)1 47 27 79 24
Mme Annie Martin
Web: www.acom.fr/gardenelysee/ - E-mail: garden.elysee@wanadoo.fr

Category ★★★★ **Rooms** 48 with air-conditioning, bath, WC, telephone, satellite TV, hairdryer, minibar and safe – 2 for disabled persons. **Price** Single 950-1300F / 144,83-198,18€, double 1050-1900F / 160,07-289,65€; extra bed +150F / 22,87€ – Special rates from Aug to Dec and weekends for the readers of this guide (excluding trade fair periods). **Meals** Breakfast (buffet) 80F / 12,20€, buffet 120F / 18,29€, served 7:00-10:30. **Credit cards** All major. **Pets** Small dogs allowed. **Facilities** Elevator, patio, laundry service, bar, room service. **Parking** 4 spaces in the hotel (150F/22,87€ /day) and rue Lauriston. **How to get there** (Map 6) Bus: 22, 30 and 82 – Metro: Boissière, Trocadéro. **Open** All year.

You must enter through a portico and walk into a courtyard full of greenery before you come upon the Garden Élysées. The very spacious ground floor is wide open to the outside. Many rooms are to be found there; in an 18th-century-inspired wood-paneled decor, the sofas and armchairs make up sitting corners where it is pleasant to sit for a chat around the fireplace. The atmosphere is just as warm in the nearby bar, which leads to the dining-room and veranda partly set in the garden, where guests also enjoy copious breakfasts. More modern, but also elegant and comfortable, the bedrooms are often sizeable. Their soft tones have been delicately brightened up by a touch of red, blue or beige. They are very luminous, with large windows opening onto the courtyard or the garden. Verdure and quiet are therefore guaranteed for all. A small luxurious hotel near the Trocadéro, where you will find thoughtful welcome and service.

Hôtel Gavarni

5, rue Gavarni - 75116 Paris
Tel. (0)1 45 24 52 82 - Fax (0)1 40 50 16 95
Mlle Nelly Rolland
Web: www.gavarni.com - E-mail: gavarni@compuserve.com

Category ★★ **Rooms** 30 with shower, WC, hairdryer, telephone, cable TV. **Price** Single 410-480F / 62,50-73,18€, double 520-540F / 79,27-82,32€; extra bed +100F / 15,24€. **Meals** Breakfast 38F / 5,80€ (free of charge on some weekends for the readers of this guide), served 6:30-12:00. **Credit cards** All major. **Pets** Dogs not allowed. **Facilities** Elevator, laundry service. **Parking** 19, rue de Passy (at 50 m). **How to get there** (Map 6) Bus: 22 and 32 – Metro: Passy – RER C: Boulainvilliers. **Open** All year.

Residential and quiet, the little rue Gavarni joins onto rue de Passy, reputed for its shopping. The Hôtel Gavarni was recently taken over by the young and very hospitable Nelly Rolland, and since then renovations have been pushing ahead. Sponged wallpaper has been put in the rooms, enhanced by a pretty frieze. The bedspreads and curtains are now bright and colorful, the floors covered with thick carpeting. One appreciates all the improvements made to the well-being of each room while forgetting the standardized small furniture and tight space of the shower rooms. All is well-maintained and now comfortable and pleasant. You should not forget the quality breakfasts, and above all, the general friendly, relaxed atmosphere. This will certainly leave you with a good impression, even though this little hotel with reasonable prices has not yet finished its improvements.

Le Hameau de Passy

48, rue de Passy - 75016 Paris
Tel. (0)1 42 88 47 55 - Fax (0)1 42 30 83 72
Mme Brepson
Web: www.hameaudepassy.com - E-mail: hameau.passy@wanadoo.fr

Category ★★ **Rooms** 32 with bath or shower, WC, telephone, cable TV – 1 for disabled persons. **Price** Single 560F / 85,37€, double 600-630F / 91,47-96,04€, triple 715F / 109€; extra bed +80F / 12,20€; –10% from Jan to Mar and –15%. in Jul to Aug. **Meals** Breakfast included, served 7:30-10:30. **Credit cards** All major. **Pets** Dogs allowed (+ 30F /4,57€). **Facilities** Garden, elevator for some bedrooms, laundry service. **Parking** 19, rue de Passy. **How to get there** (Map 6) Bus: 22, 32, 52 – Metro: La Muette, Passy – RER: Boulainvilliers. **Open** All year.

Between two boutiques on rue de Passy, a discreet passage leads you into a cul-de-sac covered with vegetation and occupied along its full length by the Hameau de Passy. Fully renovated, small modern rooms have been fixed up, and some of them can be joined together. Rooms are reached by the elevator or the spiral staircase, and they have green or blue cerused furniture and lush fabrics with geometrical motifs, a corner for writing and prints on the walls. The bathrooms are all well-equipped. All rooms enjoy the luxuriant foliage and from time to time you may find yourself "with your nose in the leaves". Whether installed in the breakfast room, relaxing in the moderately contemporary lounge bar, or sitting quietly outside, you will find it difficult to believe that you are only a few steps from the Trocadero, close to numerous museums. You won't notice any traffic noise at all.

Les Jardins du Trocadéro

35, rue Benjamin-Franklin – 75116 Paris
Tel. (0)1 53 70 17 70 – Fax (0)1 53 70 17 80
Mlle Katia Chekroun
Web: www.jardintroc.com – E-mail: jardintroc@aol.com

Category ★ ★ ★ ★ **Rooms** 12 and 5 junior suites with air-conditioning and soundproofing with bath, whirlpool, WC, telephone, satellite TV, VCR, hairdryer, minibar and safe. **Price** Single and double 790-1450F / 120,43-221,05€, junior suite on the *deuxième étage* (2-4 pers.) 1490-2350F / 227,15-358,26€ (Low season: Jul to Aug and mid Nov to end Feb). **Meals** Breakfast (buffet) 75F / 11,43€, served from 7:30; snacks avalaible. **Credit Cards** All major. **Pets** Dogs allowed. **Facilities** Elevator, laundry service, bar, room service, tea room. **How to get there** (Map 6) Bus: 22, 30, 32 and 63 – Metro: Trocadéro. **Open** All year.

Slightly set back from the Place du Trocadéro and protected by a curtain of trees that ensure its quiet and confidentiality, Les Jardins du Trocadéro occupies a choice location. This small four-star hotel created in 1994, has a limited number of rooms, which have all received the necessary care to attract an exacting clientele looking for luxury. Period furniture and quality fabrics make up the warm and classic decor, with all the modern comforts: air-conditioning, jacuzzi in the bathrooms, personalized telephones, TV and VCR. They are of various sizes but always bright. Most have a view on the Palais de Chaillot, some on the Eiffel Tower. To remain faithful to the Napoleon III style (the epoch when the building was constructed), paintings with Turkish motifs decorate the doors. Food lovers will be delighted to learn that the breakfast room becomes a tearoom in the afternoons. Both welcome and service are considerate.

Hôtel Libertel d'Argentine

1-3, rue d'Argentine
75016 Paris
Tel. (0)1 45 02 76 76 - Fax (0)1 45 02 76 00
M. Henri Courtade

Category ★★★★ **Rooms** 40 with soundproofing, telephone, bath or shower, WC, hairdryer, cable TV – 1 for disabled persons. **Price** Single and double 920-980F / 140,25-149,40€ – Special rates for the readers of this guide. **Meals** Breakfast (buffet) 75F / 11,43€, served 7:00-10:30. **Credit cards** All major. **Pets** Dogs allowed. **Facilities** Elevator, laundry service, room service. **Parking** Avenue Foch. **How to get there** (Map 3) Bus: 22, 30, 52, 73, 92 and bus pour Roissy – Metro: Argentine, Charles de Gaulle-Étoile – RER: Charles de Gaulle-Étoile. **Open** All year.

The Hôtel d'Argentine is on a small, quiet street near the Etoile. It was named after the country whose fashionable set traditionally frequented this neighborhood in the 19th century. The hotel was completely renovated by the architect Frédéric Méchiche, who designed it in the manner of a private home. The lobby is neoclassical, with fluted columns, Greek staffs, *faux marble*, and Empire mahogany furniture upholstered with Jouy fabric. In the adjacent bar, where the original rotunda ceiling and cornices have been retained, you will find 19th-century chairs, allegorical engravings, a thick carpet and complimentary tea. The bedrooms are charming, with finely striped wall fabrics, coordinated check bedspreads and calico curtains. The lovely, comfortable bathrooms are done in dark-gray and putty-colored marble. It's pleasant to enjoy a leisurely breakfast in a room (with areas for smokers and non-smokers) that is decorated in Consulate style: walls elegantly painted with large, Wedgewood-blue stripes, white pilasters antique and marble medallions. This is a very fine establishment.

Hôtel Libertel Auteuil

8-10, rue Félicien-David
75016 Paris
Tel. (0)1 40 50 57 57 – Fax (0)1 40 50 57 50
Mme Catherine Lamotte

Category ★★★ **Rooms** 94 with air-conditioning, telephone, bath or shower, WC, hairdryer, satellite TV, minibar, safe – 3 for disabled persons. **Price** (Depending on the season) single and double 721,55-1161,05F /110-177€, junior suite 1561,05F / 238€. **Meals** Breakfast (buffet) 82F / 12,50€, served 7:00-10:30. **Credit cards** All major. **Pets** Dogs allowed. **Facilities** Elevator, laundry service, room service until 11PM. **Parking** At the hotel (90F / 13,72€ /day). **How to get there** (Map 6) Bus: 22, 52, 70 and 72 – Metro: Jasmin, Mirabeau – RER: Kennedy-Radio France. **Open** All year.

Near the banks of the Seine river and the luxury shops in rue Mozart, the Libertel Auteuil was built in the 1930s style that is typical of the quarter. The decorator Frédéric Méchiche has focused on space and light; the reception area and the large lounge on the ground floor open onto the street and the patio. The white walls and the sleek, lacquered rattan furniture are highlighted by sun-yellow cushions and the Matisse, Picasso and Kline lithographs on the walls. There is also a baby grand piano which is not only used for decoration. The same elegant modernity can be found in the bedrooms with their pretty caramel-and-white striped bedspreads, coordinated drapes and beautiful bathrooms. The hotel's clients are mainly business people, due to the proximity of the Maison de la Radio and the Beaugrenelle business center. Yet you are not far from the lovely banks of the Seine and the Pont Mirabeau, luxury boutiques along the Avenue Mozart and colorful markets on the Rue de Passy. Note that on the other side of the Pont Mirabeau bridge is the restaurant *La Plage*, with a view of the French Statue of Liberty.

Hôtel Majestic

29, rue Dumont-d'Urville - 75116 Paris
Tel. (0)1 45 00 83 70 – Fax (0)1 45 00 29 48
Mme Bauerez
Web: www.majestic-hotel.com

Category ★★★★ Rooms 27 and 3 suites with air-conditioning and soundproofing, telephone, bath, WC, hairdryer, satellite TV, safe and minibar – 1 room for disabled persons. **Price** Single 1155-1485F / 176,08-226,39€, double 1485-1870F / 226,39-285,08€, suite 1760F / 268,31€ (1 pers.), 2090F / 318,62€ (2 pers.), Penthouse (1-2 pers.) 2420F /368,93€; extra bed 330F / 50,31€. **Meals** Breakfast 80F / 12,20€, served 7:00-12:00. **Credit cards** All major. **Pets** Dogs allowed. **Facilities** Elevator, laundry service, room service. **Parking** Avenue Marceau. **How to get there** (Map 6) Bus: 22 and 30 – Metro: Kléber – RER C: Charles de Gaulle-Étoile. **Open** All year.

The rue Dumont-d'Urville is a very quiet street close to Etoile. The modern façade of the Majestic does not foreshadow what you discover once you have entered: a very classical interior, highly inspired by the late 1700s. The lobby is a succession of lounge corners brightened up by carpets and tapestries. The rooms and suites are for their part much warmer. The decor, once again very classical, is also highly comfortable: king-size beds (except in the singles), well-devised storage space, impeccable bathrooms, an outlet for modems, personalized message service, air-conditioning. These are spacious rooms in which nothing has been forgotten to meet the needs the most demanding guests. Those who book the "Penthouse" on the last floor, will discover a very large apartment just as opulent and pleasant. Quite exceptional for the price. On the whole, it should be said that the prices charged at the Majestic are more than reasonable for the quality offered.

Hôtel Massenet

5 *bis*, rue Massenet - 75016 Paris
Tel. (0)1 45 24 43 03 - Fax (0)1 45 24 41 39
M. Mathieu
E-mail: hotel.massenet@wanadoo.fr

Category ★★★ **Rooms** 41 (2 with terrace, 29 with air-conditioning) with bath or shower, WC, telephone, satellite TV, minibar, 35 with hairdryer. **Price** Single 435-720F / 66,32-109,76€, double 655-810F / 99,85-123,48€; extra bed +180F / 27,44€. **Meals** Breakfast 45F / 6,86€, served 7:00-11:00. **Credit cards** All major. **Pets** Small dogs allowed. **Facilities** Elevator, laundry service, patio, bar. **Parking** 19, rue de Passy. **How to get there** (Map 6) Bus: 22, 32, 52 – Metro: Passy and La Muette – RER C: Boulainvilliers. **Open** All year.

Monsieur Mathieu was born in this hotel, which was run by his grandparents and then his parents. He he loves to tell stories of the old hotel and the Passy neighborhood when he was a child. Some bedrooms retrain their original antique furniture, while others have been recently redecorated in a more modern spirit. Most baths have also been redone. You will find pale fabrics–sometimes used as wall coverings–and beautiful engravings and paintings in the bedrooms, the corridors and the reception rooms. There is a lovely, wood-paneled dining room that opens directly onto a small patio with tables. The bedrooms overlooking the back enjoy a view of the hotel's garden as well as those of neighboring buildings. But you'd do as well with Room 70 or 71; they are on the street side, but each has a small flower-filled terrace with a table and chairs and the price is the same. There is a pleasant bar with sitting areas. The staff is attentive. A comfortable place, which has also retained the spirit of traditional hotel service.

Hôtel Nicolo

3, rue Nicolo
75116 Paris
Tel. (0)1 42 88 83 40 – Fax (0)1 42 24 45 41
Mme Ferric

Category ★★ Rooms 28 and 5 junior suites with bath or shower, WC, hairdryer, telephone and cable TV. **Price** Single 445F / 67,84€, double 500F / 76,22€, triple 575F / 87,66€, junior suite (2 pers.) 660F / 100,62€. **Meals** Breakfast 35F / 5,34€, served 7:30-10:00. **Credit cards** All major. **Pets** Dogs allowed. **Facilities** Elevator. **Parking** 19, rue de Passy. **How to get there** (Map 6) Bus: 22, 32 and 52 – Metro: Passy and La Muette – RER C: Boulainvilliers. **Open** All year.

Halfway between the Trocadéro and La Muette, a few steps from rue de Passy, you walk into a courtyard planted with trees to find the entrance of the Nicolo. The hotel is therefore very quiet, with all the rooms overlooking this green area. These are also equipped with double door entries isolating them from the long corridors with pink *toile de Jouy*. The decor is rather classic, which characterizes the entire atmosphere. They are all quite large, but if you wish to have even more room, you should book room 32 or 42: truly spacious and with have a sofa bed making them ideal for families of 4. In general, give preference to the upper floors; they are brighter. On the ground floor, near the reception area, there is a pretty lounge where breakfast is also served. As is the case in the rest of the house, the feeling of past times that reigns here makes you feel as if you were in a boarding house rather than in a hotel. Peaceful and guaranteed value for your money.

Hôtel Le Parc

55-57, avenue Raymond-Poincaré - 75116 Paris
Tel. (0)1 44 05 66 66 - Fax (0)1 44 05 66 00
M. François Delahaye
E-mail: le_parc@compuserve.com

Category ★★★★ **Rooms** 96, 17 suites and 3 duplex with air-conditioning, telephone, bath (1 with whirlpool), WC, hairdryer, satellite TV and safe – 4 for disabled persons. **Price** "Standard" 2280F / 347,58€ (1 pers.), "superieure" (1-2 pers.) 2620F / 399,42€, "prestige" (1-3 pers.) 2970F / 452,77€, junior suite (1-3 pers.) 4200F / 641,22€. **Meals** Breakfast 150F / 22,87€, served at any time. **Credit cards** All major. **Pets** Dogs allowed. **Facilities** Elevator, laundry service, fitness center, room service (24h). **Restaurant** *Le Relais du Parc.* Service 12:30-14:30, 19:30-22:30. **Parking** Avenue Raymond Poincaré. **How to get there** (Map 6) Bus: 22, 32, 52, 63 and 82 – Metro: Victor Hugo, Trocadéro. **Open** All year.

Composed of five Anglo-Norman-style buildings, the Hôtel Le Parc was designed in the style of an English manor house by the famous English decorator Nina Campbell. The beautiful Edwardian decor includes figured carpeting, quilted chintzes, four-poster beds, antique engravings and paintings. The only exception is at the reception desk: a handsome modern sculpture by Arman, who also designed the tables and sconces at the bar. Suites, rooms and lounges are all superb and offer all the comforts. Served either on the colonial-style veranda or in the garden, the gastronomic cuisine of *Le Relais du Parc* is now supervised by Laurent André. The hotel is run by a distinguished, efficient manager.

Hôtel Passy-Eiffel

10, rue de Passy – 75016 Paris
Tel. (0)1 45 25 55 66 – Fax (0)1 42 88 89 88
M. and Mme Cantuel
E-mail: passyeiffel@wanadoo.fr

Category ★★★ **Rooms** 48 and 2 suites with soundproofing (33 with air-conditioning), bath or shower, WC, telephone, satellite TV, hairdryer and minibar. **Price** Single 686-726F / 104,73-110,83€, double 702-752F / 107,17-114,80€, triple and suite 868-1060F / 132,51-161,60€. –10% from Dec to Feb and weekends; –20% in August. **Meals** Breakfast 50F / 7,62€, served 7:30-10:30. **Credit cards** All major. **Pets** Dags allowed (+ 30F / 4,57€). **Facilities** Elevator, patios, laundry service. **Parking** 19, rue de Passy. **How to get there** (Map 6) Bus: 22, 32 – Metro: Passy. **Open** All year.

The rue de Passy is a neighborhood of fashionable boutiques and many gardens, including that of the Passy Eiffel. The bedrooms at the back of the hotel, which are always in demand, enjoy a good view of the hotel's garden. They should be reserved in priority, even though those on the street have double glazing. The hotel is tastefully decorated in a rather classic style. A choice of good fabrics and carpeting brings a touch of elegance to the bedrooms, which are always comfortable and well-kept, whatever their size. Almost all the bathrooms have been renovated this year (with multi-jet showers in some single rooms). Recent work has turned numbers 41 and 51 into pleasant suites with a lounge, perfect for families (room 60 is also ideal for couples with children). Note that four rooms open directly onto the ground-floor patio. It feels good to settle down in this hospitable hotel with its pleasant dining room–veranda, full of plants, its lovely 1930s lounge and homemade honey to complete the pretty picture.

Hôtel Pergolèse

3, rue Pergolèse - 75116 Paris
Tel. (0)1 53 64 04 04 - Fax (0)1 53 64 04 40
Mme Vidalenc
Web: www.hotelpergolese.com - E-mail: pergolese@wanadoo.fr

Category ★★★★ Rooms 40 with air-conditioning, telephone, bath, WC, satellite TV, hairdryer, minibar. **Price** Single 1050-1400F / 160,07-213,43€, double 1200-1600F / 182,94-243,92€, "Pergolèse room" 1700F / 259,16€ (1 pers.), 1900F / 289,65€ (2 pers.) – Special rates weekends (excluding trade fair periods). **Meals** Breakfast 70F / 10,67€, buffet 95F / 14,48€. **Credit cards** All major. **Pets** Small dogs allowed. **Facilities** Elevator, room service. **How to get there** (Map 3) Bus: 73, 82, PC and bus for Roissy – Metro: Argentine – RER C: Porte Maillot, RER A: Charles-de-Gaulle-Etoile. **Open** All year.

Close to the Palais des Congrès, the Pergolèse is only a ten-minute walk from the Place de l'Etoile; this is a fine hotel in a quiet location. Its success owes a lot to the devotion and professionalism of Mme Vidalenc, who has called on leading contemporary designers and interior decorators, including Rena Dumas, who designed the layout and furniture. Here you forget the cliché that says that modern means cold. The entry area opens onto two lounges with superb leather armchairs, and the bar is set around a very fine carpet designed by Mac Connico In the breakfast room the illustrations of plants also painted by Mac Connico set the tone. The rooms have been cheered up with soft pastel colors matching those of the armchairs, the lamp shades and even the little rings decorating your porcelain teacups. The bathrooms in white marble are all very refined. The service and little attentions are those of a four-star hotel while they are pleasantly not too fussy.

Hôtel Raphaël-Paris

17, avenue Kléber – 75116 Paris
Tel. (0)1 53 64 32 00 – Fax (0)1 53 64 32 01
M. Alain Astier
Web: www.raphael-hotel.com – E-mail: sales@raphael-hotel.com

Category ★★★★ **Rooms and apartments** 90 with soundproofing and air-conditioning, bath, WC, telephone, hairdryer, satellite TV, minibar. **Price** Double "Charme" 2400F / 365,88€, "Boudoir" 2900F / 442,10€, "Alcove" 3900F / 595,41€, "Salon" 5050F / 770,99€, apart. by request; extra bed 450F / 68,60€. **Meals** Breakfast 140 and 180F / 21,34 and 27,44€. **Restaurant** *La Salle-Manger* gastronomic cooking. **Credit cards** All major. **Pets** Dogs allowed (+ 120F / 18,29€). **Facilities** Laundry service, room service, bar, doorman (doorman valet parking). **Parking** Avenue Marceau. **How to get there** (Map 6) Bus: 22, 30, 52, 73, 92 and bus for Roissy-Charles-de-Gaulle – Metro: Kléber – RER: Charles de Gaulle-Étoile. **Open** All year.

An authentic palace of charm, the Raphaël has its devotees and we are among them. The main gallery sets the scene: dark wooden panels, gilt, piers in an English or Louis XV style furniture. After admiring the Turner painting, you take the superb elevator that leads to the bedrooms and suites. There is a *grand siècle* atmosphere with vast spaces, painted and sculpted panelling often framing silk panels, and at times a huge alcove with superb curtains to preserve the intimacy of the bed. The colors are harmonious and cheerful, the inlaid Louis XV or Louis XVI furniture gleams with bronze. Comfort is everywhere. In fine weather, an open air panoramic restaurant completes the beautiful classic dining room. The bar continues to be a very chic meeting place, cosseted and confidential. You will find here the welcome and attention of a discreet staff. They are both courteous and distinguished, at the service of one of the most elegant addresses of the capital.

Résidence Bouquet-de-Longchamp

6, rue du Bouquet-de-Longchamp
75116 Paris
Tel. (0)1 47 04 41 71 - Fax (0)1 47 27 29 09
Mme Tamzali

Category ★★★ **Rooms** 17 with telephone, bath or shower, WC, TV, minibar and hairdyer by request. **Price** (depending on the season) Single 445-695F / 67,84-105,95€, double 485-765F / 73,94-116,62€; low season: Mid Nov to end Mar, Jul and Aug and special rates at certain periods or week-end in high season. **Meals** Breakfast 55F / 8,38€, served at any times. **Credit cards** All major. **Pets** Dogs allowed (+ 30F / 4,57€). **Facilities** Elevator, laundry service, room service 7PM to 2AM. **Parking** 65, av. Kléber. **How to get there** (Map 6) Bus: 22, 30, 32, 63 and 82 – Metro: Boissière, Iéna and Trocadéro. **Open** All year.

Its green awnings and flowered window-boxes set off the Résidence Bouquet-de-Longchamp on the small street immediately near the Trocadéro. Behind the picture windows, partially hidden by the silk of rustling curtains, one glimpses a pleasant corner-lounge which shares the ground-floor space with the reception area. Many light colors in the bedrooms, highlighted by darker-colored curtains and bedspreads, beige-lacquered furniture, small golden brass sconces. Wall fabrics are beige also, with a few sky blue exceptions. Located in the basement but basking in a well of light where green plants flourish, the breakfast room is very elegant, with comfortable medallion chairs and *moiré* wall fabric. The whole effect is perfectly maintained, soft, quiet and comfortable, convenient and, above all, affordable. These are especially interesting in the low season (but avoid Rooms 101 and 105 which give onto a blank wall). The welcome is courteous.

Hôtel Saint-James Paris

43, avenue Bugeaud – 75116 Paris
Tel. (0)1 44 05 81 81 - Fax (0)1 44 05 81 82
M. Tim Goddard
Web: www.saint-james-paris.com – E-mail: stjames@club-internet.fr

Category ★★★★ **Rooms** 24 and 24 suites, with air-conditioning, soundproofing, telephone, bath, WC, hairdryer, safe, minibar, cable TV. **Price** Single 1800-1900F / 274,41-289,65€, double 2100-2600F / 320,14-396,37€, suite 2700-4200F / 411,61-641,22€. **Meals** Breakfast 115F / 17,53€, buffet 145F / 22,11€, served 7:00-10:00 (in room at any time). **Credit cards** All major. **Pets** Dogs allowed. **Facilities** Elevator, laundry service, bar, health center, room service (24h). **Restaurant** Gastronomic – Mealtime specials 250F / 38,11€, also à la carte. **Parking** At the hotel. **How to get there** (Map 6) Bus: 52 and PC – Metro: Porte Dauphine – RER C: Avenue-Foch. **Open** All year.

It was on the initiative of the widow of President Thiers that this 19th-century private house was built in the style of a chateau. It is close to the Bois de Boulogne, but that does not prevent the Saint-James from adding its own touch of foliage, offering its guests the privilege of a large garden just a few minutes away from the Champs-Elysées. The interior has preserved the ambiance of a very select club (notably the sumptuous bar-library), and this was its role before becoming a hotel in 1992. The size of the public spaces are impressive, with high windows looking onto the garden and an oval dining room extending outdoors. Some of the rooms are in a cleverly contemporary style due to the very sure taste of designer, Andrée Putman. Those under the glass roofing of the top floor are astonishing with their terrace-gardens. Others are very British and very warm, and all have superb retro bathrooms. The cuisine is noteworthy (served under the trees in summer) while the service is just as pleasant.

Hôtel Square

3, rue de Boulainvilliers
75016 Paris
Tel. (0)1 44 14 91 90 – Fax (0)1 44 14 91 99
M. Patrick Derderian

Category ★★★★ **Rooms** 18 and 4 suites with air-conditioning, soundproofing, telephone, fax, bath, WC, hairdryer, minibar, safe, cable and satellite TV – 2 for disabled persons. **Price** Double 1400-2100F / 213,43-320,14€, suite 2300-2600F / 350,63-396,37€; special rates on week-ends. **Meals** Breakfast (buffet) 60F / 9,15€ (90F / 13,72€ in room), served 7:00-11:00. **Credit cards** All major. **Pets** Small dogs allowed. **Facilities** Elevator, bar, laundry service, room service. **Restaurant** Mealtime specials 250F / 38,11€, also à la carte. **Parking** At the hotel. **How to get there** (Map 6) Bus: 22, 52, 70 and 72 – RER C: Kennedy-Radio France. **Open** All year.

Just a few meters away from the Seine and the Maison de la Radio, you'll find this small building with its rounded forms, entirely covered with gray marble and christened the Hôtel Square. It is a perfect example of the best contemporary trends in interior decor with curved lines, soft furniture matched with ethnic items (pottery, lights, fabrics, etc.) and a touch of lively color here and there. The vast rooms have three tone schemes: gray and ivory, gold and bronze, or brick and saffran. The overall effect is one of total comfort, including the bathrooms in white marble veined with anthracite. You should also note that there is a gallery of contemporary art and a very fashionable restaurant, also used for breakfasts, on the ground floor. A very fine hotel that fully justifies what it charges.

Hôtel Trocadéro Dokhan's

117, rue Lauriston - 75116 Paris
Tel. (0)1 53 65 66 99 - Fax (0)1 53 65 66 88
Mme Corsius - M. Jamet
E-mail: hotel.trocadero.dokhans@wanadoo.fr

Category ★★★★ **Rooms** 41 and 4 suites (some with terrace) with soundproofing and air-conditioning with bath, WC, telephone, fax, outlet for modem, CD player, cable TV, hairdryer, minibar and safe – 2 rooms for disabled persons. **Price** Single and double 1900-2300F / 289,65-350,63€, suite 4500F / 687,02€. **Meals** Breakfast (buffet) 140F / 21,34€; snack availables. **Credit cards** All major. **Pets** Dogs not allowed. **Facilities** Elevator, laundry service, bar, room service. **Parking** Rue Saint-Didier. **How to get there** (Map 6) Bus: 22, 30, 32, 63 and 82 – Metro: Trocadéro. **Open** All year.

The Etoile is the district of great hotels. Although the Trocadéro Dokhan's has all the qualities to be rated among them, the term "hotel of charm" suits it best. Following a concept he is fond of, the decorator, F. Méchiche, has treated the place as a private mansion. You enter into a small courtyard full of box trees, then walk into the alcove with the reception area opening onto the *Directoire* lounge and the dining-room with 18th-century wood panelling. A nice surprise is yet to come. Once you pass through the large oak door to go up to your room, you will find a small marvel of an elevator, lined with Vuitton canvas from ancient trunks. The bedrooms are just as refined, often in pretty tones of blue (as in the "starry corner" bedroom). We need not say more about the duplex suites on the last floor, with their fireplaces for winter and terrace on the roofs for summer. To the charm and refinement can be added great comfort in order to create luxury that remains intimate.

La Villa Maillot

143, avenue de Malakoff – 75116 Paris
Tel. (0)1 53 64 52 52 – Fax (0)1 45 00 60 61
Mme Ghislaine Abinal
Web: www.lavillamaillot.fr – E-mail: resa@lavillamaillot.fr

Category ★★★★ **Rooms** 39 and 3 suites with air-conditioning, soundproofing, telephone with answering machine, bath, WC, hairdryer, satellite TV, minibar, trouser-press – 2 for disabled persons. **Price** Single 1700F / 259,16€, double 1950F / 297,28€, suite (1-4 pers.) 2500-2700F / 381,12-411,61€; extra bed 300F / 45,73€ – Special rates for week-ends (excluding trade fair periods). **Meals** Breakfast (buffet) 95F / 14,48€, buffet 120F / 18,29€, served 7:00-10:00. **Credit cards** All major. **Pets** Small dogs allowed. **Facilities** Elevator, laundry service, bar, room service. **Parking** At the hotel (6 spaces, 120F / 18,29€ /day). **How to get there** (Map 3) Bus: 73, 82, PC and Air France bus – Metro and RER C: Porte Maillot. **Open** All year.

The building was built in 1987 and was specifically designed as a hotel with large airy spaces and the most modern comfort. Breakfast is served in the lounge-bar, which extends onto a veranda. The place is adorned by a coffee table by Arman and a portrait by Tamara de Lempicka, but the dominant style is Art Deco. In the newly renovated bedrooms, more softness has been brought to the choice of decor. Its omnipresent comfort and many attentions make this hotel of discreet luxury perfect for both exacting tourists and businessmen. The latter will appreciate being able to plug in their faxes, modems and laptops. Impeccably soundproofed, the rooms are all spacious, with large windows. Those on the back overlook gardens. The bathrooms are just as perfect. A dynamic and pleasant welcome from the director and her staff, who are all keen on making your stay at the Villa Maillot the best possible.

Hôtel Ampère

102, avenue de Villiers - 75017 Paris
Tel. (0)1 44 29 17 17 - Fax (0)1 44 29 16 50
M. Chevallier
Web: www.hotelampere.com - E-mail: resa@hotelampere.com

Category ★★★ **Rooms** 102 with air-conditioning, soundproofing, telephone, bath or shower, WC, cable TV, minibar, safe, hairdryer – 3 for disabled persons. **Price** Special rates for the readers of this guide. Single 780F / 118,91€, double 875F / 133,43€, triple 965F / 147,11€. In Jul and Aug: 1 pers. 565F / 86,13€, 2 pers. 635F / 96,81€. **Meals** Breakfast (buffet) 60F / 9,15€ (free of charge for a 3-night weekend stay), served 7:15-10:00. **Credit cards** All major. **Pets** Dogs allowed (+15F / 2,28€). **Facilities** Elevator, bar (piano-bar), laundry service, patio, room service. **Restaurant** Mealtime specials from 125F / 19,06€. **Parking** Private (80F / 12,20€ /day). **How to get there** (Map 3) Bus: 84, 92, 93 – Metro and RER C: Pereire. **Open** All year.

On the corner of Place du Maréchal-Juin (Place Pereire), the Hôtel Ampere opened in 1996. This is a big-capacity hotel with a modern decor of a certain elegance rather than charm. The large and light reception area leads into the lounge (which doubles as a piano-bar at cocktail time), the dining room and an attractive garden where you can enjoy your drink. Well-maintained, the rooms are not extremely sizeable, even those intended for three people, but are well-laid out with attractive furniture designed for the hotel. They are similar, with only a change in fabric color. The avenue de Villiers is lively and so it is better to sleep on the courtyard side. The staff at reception is attentive and very efficient, handling a mainly family clientele visiting Paris.

Hôtel Arc de Triomphe Étoile

3, rue de l'Étoile - 75017 Paris
Tel. (0)1 56 68 90 00 - Fax (0)1 44 40 49 19
Mme Alvarez
E-mail: arc.triomph.etoile@worldnet.fr

Category ★★★ **Rooms** 25 with air-conditioning and soundproofing with telephone, bath or shower, WC, minibar, hairdryer, cable TV, radio and safe. **Price** Single 725-810F / 110,53-123,48€, double 790-900F / 120,43-137,20€, triple 1000F / 152,45€. **Meals** Breakfast (buffet) 65F / 9,91€ (free of charge on presentatin of this guide), served 7:00-10:00. **Credit Cards** All major. **Pets** Dogs allowed (+ 30F / 4,57€). **Facilities** Elevator, bar, laundry service. **Parking** Wagram. **How to get there** (Map 3) Bus: 22, 30, 31, 43, 52, 73, 92, 93 and Air France bus to Roissy – Metro: Ternes and Charles de Gaulle-Étoile – RER: Charles de Gaulle-Étoile. **Open** All year.

A full renovation program has rejuvenated this pleasant establishment located near the Place de l'Etoile (from which it takes its name). The reception lounge has been furnished with comfortable checked armchairs in beige and coral tones; with the library, this makes for a very convivial area. The bedrooms on the courtyard are quieter, but those on the façade are protected from the noise by double-glazing and are air-conditioned. The rooms in a corner (ending with a number 1 or 5) are larger and have a sofa that can sleep another person. Moreover, they can be combined into apartments to accommodate families with three children. Here again, the decoration is harmonious: pale wood furniture and yellow fabrics with blue motifs. The bathrooms are well-equipped. This is a good address, where the service and comfort have built up a clientele of faithful customers.

Hôtel Astrid

27, avenue Carnot – 75017 Paris
Tel. (0)1 44 09 26 00 – Fax (0)1 44 09 26 01
Mme Guillet
Web: www.hotel-astrid.com – E-mail: paris@hotel-astrid.com

Category ★★★ **Rooms** 40 with soundproofing, telephone, bath or shower, WC, hairdryer, cable TV and safe. **Price** Single 570-620F / 86,90-94,52€, double 680-800F / 103,67-121,96€, triple 895F / 136,44€, 4 pers. 950F / 144,83€ – Special rates in winter, Jul and Aug: 1 pers. 500F / 76,22€, 2 pers. 600F / 91,47€. **Meals** Breakfast included, served 7:00-10:00. **Credit cards** All major. **Pets** Dogs allowed (+35F / 5,34€). **Facilities** Elevator. **Parking** 50m. **How to get there** (Map 3) Bus: 22, 30, 31, 43, 52, 73, 92, 93 and Air France bus to Roissy – Metro: Charles de Gaulle-Étoile. **Open** All year.

Avenue Carnot is certainly the quietest in the Etoile district, but, at only 100 hundred meters from the Arc de Triomphe, it gives onto the very busy rue des Acacias. The Hotel Astrid is on this very corner. Each room has its own particular style and it was clearly with much pleasure that the owners chose all the fabrics, furniture, lamps, etc. In one room, curtains with blue leafy patterns have been matched with a fine yellow wallpaper and Directory-style furniture pieces, on which you find a small repeat in blue patina. In another room, a Provençal theme is chosen, and in a third, gilded bedsteads are used to create a romantic atmosphere much closer to the guest room at home than to the usual standard hotel. The last area to benefit from the renovation program, the rooms with showers have now been finished. Despite their small size they are pleasant, possibly a bit less personal than the others but also fully recommendable. To this well-maintained overall effect, you can add the charming view of the chestnut trees, and on the ground floor an attractive breakfast room with its large bay windows.

Hôtel de Banville

166, boulevard Berthier – 75017 Paris
Tel. (0)1 42 67 70 16 – Fax (0)1 44 40 42 77
Mme Marianne Moreau
Web: www.hotelbanville.fr – E-mail: hotelbanville@wanadoo.fr

Category ★★★ **Rooms** 38 and 1 apartment with air-conditioning, soundproofing, bath or shower, WC, telephone, satellite TV, hairdryer and safe. **Price** Single and double 695-935F / 105,95-142,54€, room with terrace and room "Théo" 1100F / 167,69€, apart. 1525F / 232,48€ – Special rates on weekends and in low season on request. **Meals** Breakfast 65F / 9,91€, diet breakfast 75F / 11,43€, healthy breakfast 85F / 12,96€, served from 6:30; snacks available. **Credit cards** All major. **Pets** Dogs allowed. **Facilities** Room service (24h), bar. **Parking** At 210, rue de Courcelles. **How to get there** (Map 3) Bus: 84, 92, 93, PC and Air France bus to Roissy at Porte Maillot – Metro and RER: Pereire. **Open** All year.

The superb Hôtel de Banville is situated in a 1930s building near the Porte Maillot and fifteen minutes away from the Champs-Élysées. Lined with plane trees, the Boulevard Berthier is fairly quiet. You are immediately won over by the elegant lounge fitted-out as in a private house with fine antique furniture and pictures. The rooms are light, spacious and open onto the trees. All deliberately different, they do have one common feature in their perfectly chosen fabrics and wallpaper (very far from the usual hotel standards), pretty furniture and, of course, fine bathrooms. They all compete in charm and comfort, reaching a pinnacle on the top floor with the exceptional *appartement de Marie* and the unique *chambre d'Amélie* whose terrace facing south looks out over all of Paris (those who can afford a small but quite reasonable extravagance should not miss it). Sensible prices and a particularly friendly welcome make this one of our favorite hotels in Paris.

Hôtel Centre-Ville Étoile

6, rue des Acacias - 75017 Paris
Tel. (0)1 58 05 10 00 - Fax (0)1 47 54 93 43
M. Michaud
E-mail: hcv@centrevillehotels.com

Category ★★★ **Rooms** 20 with air-conditioning, bath, WC, telephone, minitel, outlet for modem, cable TV, minibar and safe. **Price** Single 590-790F / 89,94-120,43€, double 690-950F / 105,19-144,83€. **Meals** Breakfast 55F / 8,38€. **Credit cards** All major. **Pets** Dogs allowed. **Facilities** Elevator, laundry service, patio, room service, shuttle to the airport by request. **Parking** At 24, rue des Acacias. **How to get there** (Map 3) Bus: 73 and bus for Roissy airport – Metro: Argentine and Charles de Gaulle-Étoile. **Open** All year.

Originally, this hotel consisted of two buildings facing each other and connected on each floor by an exterior passageway. The owners have now enclosed this space with a high, glass wall and a skylight. Serving as the reception area, the new space is bathed with natural light and beautified with lush green plants. The rest of the decor is black and white, contemporary, airy and sophisticated. Comfort is to be found in the lounge's the black leather club chairs, in the cute little dining room and in the lovely bedrooms with black lacquered designer furniture surrounded by white or brown walls. The monochrome effect elegantly sets off the brightly colored posters and luminous wall sconces. Some guests might find the rooms rather small, but they are very comfortable. Equally lovely are the small, perfectly kept bathrooms. Special mention should be made of the staff, who come around 6PM to turn down your bed covers, fill the ice bucket and, as a small finishing touch, place chocolates on your pillow.

Hôtel Champerret-Héliopolis

13, rue d'Héliopolis
75017 Paris
Tel. (0)1 47 64 92 56 – Fax (0)1 47 64 50 44
Mme Rennie - M. Ferment

Category ★★ **Rooms** 22 with telephone, bath or shower, WC, hairdryer, TV – 2 for disabled persons. **Price** Single 350-385F / 53,36-58,69€, double 450-495F / 68,60-75,46€, triple 495-580F / 75,46-88,42€. **Meals** Breakfast 38F / 5,80€, from 7:00. **Credit cards** All major. **Pets** Dogs allowed. **Facilities** Patio, bar. **Parking** Private (2 spaces), Porte de Champerret. **How to get there** (Map 3) Bus: 84, 92, 93, PC – Metro: Porte de Champerret – RER: Pereire. **Open** All year.

A white corner façade with small windows on two floors gives this hotel a homey air. Mme Rennie, the owner, who lives in Madagascar, loves sunshine and bright colors. The luxuriant decor of green plants, flowers in bright pots, and a small, colorful birdcage make the Champerret-Héliopolis seem very far from the big city. The semicircular lounge bar, furnished and decorated with personal objects and brightened by exotic green and blue cacti in the entrance, adds a holiday touch. The simple and functional bedrooms have all the comforts, but we prefer not to recommend those on the ground floor which get little light. In some, a small square balcony overlooks the patio, and the hotel has had breakfast trays especially designed to be fastened onto the wooden railings. Breakfasts are served in the rooms, in the smallish bar or at a single, much coveted table on the patio.

Hôtel Eber-Monceau

18, rue Léon-Jost
75017 Paris
Tel. (0)1 46 22 60 70 – Fax (0)1 47 63 01 01
M. Jean-Marc Eber

Category ★★★ **Rooms** 13, 3 suites and 2 duplexes (1 with terrace) with air-conditionning, bath or shower, WC, telephone, cable TV and minibar. **Price** Single and double 690-750F / 105,19-114,34€, twin 850F / 129,58€, suite (1-4 pers.) 1200F / 182,94€, duplex (1-2 pers.) 1300 and 1500F / 198,18-228,67€; extra bed. 100F / 15,24€. **Meals** Breakfast 65F / 9,91€. **Credit cards** All major. **Pets** Dogs not allowed. **Facilities** Elevator, small patio, laundry service, room service. **Parking** At 100, rue de Courcelles. **How to get there** (Map 3) Bus: 30, 31, 84 – Metro: Courcelles. **Open** All year.

The *habitués* who come back time and again to the Eber-Monceau are surely attracted by the homey atmosphere. This is largely due to the small, intimate size of the hotel and because of the lovely reception area and lounge, which is especially charming with its beautiful, polychrome beam ceiling and neo-Gothic oak fireplace. Cane chairs, decorative objects and a few paintings add further to the welcoming ambiance, as do the tiny bar and patio. Renovated this year, the bedrooms remain comfortable and are furnished with care, although those to the rear have less space and light. Therefore, since the street is very quiet and the hotel air-conditioned, you had better choose the street side. The suites (well-designed for families) and duplex rooms are larger and very pleasant. The bathrooms are impeccable and the breakfasts excellent. It should be added that M. Eber can always recommend the best restaurant for your mood of the moment.

Hôtel Étoile-Pereire

146, boulevard Pereire
75017 Paris
Tel. (0)1 42 67 60 00 – Fax (0)1 42 67 02 90
M. Pardi

Category ★★★ **Rooms** 20, 1 suite and 4 duplexes (with air-conditioning) with telephone, bath or shower, WC, cable TV, safe and minibar. **Price** Single 620-720F / 94,52-109,76€, double 810F / 123,48€, suite and duplex (1-3 pers.) 1120F / 170,74€ – Special rates Jul, Aug and weekend 2 nights (excluding trade fair periods): 1 pers. 550F / 83,85€, 2 pers. 620F / 94,52€, duplex 900F / 137,20€ (breakfast included). **Meals** Breakfast 60F / 9,15€. **Credit cards** All major. **Pets** Dogs not allowed. **Facilities** Elevator, laundry service, bar, room service. **Parking** At 30, rue Rennequin. **How to get there** (Map 3) Bus: 84, 92, 93 and bus for Roissy at Porte Maillot – Metro and RER C: Pereire. **Open** All year.

All (but one of) the bedrooms at the Étoile Pereire overlook a quiet, interior courtyard. The general layout has much character. The bedrooms vary in size. There are three steps delimiting the border between the entrance and the room itself. Otherwise, a low wall at a right angle plays this role. The blue suite with its two windows stretches in a broken line along the courtyard. The magnificent duplexes have sitting areas on the ground floor and beds upstairs. The decor is tasteful: walls covered in beige, blue or rose fabrics which match the curtains. Lithographs have been hung, often of exotic birds. Quite an accomplishment. The same can be said of the very comfortable lobby, the bar and a charming dining room where you can enjoy outstanding breakfasts, with a choice of 6 kinds of tea and 40 different preserves. An inviting, hospitable hotel

Hôtel Excelsior

16, rue Caroline
75017 Paris
Tel. (0)1 45 22 50 95 – Fax (0)1 45 22 59 88
M. Le Ralle

Category ★ ★ ★ **Rooms** 22 with soundproofing, telephone, bath or shower, WC, hairdryer, satellite TV. **Price** Single 500F / 76,22€, double 650F / 99,09€; extra bed 80F / 12,20€. **Meals** Breakfast 35F / 5,34€, served 7:15-9:30. **Credit cards** All major. **Pets** Dogs allowed. **Facilities** Elevator, drinks machine. **Parking** At 18, rue Caroline. **How to get there** (Map 4) Bus: 30 and 66 – Metro: Place de Clichy, Rome. **Open** All year.

Once through the door of the Excelsior you must not be put off by the first impression that the reception area–lounge may give you. Certainly, its Louis XIII-style furniture and the old rustic cupboard are not without charm, but the overall effect remains rather cold and stuffy. The brown tiled floor does not help. In contrast, the rooms are very much warmer and softer, often with navy-blue or raspberry draped fabrics, small furniture pieces and impeccable speckled carpeting that is matched by the headboards, pretty curtains and the printed or white *piqué* bedspreads. You often find a marble fireplace or moulded ceilings. Avoid Room 502, which is the smallest. Some look onto the street while those on the courtyard enjoy the quiet greenery of a rather "bohemian" garden which is large for Paris. The bathrooms are well-maintained and some have windows. As almost always, the breakfast room is in the basement. The welcome is friendly and relaxed.

Hôtel Flaubert

19, rue Rennequin
75017 Paris
Tel. (0)1 46 22 44 35 – Fax (0)1 43 80 32 34
M. and Mme Niceron

Category ★★ **Rooms** 37 with bath or shower, WC, telephone, TV, minibar – 1 for disabled persons. **Price** Single 460-520F / 70,13-79,27€, double 550-650F / 83,85-99,09€, triple 700F / 106,71€. **Meals** Breakfast 45F / 6,86€, served 6:30-10:00. **Credit cards** All major. **Pets** Dogs allowed. **Facilities** Elevator, patio. **Parking** Opposite the hotel. **How to get there** (Map 3) Bus: 30, 31, 43, 84, 92 and 93 – Metro: Ternes. **Open** All year.

The Flaubert is a small local hotel whose best features are found inside and beyond the reception area, on the luxuriant small patio. Here, cascades of Virginia creeper and ivy geraniums tumble down from the balconies, mingling with flower beds of aucuba, impatiens and annuals. We only recommend the few bedrooms looking out over this refreshing scene: Numbers 1 to 3, on the garden level (but without much light); and Rooms 9, 10 and 11 on the floor above, with windows opening onto the greenery. All are identically fitted-out, simple, functional and well-kept, with good bathroom facilities (although their decor could be more cheerful and sophisticated). Tiled in beautiful terra-cotta, the breakfast room has the atmosphere of a conservatory/bistro, with small bamboo chairs and green plants, offering an exotic spot from which to observe the activity on the street. Lastly, you will be charmingly received by Christiane and Michel Niceron.

Hôtel Libertel Monceau

7, rue Rennequin
75017 Paris
Tel. (0)1 47 63 07 52 – Fax (0)1 47 66 84 44
Mme Frédérique Péchenart

Category ★★★ (categorization pending) **Rooms** 25 with soundproofing, bath or shower, WC, hairdryer, telephone, minibar and cable TV. **Price** Single 918F / 140€, double 983F / 150€. From Nov to end Mar and in Jul and Aug (excluding trade fair periods and national holidays): 1 pers. 600F / 91,47€, 2 pers. 800F / 121,96€; extra bed 220F / 33,53€. **Meals** Continental breakfast 45F / 6,86€, buffet 75F / 11,43€, served 7:00-10:30. Snacks available from 80F / 12,20€. **Credit cards** All major. **Pets** Small dogs allowed. **Facilities** Elevator, bar, laundry service, room service, patio. **Parking** Wagram. **How to get there** (Map 3) Bus: 30, 31, 43, 84, 92 and 93 – Metro: Ternes, Wagram. **Open** All year.

Close to the Place des Ternes, rue Rennequin leads into avenue Wagram. The Libertel-Monceau offers 25 small sound-proofed rooms with the largest looking onto the street or over a flowery patio. Blues for some, yellows for others, but all have shimmering fabrics and mahogany style-furniture, or else simple white cane pieces. Their comfort is even furthered by ravishing bathrooms in white faience. In fine weather, we recommend that you try for numbers 104, 105 and 106; they open directly onto a small furnished terrace. Rooms 1, 2 and 3 could use a little more light. A warm bar in the British style allows you to relax in armchairs and on sofas while reading the French and foreign press. In summary, one can say that this hotel is comfortable and warm, while the attention of the service even goes as far as giving you a weather forecast with your breakfast.

Hôtel Magellan

17, rue Jean-Baptiste-Dumas
75017 Paris
Tel. (0)1 45 72 44 51 - Fax (0)1 40 68 90 36
Anne-Marie Borgen

Category ★★★ Rooms 75 with telephone, bath or shower, WC, satellite TV, outlet for PC. **Price** Single 610F / 92,99€, double 650F / 99,09€, +145F / 22,11€; extra bed. **Meals** Breakfast 45F / 6,86€, buffet 55F / 8,38€. **Credit cards** All major. **Pets** Dogs not allowed. **Facilities** Elevator, garden. **Parking** Private by reservation (85F / 12,96€). **How to get there** (Map 3) Bus: 84, 92, 93, PC and and bus for Roissy – Metro: Porte de Champerret – RER C: Pereire. **Open** All year.

The many contemporary wood panels, elegant lithographs, and small 1930s-style lounges augur well as you enter the beautiful lobby of the Magellan. Just behind it, you can glimpse the lovely garden with trees, rows of iris, rose bushes, and tables with umbrellas, where you can have drinks. The rooms are all decorated in the same way, and the standard hotel furniture in oak or burred walnut is rather old-fashioned, but the rooms are vast, bright and well-maintained. The other main attraction of the Magellan is the small pavilion in the garden and almost all the bedrooms overlook this lovely scene. The rooms are quiet, and as soon as the weather is fine, you can enjoy the garden. The welcome by the personnel is friendly and attentive.

Marmotel Étoile

34, avenue de la Grande-Armée
75017 Paris
Tel. (0)1 47 63 57 26 - Fax (0)1 45 74 25 27
M. Robert

Category ★★ Rooms 22 with telephone, bath or shower, WC, TV, minibar and safe. **Price** Single 410F / 62,50€, double 470-490F / 71,65-74,70€. In weekend and in Aug (except for trade fair periods): 1 pers. 350F / 53,36€, 2 pers. 400F / 60,98€. **Meals** Breakfast 30F / 4,57€, served 7:00-11:30, breakfast free charge for readers of the guide. **Credit cards** All major. **Pets** Dogs allowed. **Facilities** Garden. **Parking** Charles-de-Gaulle (at 500m). **How to get there** (Map 3) Bus: 22, 30, 31, 52, 73, 92 and bus Air France to Roissy – Metro: Argentine – RER: Charles de Gaulle. **Open** All year.

Almost hidden between a café and an automobile parts store, the Marmotel could easily be missed by passers-by. This very simple hotel has its *habitués*, including a good number of business people who enjoy quiet and green spaces. Having your breakfast in the flowery garden will bring you back again and again to this hotel. Of course, it is of little interest in poor weather, but if you arrive early you can sit in the hallway alongside the garden. You can also have your breakfast in your room. You won't find many two stars hotels that offer this kind of service and have this location– so close to the Arc de Triomphe. The bedrooms are spacious and have the conventional modern comforts, but their decor is only functional. For a quiet room, ask for one overlooking the garden. Rooms 112, 114, 122, 124, 132 and 134 have some noise, with their windows directly over the busy avenue de la Grande Armée. The welcome is extremely convivial and the rates very attractive.

Hôtel Médéric

4, rue Médéric
75017 Paris
Tel. (0)1 47 63 69 13 - Fax (0)1 44 40 05 33
M. Rolin

Category ★★ **Rooms** 27 with bath or shower, WC, telephone, satellite TV. **Price** Single and double 450-530F / 68,60-80,80€, twin 620-750F / 94,52-114,34€, 3-4 pers. 750F / 114,34€. **Meals** Breakfast 45F / 6,86€, served 7:00-11:00. **Credit cards** All major. **Pets** Dogs not allowed. **Facilities** Elevator. **Parking** Wagram (at 50 m). **How to get there** (Map 3) Bus: 30, 31 and 84 – Metro: Courcelles. **Open** All year.

Many passers-by on the rue Médéric stop to look in the window of this hotel's lovely breakfast room, with its *Provençal décor*. Yellow walls and tablecloths, blue-gray patinated chairs, 19th-century landscape paintings and a comfortable small lounge beckon you inside to investigate further. The bedrooms are quite pleasant; aside from the two family suites on the top floor (tall people can enjoy the view from the roof windows), the other rooms are very small. The walls are beige or tapestried in Japanese straw and are adorned with lovely mirrors and wall sconces in gilt, antiqued wrought iron. The furniture is only functional, with small beige chairs, but there are period armchairs in some rooms. The Médéric is a simple, family-style hotel and the prices are reasonable.

Hôtel de Neuville

3, rue Verniquet - 75017 Paris
Tel. (0)1 43 80 26 30 - Fax (0)1 43 80 38 55
Mme Beherec - M. Caron
E-mail: neuville@hotellerie.net

Category ★★★ **Rooms** 28 with soundproofing, telephone, bath, WC, cable TV, outlet for fax and modem. **Price** Single and double 750F / 114,34€; in low season 590F / 89,94€ (1-2 pers.). Weekends and Jul to Aug 550F / 83,85€; extra bed 150F / 22,87€. **Meals** Breakfast (buffet) 55F / 8,38€, served 7:00-11:00. **Credit cards** All major. **Pets** Dogs allowed (+60F/9,15€) **Facilities** Elevator, bar, room service. **Parking** Private, 90F / 13,72€ /day (at 20m). **How to get there** (Map 3) Bus: 53, 84, 92, 93, 94 and PC – Metro and RER C: Pereire. **Open** All year.

Just in front of the Hôtel de Neuville the very green boulevard Pereire opens up slightly to allow a small triangular space for Place Verniquet. Up a flight of steps to reach the reception lobby, you find an elegant room where light oak worked wood pieces mingle with basket seating in the 1930s spirit, and the beige marble of the bar, all creating a peaceful tone. Two steps and a pair of columns mark the bar off from the lounge. There are contemporary canvasses regularly exhibited on the walls, but the finest picture of all remains the luxurious patio which you cannot tire of looking at through the large rectangular window in the center of the lateral wall. The bedrooms were also fitted-out with taste; pleasant, functional and well-kept, they are each characterized by a pretty personal detail. Two of them have amusing beds with copper canopies, while the most luminous rooms, located on the street side, benefit from the rows of trees on the boulevard. The ground-floor breakfast room is charming in its winter garden style, and the welcome is particularly pleasant.

Hôtel Pavillon Monceau

43, rue Jouffroy-d'Abbans - 75017 Paris
Tel. (0)1 56 79 25 00 - Fax (0)1 42 12 99 38
Mme Chouchane Tasci
Web: pavillon-monceau.com - E-mail: infos@pavillon-monceau.com

Category ★★★ **Rooms** 36 and 6 suites with air-conditioning and soundproofing, telephone, bath or shower, WC, hairdryer, satellite TV, minibar and safe. **Price** Single 590-890F / 89,94-135,68€, double 690-1090F / 105,19-166,17€, junior suite (1-3 pers.) 1090-1290F / 166,17-196,66€ – Special rates on weekends all year. **Meals** Breakfast (buffet) 65F / 9,91€, served 7:00-9:30. **Credit cards** All major. **Pets** Dogs allowed. **Facilities** Elevator, bar, laundry service. **Parking** Opposite the hotel (100F / 15,24€ /day). **How to get there** (Map 3) Bus: 31, 53 and 94 – Metro: Malesherbes and Wagram. **Open** All year.

This brand-new hotel, well-anchored in the present trend, is located on the corner of two wide streets in the chic part of the 17th *arrondissement*, that is to say never far from the Parc Monceau. Therefore you should not look for its charm in the antique furniture pieces and old trunks, but in its simple elegance and cordial welcome. Warmth and modernity characterize the lounge, separated from the breakfast room by a piano often used by the guests. All around, the walls display beautiful black and white photographs of artists in Paris. Very comfortable, sober (a shade too much) and perfectly soundproofed, the bedrooms are all decorated in blue fabrics with small motifs on a background of pale yellow wallpaper. They radiate a feeling of well-being and most reflect the setting sun. Mention this guide when you reserve, and you will be greeted with a small bottle of champagne. Moreover, if you stay five days or more, the hotel will treat you to a sampling of *foie gras* in a southwest French restaurant nearby.

Hôtel Pierre

25, rue Théodore-de-Banville - 75017 Paris
Tel. (0)1 47 63 76 69 - Fax (0)1 43 80 63 96
M. Arnaud Sauve
E-mail: quality-pierre@wanadoo.fr

Category ★★★ **Rooms** 50 with soundproofing and air-conditioning, bath, WC, telephone, hairdryer, cable TV, minibar, safe – 4 for disabled persons. **Price** Single and double 920-1100F / 140,25-167,69€, "club" 1150-1350F / 175,32-205,81€; extra bed 100F / 15,24€ (free for children under 12 years). **Meals** Breakfast (buffet) 70F / 10,67€, served 6:30-10:30 (12:00 in room); snacks available: room service, meal trays. **Credit cards** All major. **Pets** Dogs allowed. **Facilities** Elevator, patio, laundry service. **Parking** At 20 m. **How to get there** (Map 3) Bus: 31 and 84 – Metro and RER C: Pereire. **Open** All year.

With a red canopied entrance, the Hôtel Pierre is a luxurious establishment on a human scale. The lobby was conceived to make the wait for a taxi or an appointment as pleasant as possible; there are several conversation corners with red or yellow velvet armchairs and a large selection of newspapers on the coffee table. Equally comfortable, the bedrooms have been recently refurbished: thick carpets, colorful curtains and bedspreads, *Directoire*-style furniture. The overall decor is not completely authentic, but there are attractive small details in the bedrooms and bathrooms. Note that the rooms overlooking the courtyard (especially those on the lower floors) benefit from a view of a charming patio with its magnolia tree and flowers. Double-glazed windows ensure a quiet night's sleep, and when you awake, you'll enjoy breakfast in a delightful room with large bay windows and floral drapes, looking out onto the garden. Professional welcome and service.

Hôtel Princesse Caroline

1 *bis*, rue Troyon - 75017 Paris
Tel. (0)1 58 05 30 00 - Fax (0)1 42 27 49 53
M. Lascaux
Web: www.hotelprincessecaroline.fr

Category ★★★ **Rooms** 63 with air-conditioning, soundproofing, telephone, bath or shower, WC, hairdryer, satellite TV, minibar, safe – 13 for disabled persons. **Price** Single 725-815F / 110,53-124,25€, double 815-1115F / 124,25-169,98€; extra bed 150F / 22,87€. **Meals** Breakfast (buffet) 75F / 11,43€, served 7:00-11:00. **Credit cards** Visa, Eurocard, MasterCard, Amex. **Pets** Dogs not allowed **Facilities** Elevator, laundry service, bar. **Parking** Wagram. **How to get there** (Map 3) Bus: 22, 30, 31, 52, 73, 92 and Air France Roissy – Metro and RER: Charles de Gaulle-Étoile. **Open** All year.

The luxurious Hôtel Princesse Caroline is on one of the few small streets (just off the Place de l'Etoile) whose tranquillity contrasts with the bustling avenues that converge on the Arc de Triomphe. It is a good example of successful renovation. In the lobby, there are several corner lounges with elegant 1930s armchairs on a beige marble floor in perfect harmony with the light-oak wall panelling. On each floor, the huge landings are also paneled in oak and have thick green carpeting that extends into the bedrooms. Regardless of size, they are appointed with comfort and taste. The bedrooms are attentively decorated with cherry-wood furniture in a Louis XVI or *Directoire* style, of good quality but unmistakably of recent origin. The baths are immaculate. There is a pleasant view on the courtyard side because the pale brick buildings opposite are at a good distance, and these rooms are totally quiet. Breakfast is served in a bright basement room just as beautifully designed.

Hôtel Regent's Garden

6, rue Pierre-Demours – 75017 Paris
Tel. (0)1 45 74 07 30 – Fax (0)1 40 55 01 42
M. Condy
E-mail: hotel.regents.garden@wanadoo.fr

Category ★★★ **Rooms** 39 with air-conditioning, telephone, bath or shower, WC, hairdryer, cable TV, outlet for PC and minibar. **Price** "Standard" 760F / 115,86€ (1 pers.), 800F / 121,96€ (2 pers.), "médium" (1-2 pers.) 1060F/161,60€, "de luxe" (1-2 pers.) 1400F / 213,43€; –15% In Jan, Feb and Aug. **Meals** Breakfast 55F / 8,38€. **Credit cards** All major. **Pets** Dogs not allowed. **Facilities** Elevator, laundry service, garden. **Parking** Private 60F / 9,15€ /day (8 cars) or public (at 30m). **How to get there** (Map 3) Bus: 43, 92, 93, PC and Air France bus for Roissy – Metro: Charles de Gaulle-Étoile, Ternes. **Open** All year.

Behind the avenue des Ternes, this is the beautiful mansion that Napoleon III built for his doctor. A flight of steps leads up to an elegant lobby occupied by the reception area and the lounge. This opens onto a large garden. The rooms are distributed around large landings. Half overlook the garden while the others are soundproofed with double-glazing and furthermore protected from the street by an entrance courtyard planted with trees. All the rooms have high ceilings; they vary in size but are never small (some are even huge) and they all are extremely comfortable and pleasant. Fully renovated in 1988, they have acquired a tasteful, up-to-date decoration with the classical refinement that has always made up their charm. The bathrooms are new and just as well-done. In nice weather, breakfast is served in the garden quickly making you forget that you are in Paris, two minutes from the Etoile. This beautiful hotel also provides excellent value for your money.

Hôtel Tilsitt Étoile

23, rue Brey – 75017 Paris
Tel. (0)1 43 80 39 71 – Fax (0)1 47 66 37 63
Christine Lafosse and Stéphanie Batten
Web: www.tilsitt.com – E-mail: info@tilsitt.com

Category ★★★ Rooms 38 (2 with terrace) with air-conditioning and soundproofing, bath or shower, WC, telephone, satellite TV, safe and minibar. **Price** Single 610-735F / 92,99-112,05€, double 850F / 129,58€, junior suite (2-3 pers.) 990F / 150,92€, junior suite (2-3 pers.) 990F / 150,92€; –10% Jul to Aug, from Nov 15 to end Feb and weekends (except in trade fair periods). **Meals** Breakfast 65F / 9,91€. **Credit cards** All major. **Pets** Dogs allowed. **Facilities** Elevator, laundry service, room service, shuttle service to airport. **Parking** Wagram. **How to get there** (Map 3) Bus: 22, 30, 31, 43, 52, 73, 92 and bus to Roissy airport – Metro: Ternes, Charles de Gaulle-Étoile – RER: Charles de Gaulle-Étoile. **Open** All year.

The Rue Brey is small and discreet but only a few paces from the Arc de Triomphe and Champs-Élysées, and just the kind of place to look for in a quiet central hotel. Christine Lafosse has managed to create an atmosphere both modern and peaceful by using her taste and practical skills. You will appreciate the size of the reception lounge with its bar and pearl gray wood panelling which integrates mirrors and bay windows exploiting the space of the room to the maximum. It has armchairs in a 1930s style set around octagonal coffee tables and forming various small corners for drinks. The rooms are all comfortable, even though they are often small. The pretty colors make them quite cheerful (the largest are automatically given to people on longer stays). It should be added that two rooms on the ground floor have their own private little terrace. The brightly colored breakfast room is very pleasant. The hotel as a whole is very well kept, and the service particularly attentive.

Ermitage Hôtel

24, rue Lamarck
75018 Paris
Tel. (0)1 42 64 79 22 – Fax (0)1 42 64 10 33
Famille Canipel

Category ★★ **Rooms** 12 with bath or shower, WC, telephone, hairdryer. **Price** Single 450F / 68,60€, double 510F / 77,75€, triple 640F / 97,57€, 4 pers. 740F / 112,81€; small bedroom with shower and WC outside the room: 390F / 59,46€ (2 pers.). **Meals** Breakfast included, served 7:00-9:00. **Credit cards** Not accepted. **Pets** Small dogs allowed. **Facilities** Terrace. **Parking** 20, rue Lamarck. **How to get there** (Map 4) Bus: 80, 85, Montmartrobus – Metro: Lamarck-Caulaincourt. **Open** All year.

This mansion was built in the reign of Napoléon III for "a beloved lady." From the entranceway, the frescos by Roland du Buc evoke Montmartre scenes from right outside the door: steep streets and famous stairways that take you up to the vineyards, the Montmartre Museum and, of course, Sacré Cœur, a short distance away. For 25 years, the Ermitage has been a family-style hotel, with only twelve bedrooms, decorated as if they were intended for friends: English fabrics (generally floral) on the walls, alcove beds in two of the large rooms, 1900s-style or more contemporary furniture. The small bathrooms have all been renovated, except for that of the single room. Seven rooms overlook the garden; those on the ground floor are directly on the garden and are seized upon in good weather when breakfast can be served there. The rooms upstairs have a magnificent panorama over Paris. The small lounge with its old kneading trough and *Provençal* buffet is also at your disposal. The whole effect is very well cared-for and we felt at home here.

Hôtel Prima Lepic

29, rue Lepic
75018 Paris
Tel. (0)1 46 06 44 64 – Fax (0)1 46 06 66 11
Mme Renouf

Category ★★ **Rooms** 35 and 3 suites with soundproofing, bath or shower, WC, telephone, TV, hairdryer. **Price** Single 350-380F / 53,36-58,01€, double 400-440F / 60,9-67,08€, triple 500F / 76,22€, 4 pers. 600F / 91,47€, 5 pers. 700F / 106,71€. **Meals** Breakfast (buffet) 30F / 4,57€, served 8:00-10:30. **Credit cards** Visa, Eurocard, MasterCard. **Pets** Dogs allowed. **Facilities** Elevator, drinks machine. **Parking** Impasse Marie Blanche. **How to get there** (Map 4) Bus: 30, 54, 68, 74, 80, 95 and Montmartrobus – Metro: Blanche and Abbesses. **Open** All year.

The rue Lepic bustles with an lively outdoor food market, but the entrance to this Montmartre hotel is very discrete. The ground floor, which is illuminated by a skylight, is occupied by the reception area, a small corner lounge and a large breakfast room with garden furniture in rococo wrought iron, green plants, and frescos depicting the famous sites of the neighborhood. The bedrooms on both the courtyard and the street side are bright, and have lovely wallpaper–including Laura Ashley designs in the most recent rooms–and white *piqué* bedspreads. They are tasteful, and most have a good size. In addition to the rattan furniture, you will find period furniture that Madame Renouf enjoys bringing home from antiques markets: small Louis Philippe and Louis XVI wardrobes, antique tables. Some rooms have a lovely headboard, others a bed canopy that harmonizes with the curtains. The bathrooms are not in their prime but are nevertheless adequate. Very reasonable prices.

Hôtel Regyn's Montmartre

18, place des Abbesses - 75018 Paris
Tel. (0)1 42 54 45 21 - Fax (0)1 42 23 76 69
M. Michel Cadin
E-mail: hotelreg@club-internet.fr

Category ★★ **Rooms** 22 with bath or shower, WC, telephone, TV, hairdryer and safe. **Price** Single 385-400F / 58,69-60,98€, double 435-465F / 66,32-70,89€; extra pers. +30%, free for children under 12 years; "Carte club" of the hotel: 11th night free and many personalized services. **Meals** Breakfast 40 and 45F / 6,10 and 6,86€, served at any time. **Credit cards** Visa, Eurocard, MasterCard, Amex. **Pets** Dogs allowed. **Facilities** Elevator, laundry service. **Parking** Impasse Marie Blanche. **How to get there** (Map 4) Bus: 30, 54, 67, Montmartrobus – Metro: Abbesses. **Open** All year.

On the Place des Abbesses, the Regyn's is the ideal base for visiting Montmartre; the owner, Michel Cadin, is very fond of his neighborhood and he founded the association "A Village In Paris, Montmartre," which publishes a small guide, organizes events and promotes the preservation of the quarter. You immediately "get the picture" from the frescoes in the entry. The bedrooms are functional, bright and well-kept, with many small details that add to your comfort and pleasure: double-glazed windows on the street side, good beds, a corner for writing, stylized bronze light fixtures, and immaculate bathrooms. In most of them soft tones set off the elegant curtains and bedspreads sewn by Michel (the *premier* and *cinquième étages* have just been redone in *toile de Jouy*). Most rooms overlook the tree-covered square and the Saint-Jean L'Évangéliste Church, which is a chef d'œuvre of Art Nouveau; those on the *quatrième* and *cinquième étages* enjoy a panoramic view of Paris. Seven rooms overlook the courtyard–garden, and Room 50 has a view of Sacré Cœur. The welcome is youthful and energetic.

276

Terrass' Hôtel

12, rue Joseph-de-Maistre
75018 Paris
Tel. (0)1 46 06 72 85 – Fax (0)1 42 52 29 11
M. Binet

Category ★★★★ **Rooms** 88 and 13 suites with air-conditioning and soundproofing (2 with terrace) with bath or shower, WC, telephone, satellite TV, hairdryer and minibar. **Price** "Confort" 1160F / 176,84€ (1 pers.), 1390F / 211,90€ (2 pers.), "supérieure" 1320F / 201,23€ (1 pers.), 1540F / 234,77€ (2 pers.), suite (1-3 pers.) 1860F / 283,56€; extra bed +450F / 68,60€. **Meals** Breakfast (buffet) included, served 6:15-10:30 (continental breakfast in room at any time). **Credit cards** All major. **Pets** Dogs allowed. **Facilities** Panoramic terrace, elevator, laundry service, individual safes at reception, bar. **Restaurant** Mealtime specials 135 and 168F / 20,58 and 25,64€, also à la carte. **Parking** Impasse Marie-Blanche. **How to get there** (Map 4) Bus: 80, 95 – Metro: Place-de-Clichy. **Open** All year.

Facing the Montmartre cemetery, this hotel offers guests an extraordinary garden and terrace restaurant with a splendid view over the rooftops of the capital. You can enjoy gourmet meals there. Pleasantly decorated in a Provençal style, the ground floor restaurant also serves lunch or dinner, as well as an excellent breakfast-brunch. The reception area has numerous corner lounges and a snug bar with a fireplace. Almost all the bedrooms and suites have been renovated (the remaining 15 will be done soon). The whole effect is very comfortable, in a rather classic decor with a beautiful choice of bright colored fabrics and ingenious fittings. Those called "superior" are larger than "comfort", and the suites are really huge. From the *quatrième étage* up, you will enjoy a magnificent view of Paris if you stay on the street side. Welcome and service are very professional. A beautiful hotel with good value.

Hôtel Le Laumière

4, rue Petit
75019 Paris
Tel. (0)1 42 06 10 77 - Fax (0)1 42 06 72 50
Agnès and Marie Desprat

Category ★★ **Rooms** 54 (4 with balcony) with telephone, bath or shower, WC, satellite TV. **Price** Single 295-365F / 44,97-55,64€, double 300-390F / 45,73-59,46€, triple 395F / 60,22€. **Meals** Breakfast 34F / 5,18€, served 6:45-10:30. **Credit cards** Visa, Eurocard, MasterCard. **Pets** Dogs allowed. **Facilites** Elevator, bar, garden. **Parking** In hotel (45F / 6,86€ /day). **How to get there** (Map 5) Bus: 60 and 75 – Metro: Laumière. **Open** All year.

Located near the Parc des Buttes-Chaumont and the Cité des Sciences et de la Musique, the Laumière is run by two charming sisters. Since 1993 they have totally renewed their hotel. The lounge and dining room, particularly well achieved, open onto a lovely garden where there are a few tables for serving breakfast in nice weather. Half of the rooms overlook this flowery garden. These are the ones we recommend because they are quiet and, above all, more spacious (those ending in 2 not quite as much so). On the *premier étage* the rooms also have furnished balconies, and you should ask for these in priority if you reserve in advance (numbers 12, 14, 16 and 18). Avoid the rooms on the street; they are small (only usable as singles) and their only interest is the price. All the rooms are bright and colorful, with functional furniture and well-kept bathrooms. Outlying, but with quick access by bus or metro, the Laumière is a very recommendable hotel at really good rates.

Résidence Hôtel Villa Escudiers

64, rue Escudier
Tel. (0)1 48 25 55 33 – Fax (0)1 46 03 74 38
92100 Boulogne
Mme Véra Saint Guilhem

Studios and apartments 19 with soundproofing, telephone, bath or shower, WC, satellite TV and kitchenette. **Price** (1-2 pers.) nightly, weekly or monthly rates for studios and apart.: 480-660F, 432-594F and 336-462F / 73,18-100,62€, 65,85-90,55€ and 51,22-70,43€, "large living room" 750F, 675F and 525F / 114,34€, 102,90€ and 80,04€, apart. 880-1200F, 792-1080F and 616-840F / 134,16-182,94€, 120,73-164,64€ and 93,90-128,06€; extra bed 100F / 15,24€. **Meals** Breakfast 55F / 8,38€, served 7:00-12:00. **Credit Cards** Amex, Visa, Eurocard, MasterCard. **Pets** Dogs not allowed. **Facilities** Laundry service, garden, room service. **Parking** Private (50F / 7,62€ /day). **How to get there** (Map 9) Bus: 52 – Metro: Boulogne-Jean Jaurès. **Open** All year.

Two hundred meters from a metro station leading directly to the center of Paris, this villa is a good surprise which you discover once you go through the entrance of a modern building. There, suddenly, nature takes back its rights and the chirp of birds replaces the noise of cars. A small, elegant building from the late 1800s has been transformed into a residential hotel, mainly aimed at weekly stays but you can just as well book for the night if there is room. All the bedrooms, studios and apartments are pleasantly sizeable and enjoy a kitchenette corner. The decoration blends English pine furniture, beige carpeting and various fabrics where blue is the dominating color. Since there is no special area for breakfast, it is served in your room. There is a small and pleasant lounge with a fireplace. A charming and convivial address, even though you might not always find someone at the reception desk.

Hôtel George Sand

18, avenue Marceau
92400 Courbevoie - La Défense
Tel. (0)1 43 33 57 04 - Fax (0)1 47 88 59 38
Mme Teil

Category ★★★ **Rooms** 31 with telephone, bath or shower, WC, TV, minibar. **Price** Single and double 465-480F / 70,89-73,18€ (with shower), 495-510F / 75,46-77,75€ (with bath); weekends and in Aug: 350F / 53,36€ (1-2 pers.). **Meals** Breakfast (buffet) 50F / 7,62€, served 7:00-11:00. **Credit cards** All major. **Pets** Dogs allowed. **Facilities** Elevator, laundry service, room service, patio, shuttle to La Défense. **Parking** At 30m (7 places, 30F / 4,57€ /night). **How to get there** (Map 3) Bus: 176 – Metro and RER: La Défense – Rail station: Gare Saint-Lazare to Courbevoie. **Open** All year.

The George Sand is fifteen-minute walk from the Grande Arche of La Défense; with its offices and business complex, this modern quarter today is an important part of the capital. Named after the writer George Sand, the hotel is a veritable small museum in homage to her. In a romantic 19th-century decor, the lounge is beautified with antiques and decorative objects of her time: sculptures by David d'Angers and Jean-Baptiste Clesinger, a rare pastel portrait of George Sand, several books, a portrait of Liszt and lastly, a bust of Chopin (whose music will add a note of enjoyment to your breakfast). The bedrooms are decorated in the style of the writer's country house at Nohan with floral wallpaper, convenient cupboards in an alcove, antique furniture and Italian style frescoes in the small bathrooms. There are comfortable amenities and useful services for business people staying at the hotel. The breakfasts and Mme Teil's wonderful welcome are well in tune with the atmosphere of this house as discreet as it is irresistible.

Le Jardin de Neuilly

5, rue Paul-Déroulède
92200 Neuilly-sur-Seine
Tel. (0)1 46 24 51 62 - Fax (0)1 46 37 14 60 - Mme Rouah
Web: hotel-jardin-neuilly.com - E-mail: hotel.jardin.de.neuilly@wanadoo.fr

Category ★★★ **Rooms** 30 with soundproofing and air-conditioning, bath or shower, WC, telephone, cable TV, hairdryer, safe, minibar. **Price** Single and double 700F, 1100F and 1200F / 106,71€, 167,69€ and 182,94€. **Meals** Breakfast 95F / 14,48€, served 7:30-10:30; snacks available. **Credit cards** Amex, Visa, Eurocard, MasterCard. **Pets** Small dogs allowed. **Facilities** Garden, room service, bar. **Parking** Nearby. **How to get there** (Map 3) Bus: 73, 82 and bus to Roissy (Porte Maillot) – Metro: Sablons, Porte-Maillot. **Open** All year.

This former private residence, separated from the street by a pretty garden, now offers an ideal base for those who attend the nearby convention center but want a charming, quiet hotel for the evenings. Spacious, even though a little impersonal, the reception area does not lack charm and leads into a lounge soberly fitted-out in an 18th-century-style. The rooms are warmer – some of them elegant, others more provincial – and all are different but very comfortable and personalized with antique furniture pieces. The *standard* rooms are a little small for their price, but conversely the *luxes* are often large. The marble bathrooms are modern and functional. A very attractive connecting veranda runs beside the, garden and can be enjoyed in all seasons, notably when breakfast is served outside on elegant groupings of tables and chairs in cane and wrought iron. You should note that the hotel is particularly quiet on weekends, when Neuilly is deserted by its inhabitants.

Hôtel Princesse Isabelle

72, rue Jean-Jaurès
92800 Puteaux
Tel. (0)1 47 78 80 06 - Fax (0)1 47 75 25 20
M. Philippe Vaurs

Category ★★★ **Rooms** 35 and 1 suite with soundproofing and air-conditioning, telephone, bath or shower, WC, hairdryer, safe, minibar, cable TV. **Price** Single and double 725F / 110,53€, 580F / 88,42€, suite (max. 5 pers.) 1200F / 182,94€; extra bed 100F / 15,24€. **Meals** Breakfast (buffet) 60F / 9,15€, served 7:00-10:00. **Credit cards** All major. **Pets** Dogs allowed. **Facilities** Elevator, laundry service, bar, patio, room service, fitness center. **Parking** 20 spaces. **How to get there** (Map 3) Bus: 73 — Metro: La Défense – RER: Grande Arche. **Open** All year.

Behind a rather gray façade this hotel hides a much more attractive interior where you find a bourgeois–decorated lounge bar and a selection of rooms very different in size and styling. Our favorites are on the ground floor in the two small buildings which face each other, reached via a flowery alleyway behind the hotel. We also liked those in the annex (apart from no. 703), located across the road and around the courtyard of the Hôtel Le Dauphin which is under same ownership. The small rooms of the main building are more classical and pleasant, especially on the courtyard side. Their decor is cozy with light oak worked wood, wall fabrics and small pictures, but the furniture, often white-lacquered, is now rather out-of-date. We should also refer to a huge family suite with lounge and kitchenette, along with a vast communal terrace on the courtyard side, ideal for having a drink or reading in the sunshine. Breakfasts are served inside or in a charming garden on the Hôtel Le Dauphin side.

Syjac Hôtel

20, quai de Dion-Bouton
92800 Puteaux
Tel. (0)1 42 04 03 04 - Fax (0)1 45 06 78 69
M. Olivier Lesaffre

Category ★★★ **Rooms** 29, 1 suite and 3 duplexes with soundproofing, telephone, bath or shower, WC, hairdryer, safe, minibar, satellite TV – 2 for disabled persons. **Price** Single 570-670F / 86,90-102,14€, double 670-750F / 102,14-114,34€, triple 850F / 129,58€, duplex 980F / 149,40€, suite (1-5 pers.) 1500F / 228,67€. **Meals** Breakfast (buffet) 60F / 9,15€, served 7:00-10:00. **Credit cards** All major. **Pets** Dogs allowed. **Facilities** Elevator, laundry service, bar, patio, room service, sauna. **Parking** Godefroy. **How to get there** (Map 3) Bus: 73 – Metro: La Défense. **Open** All year.

Beside the Seine, the Quai de Dion-Bouton is a very busy road, but the Hôtel Syjac has protected itself effectively from such a noisy background, and you reach it via a small counter-alley just before the Pont de Puteaux. The entry hall brings the visitor into a very attractive lounge with an open fireplace. Furnished and abundantly decorated as in a private house, it is completed by a small bar opening onto a patio. Comfortable and serene, the rooms are generally more standard but with attractive small bathrooms, and we recommend those giving onto the courtyard. Very successful, the apartments have a more personalized decor seen perfectly in the corner lounges and open fireplaces for winter use. You will also appreciate the elegant breakfast room with an abundant buffet on the ground floor and decorated with a vast Italian seascape as a *trompe-l'œil*. Lastly, for relaxing and keeping fit, there is a sauna and a fully equipped work-out room.

RIVE GAUCHE

JARDIN DES PLANTES - LES GOBELINS

SAINT-GERMAIN-DES-PRÉS

FAUBOURG SAINT - GERMAIN

I N V A L I D E S - T O U R   E I F F E L

M   O   N   T   P   A   R   N   A   S   S   E

P A R C   M O N T S O U R I S

P O R T E   D ' O R L É A N S   -   P L A I S A N C E

G   R   E   N   E   L   L   E

P A S T E U R   -   V A U G I R A R D

RIVE DROITE

C H Â T E L E T   -   L E S   H A L L E S

I L E   S A I N T - L O U I S

M A R A I S

L O U V R E - T U I L E R I E S

É T O I L E - C H A M P S - É L Y S É E S

PORTE MAILLOT - LA DÉFENSE

PASSY - TROCADÉRO

PLACE VICTOR HUGO

AUTEUIL - MAISON DE LA RADIO

BASTILLE - NATION - GARE DE LYON

Index of Hotels with Low Rates

XIE ARRONDISSEMENT

XIIE ARRONDISSEMENT

XIIIE ARRONDISSEMENT

XIVE ARRONDISSEMENT

XVE ARRONDISSEMENT

XVIᴱ ARRONDISSEMENT

XVIIᴱ ARRONDISSEMENT

XVIIIᴱ ARRONDISSEMENT

XIXᴱ ARRONDISSEMENT

BOULOGNE – NEUILLY – LA DÉFENSE

HOTELS WITH RESTAURANT

In addition, most of the hotels chosen for this guide offer small tray meals served in the rooms.

INDEX OF HOTELS IN ALPHABETICAL ORDER

O

P

Q

R

HUNTER RIVAGES
4TH EDITION

HOTELS AND COUNTRY INNS
of Character and Charm
IN FRANCE

• WITH COLOR MAPS AND PHOTOS •

HUNTER RIVAGES

4TH EDITION

BED AND
BREAKFASTS
of Character and Charm
IN FRANCE

• WITH COLOR MAPS AND PHOTOS •

HUNTER RIVAGES

3RD EDITION

HOTELS AND COUNTRY INNS
of Character and Charm
IN SPAIN

• WITH COLOR MAPS AND PHOTOS •

HUNTER RIVAGES
3RD EDITION

HOTELS AND COUNTRY INNS
of Character and Charm
IN PORTUGAL

• WITH COLOR MAPS AND PHOTOS •

HUNTER RIVAGES GUIDES

The Guides Europeans Use.

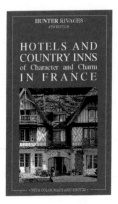

US $ 22.95
ISBN 1-55650-899-9

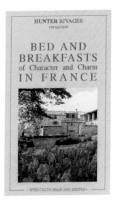

US $ 19.95
ISBN 1-55650-902-2

US $ 16.95
ISBN 1-55650-901-4

US $ 22.95
ISBN 1-55650-900-6

US $ 18.95
ISBN 1-55650-903-0

US $ 16.95
ISBN 1-55650-904-9

Notes

Notes

Notes